I0831300

TAMIL ORATORY AND THE DRAVIDIAN AESTHETIC

CULTURES OF HISTORY

CULTURES OF HISTORY

NICHOLAS DIRKS, SERIES EDITOR

The death of history, reported at the end of the twentieth century, was clearly premature. It has become a hotly contested battleground in struggles over identity, citizenship, and claims of recognition and rights. Each new national history proclaims itself as ancient and universal, while the contingent character of its focus raises questions about the universality and objectivity of any historical tradition. Globalization and the American hegemony have created cultural, social, local, and national backlashes. Cultures of History is a new series of books that investigates the forms, understandings, genres, and histories of history, taking history as the primary text of modern life and the foundational basis for state, society, and nation.

Shail Mayaram, *Against History, Against State: Counterperspectives from the Margins*

Tapati Guha-Thakurta, *Monuments, Objects, Histories: Institutions of Art in Colonial and Postcolonial India*

Charles Hirschkind, *The Ethical Soundscape: Cassette Sermons and Islamic Counterpublics*

Ahmad H. Sa'di and Lila Abu-Lughod, editors, *Nakba: Palestine, 1948, and the Claims of Memory*

Prachi Deshpande, *Creative Pasts: Historical Memory and Identity in Western India, 1700–1960*

Todd Presner, *Mobile Modernity: Germans, Jews, Trains*

Laura Bear, *Lines of the Nation: Indian Railway Workers, Bureaucracy, and the Intimate Historical Self*

Vazira Fazila-Yacoobali Zamindar, *The Long Partition and the Making of Modern South Asia: Refugees, Boundaries, Histories*

TAMIL ORATORY
and the
DRAVIDIAN AESTHETIC

[DEMOCRATIC PRACTICE IN SOUTH INDIA]

Bernard Bate

COLUMBIA UNIVERSITY PRESS

NEW YORK

Columbia University Press
Publishers Since 1893
New York Chichester, West Sussex

Library of Congress Cataloging-in-Publication Data
Bate, Bernard.
Tamil oratory and the Dravidian aesthetic : democratic practice in south India / Bernard Bate.
p. cm.
Includes bibliographical references and index.
ISBN 978-0-231-14756-9 (cloth : alk. paper)—
ISBN 978-0-231-51940-3 (ebook)
1. Folk literature, Tamil—India—Madurai. 2. Epic poetry, Tamil—India—Madurai. 3. Speeches, addresses, etc., Tamil—India—Madurai. 4. Tamil language—India—Madurai—Rhetoric. 5. Politics and culture—India—Madurai. 6. Language and culture—India—Madurai. 7. Madurai (India)—Politics and government.
1. Title.
PL4758.85.M29B38 2009
398.2'0494811—dc22 2009020689

∞

Columbia University Press books are printed on permanent and durable acid-free paper.
This book is printed on paper with recycled content.

Printed in the United States of America

In memory of N. G. M. Kavitha, *navalar*

CONTENTS

FIGURES AND TABLES

PREFACE

The tradition of all the dead generations weighs like a nightmare on the brain of the living. And just when they seem engaged in revolutionizing themselves and things, in creating something that has never yet existed, precisely in such periods of revolutionary crisis they anxiously conjure up the spirits of the past to their service and borrow from them names, battle cries, and costumes in order to present the new scene of world history in this time-honored disguise and this borrowed language.

—KARL MARX, *THE EIGHTEENTH BRUMAIRE OF LOUIS BONAPARTE*, 1852

THE NEWNESS OF MADURAI

India is very old. Geologists tell us that the entire Indian subcontinent was a part of southern Africa some one hundred fifty million years ago. It crossed what is now the Indian Ocean and smashed into Asia twenty to forty million years ago raising up the Himalayan Mountains in the process. They are still rising today.

Ordinary people in Tamilnadu have different senses of this antiquity. For instance, surrounding the ancient city of Madurai in the southernmost part of the peninsula are granite hills whose stone first formed in Africa. People say they are the petrified remains of great demons—elephant, snake, cow—whom the Lord Siva defeated in the time of the *puranas*, the old stories. On some of those hills are caves, stone beds, ancient writings, and beautiful images of Mahavira, the founder of Jainism, carved twelve hundred years ago by ascetics waiting to die. (There are no Jains there now.) Construction sites for Madurai's new big buildings with their deep foundations regularly reveal heartbreaking layers of human effort, suggesting that there were many others here long before. Everywhere one looks, it seems, are traces of people long gone, erased by people gone almost as long.

It is that sense of layers, of depths, of history laminated over history

FIGURE 1 India, Tamilnadu, and major metropolitan cities

melded with stories, riddles, proverbs, and stone that permeate one's sense of the place. Reading an ancient Tamil text has this same quality: an anthology of poems will date perhaps to the first–third century C.E., the period of the Tamil *sangams*, or "academies." A commentator's exegesis composed six centuries later will appear just below the original verse. Another commentary written in the fourteenth century will illuminate the first commentary for his contemporaries. And nineteenth- or twentieth-century Tamil prose frames this archaeology, all of it bound into that most modern of objects, a printed book. History laminated over history, readings of readings of readings all culminating in an ancient text bound in a modern form whose very presence indicates to us just how old Tamil is, just how long people have been writing and speaking in Tamil.

At the same time, a great deal of what we see—or hear—as old in Tamilnadu, and India more generally, is really very new. To put it even more pointedly, a great deal of the very new things in India have that feel of very old things layered with history. As it turns out, these very new things appear to make claims regarding the essences of the Tamil people. For instance, perhaps the very first thing a student will read of Madurai, or what a visitor or pilgrim will learn in a tourist map and guide, is that the city is centered upon the great temple of the Goddess Meenakshi, Lord Siva's consort, almost universally said to be Madurai's queen. Everything about the city confirms this basic fact: streets appear to radiate out from the temple in concentric circles. And the high point of any year is the annual festival in the Tamil month of Chittirai (April/May), in which the goddess reenacts her Conquering the Lords of the Eight Directions (*dik vijya*) and her marriage to Lord Siva. Everything about contemporary Madurai—from the granite hills surrounding the city to its spatial layout and temporal rhythms—confirms that the goddess Meenakshi has always been queen, has always resided at Madurai's core, and has always defined it. We might see the city, then, as an embodiment of antiquity, a sacred center, and an icon of the centrality of religion in Tamil—and, more broadly, Indian—thought and practice.

But we would be wrong. The temple site is indeed ancient, perhaps even prehistoric. It is mentioned in the earliest texts we have, including one of Tamil's greatest literary achievements, the sixth-century epic *Tale of the Anklet* (*Silappathikaram*), which tells the tragic story of Kannaki, her wayward husband, Kovalan, their journey to Madurai, his murder, her wrath, the city's destruction, and her ultimate apotheosis. The *Tale of the Anklet* also tells of a palace, a king, a living human sovereign who, at least in the *Tale*, eclipsed the living goddess in import. Present-day structures, palace and temple both, and the layout of the old city itself date mostly from the Nayakar period (sixteenth and seventeenth centuries), and they have been modified dramatically over the past two hundred years. The British tore down the ancient walls in the early part of the nineteenth century—for sanitary reasons, we're told. And for the safety of Madurai's inhabitants, they razed most of the vast crumbling palace complex that had been the center of the city's activity prior to that time. A beautiful remnant of that palace still exists today. The city's tourist authorities stage a historical sound-and-light show featuring segments of Kannaki's *Tale* there every evening.

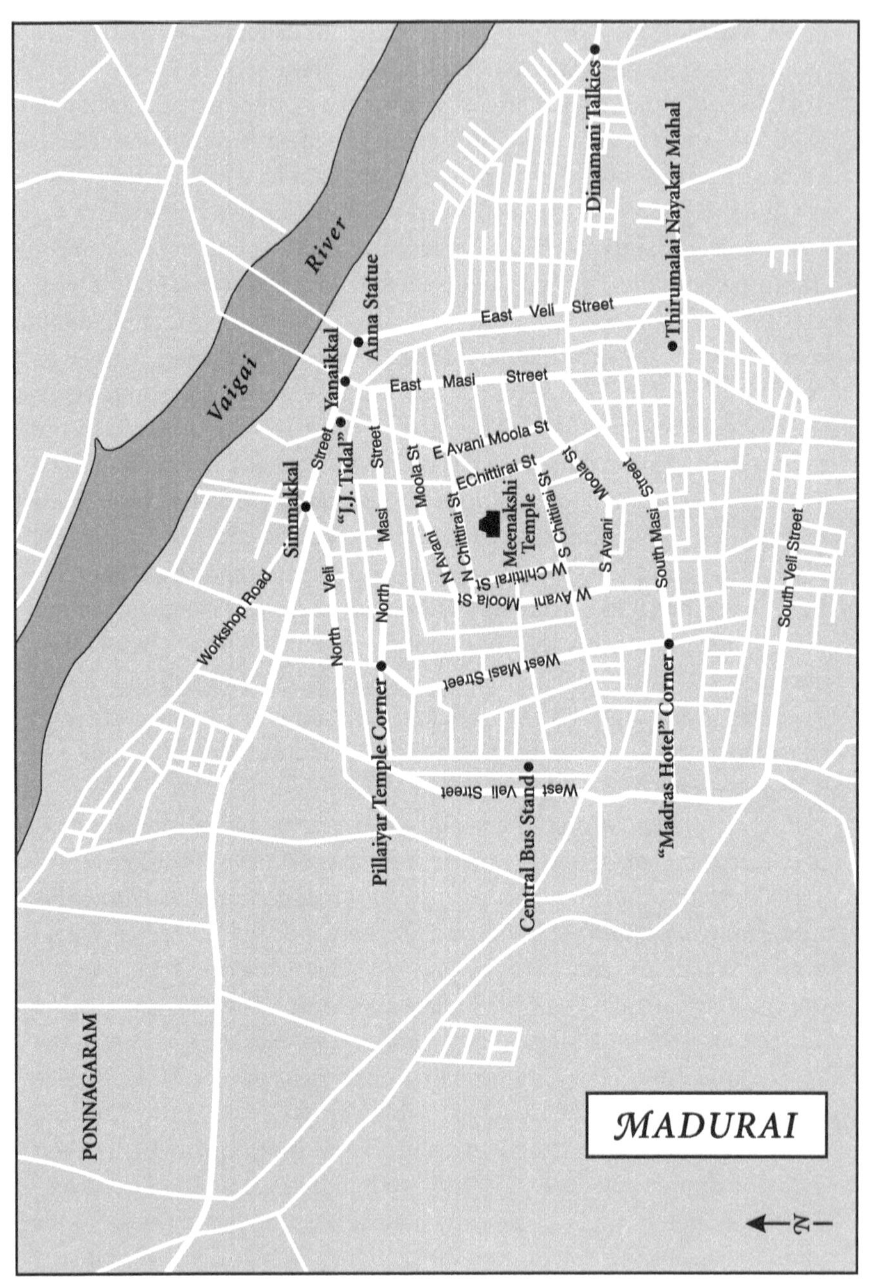

FIGURE 2 Map of Madurai, Old Town

The sense of Madurai's sacred temple center—and the claims that the goddess has always ruled the city, that religion always trumped politics, and the antiquity of all of it—is a new thing. In this the idea of Madurai is like the idea of Tamil. It is old—indeed, it has one of the world's oldest continuous literary traditions. So it is not that Tamil is not old, it is simply that oldness itself was brought to bear in a very new way. During the second half of the twentieth century Tamil oratory began to sound very old, to use ancient words, to embody ancient tropes and figures—all to articulate a modern, democratic polity. In other words, the old things of Tamil emerged at the very moment that Tamils began to do something very new: they began to imagine themselves as a nation, as a people, as a public, and as a political economy, all on a mass scale.

THE NEWNESS OF OLD THINGS

This is a book about the newness of old things. It concerns an oratorical revolution, a transformation of oratorical style linked to larger transformations in society at large. It explores the aesthetics and ideologies of Tamil oratory and its vital relationship to one of the key institutions of modern society, democracy. Hence, this book also concerns the centrality of language within the modern human condition in general.

Though Tamil oratory (*medaitamil*) is relatively new in South India, the Dravidianist (or Tamil nationalist) style suggests an ancient mode of speaking by its use of archaic forms of Tamil modeled principally on the written word. During the first half of the twentieth century a first generation of political orators in Tamil addressed audiences in halls and streets in what Tamil people call "ordinary" (*nadaimurai*), "bent" (*kodun*), or "vulgar" (*kochai*) Tamil. With the advent of mass democratic politics in the 1940s, orators shifted from such common registers of spoken Tamil to a speech genre called "fine" or "beautiful" Tamil (*centamil*) in an elocutionary revolution: this new, archaic, and distinctly literary mode of speech distinguished the new democrats who deployed it from a previous generation of relatively plainspoken politicians.

The *centamil* revolution also distinguished its practitioners as people different in kind from their public, a seemingly counterintuitive strategy for democratic politicians appealing to a rural, illiterate and politically active electorate. Why did such a move make sense? The new and archaic oratory was developed by politicians within the production of what we will call throughout the book the *Dravidianist political paradigm*. In this paradigm signs of an ancient and original Tamil-speaking civilization, independent of what was considered the relatively more recent Sanskrit-speaking, Indo-Aryan, North Indian, and Brahmin-dominated civilization, were widely deployed in the production of their democratic political power (chapter 1). When politicians spoke in a literary and archaic Tamil, they embodied ancient kings and gods addressing their people in heroic orations that had no historical antecedents (chapter 2); they processed through streets likes gods being taken on procession, or reviewed processions as kings receiving their gods, they made pilgrimages modeled on religious ones, and conducted elaborate public meetings that operated on the same logic as worship (chapter 3); they deployed literary tropes and ancient figures of speech peculiar to Tamil, demonstrating a kind of spectacular literacy in order to embody a culturally and historically authentic mode of political patronage (chapter 4). Likewise, the people praised their leaders on the oratorical stage, in heartfelt poetry that filled newspapers, on posters plastered throughout towns, on ceremonial arches, and on sixty-foot images called "cutouts" erected to welcome them (chapter 5). Finally, the Dravidianists produced a political paradigm shot through with signs of feminine energy, another counterintuitive move in an overwhelmingly masculine public sphere: the political space of male action and male concerns was aestheticized by signs of the feminine drawn from a broad range of cultural resources, including Ayurvedic medicine, literature, and worship (chapters 6, 7). But again, such a feminizing move also pointed to an antiquity, a refinement, a cultivation, and an authenticity that would Tamilize a Tamil modernity and produce a deeply democratic paradigm with a pan-Indic aesthetic of power.

To speak, then, in a highly stylized and literate genre on a populist stage was to embody an imagined past of a pure and ancient Tamil civilization. The Dravidianists' language was but another sign of the Tamil longue durée and their intimate connection to it. And even in what is sometimes called a populist movement, the deployment of a distinctly literary speech genre makes perfect sense once we understand language not merely as the communication of denotational sense but as the practical and phenomenological becoming of social and historical worlds and the primary medium of a people's aesthetic attachment to them.

In a larger sense this book argues that the spectacular literacy of the *centamil* revolution and other practices of the Dravidianist political paradigm were elements of the modernization of Indian society. In this case, modernity took the form of an invented tradition, a neoclassicism, the framing of which as a nation and as a people was entirely new, though the content was quite old. In this the *centamil* revolution and its associated forms in the Dravidianist paradigm suggests that modernity is not the mere succession of tradition, but rather that the production of tradition is a primary modality of modernity, a new newness, albeit a newness of old things.

THE ANTIQUITY OF KAVITHA'S LOVE

N. G. M. Kavitha was an orator whom I heard speak once in 1995 and spoke to a few weeks later in an interview she initiated. I never spoke to her again. When I went back to look for her in August 2000, I was told by one of her mentors, Parvathi Annamalai, that she had been killed just a few weeks earlier on 5 August in a bus accident as she was returning from a visit to her goddess. She died a few years after her political party had won an election. But despite her hopes and efforts, she did not receive the kind of attention from the leadership that she had hoped for: no position, no honors, no stability for her family. Mrs. Parvathi—a very sharp elderly woman with decades of political experience—told me to write about her, to tell people about her life, that things didn't work out for her. And Kavitha herself had asked me to write about her, that people should know that it was "like this for a woman." So this project, which the people I was writing about did not always welcome, was licensed by Kavitha and by one of her mentors.

But more than that, as I wrote and thought about Tamil oratory over the years I kept coming back to that one speech and that one interaction. I realized that in that speech burned the purest ideal of the poet-politician: she was the Dravidianist orator par excellence. And in Kavitha's love burned the hopes and desires of thousands of people who orated on stages, who put up posters and cutouts, who published poetry in newspapers, who dreamed of their leaders and what they might become. As her speech kept coming back to me, it will return again and again in this book in order to illustrate this poesy and this love. Like Madurai, like Tamil itself, Kavitha's love is an ancient thing, one that has been cultivated in every prayer to every god and goddess in the Tamil world—probably across India—for thousands of years. As it turns out, though, it was also cultivated in the very style of the Dravidianist paradigm as the mode of modern democratic campaigning and a modern democratic subjectivity that found its expression in poesy, prayers, and dreams.

Finally, her womanhood was by no means irrelevant to the project. In fact it was her womanhood that forefronted the gendering of the larger system, that enabled the gendered quality of Tamil oratory to stand in relief. On the advice and insistence of feminist scholars prior to my fieldwork, I listened to the voices of women in an overwhelmingly male sphere of action, and was able to see the gendered foundations of the system as a whole. As Joan Scott put it, to attend to the voices of women is not to write women's history, but to write history in all its fullness. Attending to the voice of Kavitha enabled a fuller account of the ethnography of contemporary Tamil oratory, and indeed came to define it for me.

ACKNOWLEDGMENTS

THIS BOOK developed through a fertile cross-pollination of ideas gathered in near-seasonal migrations among Chicago, Madison, Madurai, and Chennai between 1986 and 2000. Since then it has been transformed and completed in continued correspondence, travel, conferencing, and especially teaching. Paul Friedrich, my dissertation guide at the University of Chicago, served as an engaged sage in every respect, offered attentive and helpful guidance from beginning to end, and modeled a freedom of intellectual inquiry and curiosity unfettered by disciplinary boundaries. Paul also modeled a generosity of guidance and encouraged me to work closely with James Fernandez, John Kelly, McKim Marriott, A. K. Ramanujan, and Milton Singer. During that time the teaching of Bernard Cohn, Norman Cutler, Nancy Munn, Marshall Sahlins, and Michael Silverstein contributed critical elements to the scholarship represented here. Conversations with, and interventions by, Arjun Appadurai, Carol Breckenridge, and Valentine Daniel continued during my transition from Chicago to New Haven. In Madurai my understanding of Tamil and Tamil society developed during close interactions with two teachers, first with Ku. Paramasivam of the American College and the American Institute of Indian Studies and later with Tho. Paramasivan of Thiyagaraja College and Manonmaniyam Sundaranar University.

The field research period in Madurai between 1992 and 1995 provided one of the most stimulating intellectual environments of my life—in intensity of discussion, thought, and argument, the level of intellectual energy and passion rivaled only my experience at the University of Chicago. One of the primary sites of that experience was the Raffic Gallery, where a loose grouping of university and nonuniversity intellectuals, artists, actors, playwrights, and activists gathered for fellowship and discussions; among these were Raffic Ahmed, Sundar Kali, Artist Babu, Sivakumar, Arouna, and Logu. The rooftop of the New Century Bookhouse sponsored almost weekly debates, speech competitions, literary meetings, and general gatherings of thinkers and organizations interested in the critical discussion of life, culture, and politics in Tamil society. A third organizational site of fellowship was the Excellent Tutorial Center, where gathered three men who, more than any others, provided warm counsel, friendship, and insight into stage speaking: the Tamil teachers S. Sendhuran and A. Ganesan of the Sethupathi and Labour Schools, respectively, and G. Gnanasambandan, professor of Tamil, Thiyagaraja College.

I was a frequent visitor at Madurai Kamaraj University, American College, and Thiyagaraja College, where I benefited from regular discussions with Solomon Poppaiya, Samuel Sudanandha, Saraswathi Venugopal, and T. S. Natarajan (with whom I studied Tamil grammar and poetics in formal tuition in 1994 and 1995). Highlights of many trips to Chennai involved fruitful meetings with A. R. Venkatachalapathy and M. S. S. Pandian of the Madras Institute of Development Studies and T. Arasu of the Tamil Studies Department at Madras University. I was sheltered on numerous sojourns in Chennai and kept nourished in mind, body, and spirit by Aruna R. and Prabhakar. Among the many, many people who helped me in Madurai are Parvathi Annamalai, R. Gandhi, Nagendiran, P. M. Mannan, Thengaikadai Mariyappan, and M. Occubalu.

Anbuselvi, S. Shaik Ismail, Krishnaswamy, and R. Ulaganathan served as assistants and collaborators over the course of the field research period; A. Chandran, S. Jayaraman, A. Pandiyammal, M. Poongodi, and P. Ramadevi made transcriptions of speeches and other events.

Norman Cutler, Michael McGovern, M. S. S. Pandian, and A. R. Venkatachalapathy made complete readings of this work at one time or another and offered substantial comments, for which I am very grateful. Mattison Mines and Michael Silverstein made several very close readings of the manuscript as reviewers for Columbia University Press and provided copious comments and suggestions, which informed the final rounds of writing, editing, and ordering of the material in the book. I was very fortunate to have such responsive, responsible, and engaged readers. Of course, I sometimes did not follow their guidance; all errors and infelicities in the text are mine.

People who offered comments and critiques on specific chapters, or who otherwise substantially engaged me with their thoughts in the field or in write-up, include Ira Bashkow, Richard Bauman, Veronique Benei, Kate Bjork, Dominic Boyer, Dipesh Chakrabarty, Kamari Clarke, Frank Cody, Steve Coleman, Whitney Cox, Joseph Errington, Tania Forte, Susan Gal, Carol Greenhouse, Arjun Guneratne, Akhil Gupta, Thomas Blom Hanson, Adi Hastings, Sarah Hodges, Steve Hughes, Jennifer Jackson, Sam Kaplan, Webb Keane, William W. Kelly, C. S. Lakshmi, Sarah Lamb, Alaina Lemon, Paul Liffman, Paul Manning, Flagg Miller, Diane Mines, Lisa Mitchell, Osamu Note, Sheldon Pollock, Gloria Raheja, Dhooleka Raj, Sumathi Ramaswamy, Velcheru Narayana Rao, Stuart Rockefeller, Mary Scoggin, Michael Scott, Susan Seizer, Martha Selby, Aliza Shvartz, Ravi Sriramachandran, Gregory Starrett, Thomas Trautmann, Margaret Trawick, Elizabeth Vann, Amanda Weidman, Blake Wentworth, Laura Wexler, and Eric Worby. Special thanks to Joshua Kellman in Chicago and Christopher Greene in New Haven. Diane Mines was a fellow traveler from the beginning in Chicago, over many years in Tamilnadu and back again, and her visions of what we do as scholars of Tamil and Tamil society are very much a part of this book. Tania Forte was a spiritual, intellectual, and ethical collaborator and guide in life and in scholarship; her thoughts, too, find themselves on almost every page as her loss haunts me almost every day.

Joseph Elder of the University of Wisconsin created and headed up the institutions that provided the infrastructure for me to become a student of Tamil; like dozens of my contemporaries, my scholarship is a product of his fifty-plus years of forging intellectual ties and fostering good will between the peoples of the United States and India.

Financial support was provided by a Century Scholarship, FLAS (Title VI) Fellowships, and by the Committee for South Asian Studies at the University of Chicago, and language training and junior research fellowships by the American Institute of Indian Studies, a Fulbright-Hays Doctoral Dissertation Abroad Fellowship, and by a Charlotte W. Newcombe Dissertation Fellowship. In India institutional affiliation was generously extended by Dr. G. John Samuels and Dr. Shanmugam Pillai of the Institute of Asian Studies, Madras. Our family also benefited from generous support from my parents, Joan Dexter and Frank Lewis Bate, and parents-in-law, Doris Jo and Phil Fisher.

At Columbia University Press, my long-suffering editor, Anne Routon, deserves special thanks for shepherding the manuscript through the system, lining up the staff necessary to finish and polish the work, and generally being a professional of good cheer and even better patience. A skillful copy editor, Kerri Sullivan went through the text with extraordinary care, and Chris Brest produced the maps of India and Madurai shortly before leaving us in an untimely death.

Elements of chapters 1 and 2 appeared in "Shifting Subjects: Elocutionary Revolution in Eighteenth-Century America and Twentieth-Century India," *Language and Communication* 24.4:337–352 (2004). Chapter 4 was previously published in Spanish as "El juego del tropo en la práctica política tamil: De vita, luz de luna, y jazmín," translated by Ariel Silva, in *La tropología y la figuración del pensiamento in la acción social* , a special issue of *Revista de antropología social* (Madrid) 15:85–112, edited by James Fernandez (2006). And some of the images and poems in chapter 5 were published in "Political Praise in Tamil Newspapers: The Poetry and Iconography of Democratic Power," in Diane Mines and Sarah Lamb, eds., *Everyday Life in South Asia* (2002), pp. 308–325.

Over many, many years in Madurai the extended family of S. Shaik Dawood and S. Bathool Begum treated us as their own children and grandchildren. My family and I lived with them as an extended family for more than nine months in 1992 and 1993. Their eldest son, S. Shaik Samsudeen, my first friend in India, helped in many ways, including introducing me to people who became critical to this research. Their second son, S. Shaik Ismail, accompanied me to public meetings, worked the recording equipment, and generally kept me company on many long nights of research.

Catherine Fisher has put up with such a partner as me for far longer than most women would, and I am grateful that she did. She kept our boy, Noah, healthy over several years in India and gave birth to two girls, Isabel and Clio. It was not always easy. But as this book went to press she was headed back to India again for another year of teaching, living, and traveling in Tamilnadu with our children—of being persons the Tamil way.

A NOTE ON TAMIL WORDS

FOR THE purposes of simplicity, the spelling style adopted in this book is based on current (and sometimes inconsistent) fashions of writing Tamil in English. Most words are rendered according to the fairly intuitive conventions used in journalism and scholarly writing in Tamilnadu today; personal and place names, of course, are rendered as the people who have or live in them have chosen to do so. In some words this style nullifies certain key phonological distinctions in Tamil such as short and long vowels, *nadu* (center) vs. *nadu* (country), and dental and retroflex consonants, *pathini* (wife) vs. *pattini* (hunger). Following such spelling styles also leads to inconsistencies: for instance, the voiced retroflex approximant at the end of the word *Tamil*, sometimes written as *zh*, is consistently used only in some words, e.g., *kazhagam* "association," or *mozhi* "language," but not generally for *Tamizh*. Though distinctions between words or styles of speaking in Tamil, where relevant, are made clear, the most commonly used Tamil terms are found in the glossary, where I also provide a more precise transcription based on the format used by the University of Madras Lexicon.

I follow Robert Moore's (2000:293–297) transcription style for indicating reported speech, especially in the interviews of chapters 1 and 2: the speech of the here and now of the interview is flush left, with reported speech indented one column. For interlinear transcriptions and grammatical explication, I use the following abbreviations:

acc	accusative
adj	adjective
adv	adverb

ajp	adjectival participle
assc	associative
avp	adverbial participle
cont	continuous
dat	dative
F/fut	future tense
gen	genitive
inf	infinitive
int	interrogative
loc	locative
n.	noun
neg	negative
nr	nonrational
pl	plural
pos	possessive
P/pr	present tense
Pt/pst	past tense
sg	singular
vn	verbal noun
voc	vocative

TAMIL ORATORY AND THE DRAVIDIAN AESTHETIC

INTRODUCTIONS

THE DRAVIDIAN AESTHETIC AND "PROPER" TAMIL

This book asks why democratic Tamil politicians speak in a way that strikes many as literary and ancient. They climb onto the speaking stages set up on the streets of cities, towns, and villages, and they speak in a proper, highly elaborate register of Tamil (*centamil*), a literary—or perhaps better, *scriptural*—language pervaded with archaic forms—lexically (i.e., in words), morphologically (in the meaningful elements of words), syntactically (in the arrangements of words), and poetically (in the meaningful organization of the messages themselves and in the deployment of tropes). As a scriptural register of Tamil, *centamil* contrasts with the Tamil of everyday life (and the Tamil of ordinary people), known as "common Tamil" (*nadaimuraitamil*), or in the more pejorative and widespread terms, "vulgar Tamil" (*kochaitamil*) or "bent Tamil" (*koduntamil*). The literary sophistication of the *centamil* revolution—this spectacular literacy—ensured that Dravidianist politicians would achieve for themselves a distinction both from their political opponents and, interestingly, from the electorate.

The *Dravidianist political paradigm*,[1] a utopian and charismatic form of political campaigning, was developed in the 1940s and '50s by a series of political leaders, philosophers, film actors, orators, playwrights, and poets. The paradigm grew from solemn beginnings in the philosophical and political non-Brahmin movement of Periyar E. V. Ramaswamy (1879–1973), who, beginning in the 1920s, defied the oppression of women and subaltern castes under what he argued was a pan-Indic, Sanskritic, North Indian, and Brahmin-dominated civilization (Arnold 1977; Arooran 1980; Chandrababu 1993; Geetha and Rajadurai 1998; Hardgrave 1965; Irshick 1969; Pandian 1994, 1996a, 1996b, 2007; Price 1996a, 1996b; Ram 1977; Ramaswamy 1993, 1997; Sivathamby 1995; Subramanian 1999; Venkatachalapathy 1995a, 2006; Washbrook 1989). The movement had its foundations in a new imaginary of the ancient distinction of the Tamil, or Dravidian, civilization from the larger and more dominant Indo-Aryan one; this imaginary is built upon the Tamil literary tradition, which stretches back to the period of the Sangam poetic anthologies and grammar, first–third centuries C.E. Combining literary evidence with new interpretations of archaeological materials from the Indus river valley, scholars suggested that the Tamil civilization had even earlier roots than the Aryans, who were thought to have invaded the subcontinent ca. 1500 B.C.E.[2] Based on evidence from ancient Tamil literature, which showed no evidence of Aryan influence,[3] it was the Aryans, they said, who imposed such social evils as the caste system and the subjugation of women and imposed a reign of Brahminical tradition that lasted for thousands of years. North Indians were the inheritors of that tradition, and the Congress Party was dominated by North Indians. The Dravidian movement was organized to counter precisely that.

In this respect Periyar's Dravida Kazhagam, or Dravidian Association (DK), was a classically modernist movement in the sense of distinguishing itself from what it considered a moribund "tradition" (i.e., Brahminism) and proposing a new, enlightenment-based philosophy of self-respect (*suyamariyathai*) and rationalism (*pakkutharivu*) that would wipe away the irrationalities of caste and gender oppression. Though Periyar himself asserted that he wasn't concerned about any particular language, the movement also promoted Tamil as a national language in the face of the growing importance of Hindustani (Hindi/Urdu) within the Indian National Congress Party (Brass 1990, 1974; Lelyveld 1993; Washbrook 1989). In its earliest phase the movement called for a separate nation called Dravidastan or Dravidanadu. For many of the DK, then, 15 August 1947, India's day of independence, was dubbed a *dukka nal*, a "day of sorrow," for that was the day on which the Tamil people traded the British Raj for North Indian rule. While Periyar and members of the DK never entered formal party politics, the philosophical tone and cultural nationalism of the DK was taken up in the literary *cum* oratorical virtuosity of people such as Ariñar ("The Learned") C. N. Annadurai (1909–1969) and Kalaiñar ("The Artist") Mu. Karunanidhi (1924–), who established the first democratic political party of the Dravidianist paradigm in the 1940s, the

Dravida Munnetra Kazhagham (DMK), or the Dravidian Progress Association, and couched their politics in the promotion of the Tamil language and civilization. Though the DMK continued to defend the Tamil language—and several anti-Hindi agitations and full-blown riots erupted over the years—Ariñar Annadurai formally renounced the nationalist goals of the movement after his election to the Indian Parliament in 1962.

The Dravidianist paradigm reached an apogee, as it were, in the wild excesses associated with the patronage of a cinema actor-turned-god, M. G. Ramachandran (MGR, 1917–1987), whose patronage was bodily and involved fantasies of the body (Dickey 1993a, 1993b; Hardgrave 1975; Pandian 1992a, 1992b; Ramaswamy 1993). In 1972 MGR broke away from Kalaiñar Karunanidhi and the DMK to establish the second major Dravidian party, one named in memory of Ariñar Annadurai, the All-India Annadurai Dravidian Progress Association (AIADMK). Piercings, barefoot pilgrimages, prostrations at his feet, and other austerities characterized some extreme forms of political patronage when he was alive; self-immolations and the erection of permanent temples occurred when he died (Dickey 1993a; Hardgrave 1975). MGR embodied in the minds of his audiences a combination of heroism, goodness, regal largesse, Dravidian divinity, and masculine beauty that would bring him to power in 1977 and keep him, and his political descendants, there almost continuously until 2006. His death in 1988 left Tamilnadu with his consort, the extraordinary "Revolutionary Leader" (*Puratchi Talaivi*) Dr. J. Jayalalitha (1948–); during her multiple terms (1991–1996, 2001, 2002–2006) the charismatic patronage, indeed devotion, of MGR was routinized as standard political practice. That paradigm was taken up by all the Dravidian parties, including the second major breakaway from the DMK, Vai. Gopalswamy's—or Vaiko's—Renaissance (*Marumalarchi*) Dravidian Progress Association (MDMK) in 1994. By that time, it had even been taken up by the all-India Congress-I, one of the main rivals to Dravidian regionalism in general. As we will see, the devotional model deployed as a mode of political patronage also embodied the kind of antiquity and authenticity associated with the *centamil* revolution.

Inherent within the distinction achieved by the Dravidianists was an aesthetic opposition between "refinedness" (*cemmai*), as marked by literary style and citation, and vernacular "vulgarity" (*kochai*); following Michel de Certeau (1984: xix), we will call this a "proper" distinction among human beings. The "proper"[4] is a hierarchical *cum* aesthetic distinction, the standard of which is based on the practices and evaluations of people located in a place of privileged evaluation, some hegemonic center. Certain status groups or classes within any society control the institutional modes of semeiosocial—that is, social, cultural, and political-economic—production. Regardless of one's position within a semeiosocial field, the "proper" is a social fact producing a seemingly natural order of aesthetic evaluation in which persons, collectivities, and practices are acceptable or not, beautiful or ugly, attractive or repulsive, "refined" (*cemmai*) or "vulgar" (*kochai*). Such an aesthetic appears to us as written in universal law, laws to be propagated in orthodoxy, challenged in heterodoxy, or, most commonly, viscerally experienced as a part of a *doxic*[5] encounter with the world (Bourdieu 1977:159–197). Social and cultural evaluation is, more often than not, a doxic experience, a bodily response.

Though the term is used variously (and erroneously as a synonym for "beauty") we will use *aesthetic* to refer to such gut, embodied, doxic responses, positive and negative. It is a first and unconscious response to phenomena in the world, a sense of the *suchness of things*, to deploy the language of the American pragmatist C. S. Peirce (1955 [1940]:81). Much of what we think of as human culture operates in terms of this suchness, from the senses of what we find attractive or repulsive in social interaction (e.g., styles of greeting, dialects, clothing, hairstyles, etc.) to the organization of domestic and public space and the ways men and women move through and animate such spaces. Pierre Bourdieu used the term *bodily hexis* to refer to this structure of our embodied responses to the world, how culture (or *habitus*, in his terminology) is embodied in the practices of everyday life in our bodies and our aesthetics.[6]

We have a tendency to assume that because emotions are associated with the body, emotional responses to the world are natural and therefore universal. But the aesthetic response to the world is no less culturally and historically specific. As Raymond Williams put it (1977:128–135), every society produces a *structure of feelings* that is tied to the larger socioeconomic and political structures in which people act. As many have argued (Lutz and Abu-Lughod 1990; Lynch 1990; Rebhun 1999; Trawick 1990), such complex systems of emotional responses are cultural systems that are massively structured by language and the ways that we speak of them. This is not to claim that language merely structures thought and emotion, as in a kind of brute structural determinism, what linguists sometimes call naïve Whorfian relativism (Whorf 1956 [1939]; cf. Friedrich 1979a; Leavitt 2005; Lucy 1992; Silverstein 2000). It is to claim, rather, that our apperceptions of language practice itself operate largely on an aesthetic level and not (merely) on an ideological one (cf. Sapir 1995 [1927]; Bourdieu 1977:159–177).

It is this aesthetic sense of sheer *being* or *becoming* (Bakhtin 1981) within culturally and historically contingent modalities of communication in which the world is felt and, sometimes when pressed, known. At the very least, it is never *anaesthetic*, a term we have difficulty separating from some notion of corporeality.

At the opposite phenomenological extreme from the aesthetic is the *ideological*, that is, the more or less articulated, more or less articulable, and more or less systematized or lawlike aspects of the apperception of language. This opposition finds a long and varied discussion in anthropological literature. Gregory Bateson is the first to make such a distinction between what he called a culture's *ethos*, the embodied emotional and affective elements of human life, and its *eidos*, the cognitive and more logical plane of ideological perception and discourse (Bateson 1958 [1936]:21–34, 198–256). Victor Turner made a similar distinction between what he called the *orectic*[7] and the *ideological* poles of cultural life (Turner 1974:55–56), the bodily and sensory on the one hand and the rational and logical on the other. Of course Bourdieu's opposition, discussed above, between the realm of *doxa* (the naturalized, embodied, and undebatable) and the realm of *orthodox* and *heterodox* ideological positions (which, by their very nature, are debatable) represents a parallel opposition to the one offered here between the aesthetic and the ideological (Bourdieu 1977:164). And this same parallel is articulated in C. S. Peirce's distinction between a phenomenological First (that *suchness* of the world) and a phenomenological Third, the lawlike, systematized, and articulable understandings of things (Pierce 1955 [1940]:74–97).

The distinction between the ideological and the aesthetic under the encompassing term of *phenomenology* contributes to a discussion within linguistic anthropology under the rubric of language ideology (Silverstein 1979; Woolard and Schieffelin 1994; Gal and Irvine 1995; Schieffelin, Woolard, and Kroskrity 1998; Kroskrity 2000). These scholars demonstrate how social action—in particular political action—unfolds according to the ideas—or "ideologies"—people have regarding the nature of communication itself. For the language ideologists, the hypernym (or most encompassing category) is ideology, i.e., all those cultural ideas and beliefs, conscious and unconscious, about the nature and functionality of language and its relationship to social, political, and moral order. In this respect, *ideology* is another term for a system of semeiosocial meaningfulness of social and cultural order that emphasizes the political and economic, a kind of Gramscian understanding of the term. Gramsci's ideology "in its highest sense" (1971:328), involves "a conception of the world that is implicitly manifest in art, in law, in economic activity and in all manifestations of individual and collective life"[8]—that is to say, culture. He warns of the dangers of the term as it has been used to denote "both the necessary superstructure of a particular structure and the arbitrary elucubrations of particular individuals" (1971:376). At the same time he avoids the vulgar materialist perspective that would relegate ideology to purely superstructural phenomena. In the sense of ideology as the totality of the phenomenological apperception of the world, he writes, "precisely material forces are the content and ideologies are the form, though this distinction between form and content has purely didactic value, since the material forces would be inconceivable historically without form and ideologies would be individual fancies without the material forces" (1971:377).

Now some of those fancies may be just the thing we look for as anthropologists. And after carefully considering them within the semeiosocial fields of their production we might find them not so fantastic after all. This is one of the strong contributions of the language ideology position, which takes seriously the "arbitrary elucubrations" and "secondary explanations" that previous generations of linguists and social theorists dismissed as irrelevant to the study of language. But do we wish to equate ideology with culture? Might we reserve the term *ideology* for something more specific? In this book I choose to make a distinction between ideology and aesthetic as two modalities of the hypernymic *phenomenology* of communicative practice.[9] This is not to say that phenomenology can be neatly characterized as either ideological or aesthetic: indeed, any apperception of linguistic phenomena partakes of both simultaneously (though, as Sapir observed, far more on the aesthetic and doxic level than on the ideological one). The "proper" is the product of both aesthetic and ideology, one being transformed into the other, from the *suchness of things* inhering within a structure of feeling to a universal theory of the human condition in its broadest sense—and back again. People may make ideological, systematic statements regarding the nature of linguistic action on the basis of how we feel about some genre, or dialect, or term, or joke, etc. Likewise, we may feel at a gut level something about what someone says, and upon reflection or third-person analysis realize that we felt that way based on a previously learned ideological element of the "proper." In this way ideologies may be transformed into aesthetics and aesthetics into ideologies. We may even have aesthetic responses to ideologies and vice versa.

Finally, rather than imagining the ideological and the aesthetic as two poles of a binary opposition, we might think of any apperception as having at its core an aesthetic element with a more or less articulable ideology in a more or less derived and external position, like concentric circles of increasingly more encompassing ideologies surrounding a deep core of affective, embodied response. I would suggest that this is how the phenomenology of proper forms of language work, as the systematic ideological operations of formal grammar and institutionalized schooling built upon the embodiment of what feels correct or incorrect, pure and corrupt, grammatical and ungrammatical, refined and vulgar, *cemmai* and *kochai*. And not incidentally, such judgments about language often correspond to judgments made about entire classes of people.

FROM DIGLOSSIA TO HETEROGLOSSIA

Diglossia

The phenomenological opposition between *centamil* and *kochaitamil* has traditionally been interpreted as a binary opposition between the written and the spoken, between that form of Tamil that has been regularized, grammaticalized, and thereby essentialized as the "pure" (*tuya*) or "original" Tamil and spoken varieties that are considered impure, incorrect—"bent"—by most teachers and commentators.[10] This opposition between the written and the spoken has been theorized largely through the concept of diglossia (Ferguson [1959], Fishman 1967; cf. Britto 1986; Schiffman 1997). Diglossia refers to a division in some languages between two dramatically different varieties, the High (H) and thee Low (L), usually (but not necessarily) corresponding to the written and oral "standards" of a language. Arabic is the canonical example as it involves a written Koranic standard (*al-fusha*) and multiple local spoken "dialects" (*al-'ammiyya*), some of which are mutually unintelligible (e.g., Maghrebi and Levantine; Messick 1993:156). Greek, too, is often cited in its opposition between the literary H *katharevousa* and the L *demotiki* spoken by ordinary folks on the streets and in their homes.

According to Charles Fergusson's original discussion of the phenomena in 1959, diglossia is

> a relatively stable language situation in which, in addition to the primary dialects of the language (which may include a standard or regional standards), there is a very divergent, highly codified (often grammatically more complex) superposed variety, the vehicle of a large and respected body of written literature, either of an earlier period or in another speech com-

> munity, which is learned largely by formal education and is used for most written and formal spoken purposes but is not used by any section of the community for ordinary conversation. (Ferguson [1959]:336)

Interestingly, most of the examples that Ferguson cites for the H form are oratorical: sermons, speeches in parliament, political speeches, university lectures, and news broadcasts—modes of speaking that interpellate (address and thereby instantiate) audiences. Instances of the L form include instructions to servants or workmen, conversation with family members or friends, folk literature, or captions on political cartoons (Ferguson [1959]:329). The H/L opposition corresponds to class and prestige distinctions, to ideas of refinement and corruption, to the classical and the folk, and to temporalities of literary heritage and antiquity versus a contemporary world that is not as pure as the classical ideal. In this original formulation, the opposition between H and L is said to be stable over long periods of time.

Joshua Fishman (1967) extended Ferguson's concept to account for societies with pervasive bilingualism and in so doing complicated the notion of monolingualism as the natural linguistic state of human beings (as Americans, for instance, have a tendency to assume[11]). Human beings in complex societies have multiple compartmentalized roles that have associated with them linguistic *role repertoires*, a range of varieties in terms of either different languages or H/L varieties of the same language (or both). Examples of societies with multiple languages include those societies within what Sheldon Pollock (1996, 2006) called the Sanskrit Cosmopolis, in which Sanskrit was used as the language of state, worship, literature, and the imagination of large-scale cosmological order from around the third to the fifteenth centuries C.E. across a vast territory—from Afghanistan through India and Southeast Asia; all other languages, what Pollock calls vernaculars (e.g., Kannada, Tamil, Bangla, Thai, Javanese, etc.), were used for local or intraregional communication. Similarly, Europe's cosmopolitan languages, first Greek and then Latin, were used for all trans- and intralinguistic intellectual, ecclesiastic, government, and bureaucratic communications during roughly the same period as Sanskrit cosmopolitanism. Vernacular languages (e.g., Italian, French, German, etc.) were used in informal or domestic settings just as their South and Southeast Asian counterparts were.

In contemporary times, many colonial and postcolonial societies of Africa, Asia, and South America are characterized by dual-language systems involving most often Spanish, English, French, and Russian: Fishman cites Paraguay, for instance, in which the majority of the population speaks both Spanish (H) and Guarani (L). In fact, writes Fishman, when we include such situations, "many modern speech communities that are normally thought of as monolingual are, rather, marked by both diglossia and bilingualism if their several registers . . . are viewed as separate varieties of language" (Fishman 1967:32). The difference between them, he thought, was that bilingualism is considered an element of role repertoires of individual speakers whereas diglossia is a "characteristic of linguistic organization at the socio-cultural level" (1967:34). (We will return to this point below.)

One can easily characterize Tamil society this way, as having many bi- (and multi-) lingual speakers and a wide range of different Tamil-internal varieties corresponding to a massively complex sociocultural organization. Sanskrit, though significantly reduced from its supreme status in the Sanskrit Cosmopolis, is used by Brahmin (and other) priests to conduct the worship of pan-Indic, or Brahminical, deities (such as Siva or Vishnu). But more vital in the Tamil world today is English—and to a somewhat lesser though growing extent, Hindi—as the H language for business and elite education. Register shifts within the language are also quite marked in Tamil. Kamil Zvelebil (1963), for instance, suggested that there are three varieties—or "levels"—of Tamil speech: *standard literary* (*centamil*); *standard colloquial*, based on the higher status, non-Brahmin speech of central Tamilnadu (including Madurai); and *substandard colloquial*, which includes all regional and community-based varieties—what higher-status people would generally call *kochaittamizh*.[12] M. Shanmugam Pillai (1965) also made a threefold division but identified what Zvelebil calls *centamil* as both *literary Tamil*, or formal written *centamil*, and *Pandit Tamil*, the oral counterpart to *centamil* spoken in formal addresses (speeches or lectures), which is marked by archaic lexical and inflectional forms and close adherence to written standards (such as Dravidianist oratory). Finally, Britto (1986) identified four varieties: (1) *substandard colloquial Tamil*, (2) *standard colloquial*, (3) *literary Tamil*, and (4) classical or *Pandit Tamil* (i.e., spoken *centamil* or "stage Tamil," *medaitamil*), also based on literary standards (Andronov 1969). "Substandard colloquial Tamil" is composed of all other regional, caste-based, or otherwise marked dialects and features that educated middle-class people tend to drop in professional and mixed contexts (Annamalai 1976, 1980; Gnanasundaram 1980).

A striking discussion of the value differences among H and L varieties in practice is Arokianathan's study of Tamil variation in radio programs (1982). Arokianathan identified three varieties of Tamil in radio programs:

two varieties of H, which he called "literary Tamil," marked by a preponderance of either literary Sanskrit or Tamil terms; and one generic L, called "colloquial," which varied according to program type—"discourses," which involved learned conversations on music, literature, and politics; "plays," both sociological and mythological; and "spots," short commercial and public service announcements and skits. When placed in a diagram (see table 1), Arokianathan's data reveal a striking complementary distribution of literary and colloquial varieties, suggesting the differential values of the several types of spoken Tamil. Dravidianist oratory falls into the place of political plays on the radio and shares features with literary discourses, mythological plays, and commercial advertisements. Political speech is opposed, on the one hand, to musical and religious discourses, which, due to the "classical" traditions of Karnatic music and religious literature, tend to be articulated with a more Sanskrit-based vocabulary. On the other hand, political discourse is also opposed to "colloquial" Tamil, which finds its expression in plays depicting the problems and situations of everyday life.

What is important to see here, though, is that political discourse of the sort that Arokianathan heard in the late 1970s and early 1980s was articulated well within the Dravidianist period. As already mentioned and as will be discussed at length in chapters 1 and 2, some of the earliest stage speakers in the political realm did not use *centamil* in their speeches but rather a Tamil that was not marked off as scriptural. When former Congress leaders C. Rajagopalachari (1878–1972) and Peruntalavar K. Kamaraj (1903–1975) spoke, their language did not share features with mythological and literary discourses and plays.

Diglossic Distortions

Though diglossia has been useful for theorizing semeiosocial difference within complex societies, the periodization of the features of formal oratory suggests something we might otherwise overlook when working solely according to the concept of diglossia, something that points us to an entirely different framing of a linguistically plural situation. The idea of the long-term stability of the concept of Tamil diglossia overlooks the fact that Tamil's deep literary archive was deployed as an element of the Dravidianist paradigm. In this, it is no accident that two of the four examples of diglossic languages that Ferguson cites are those with similarly long literary traditions: Greek and Arabic. Conventional philological dating puts the first literary and grammatical productions of Tamil sometime in

TABLE 1 Tamil Variation in Radio Programs

Program Type	Discourses			Plays			Spots	
Program Topic	Music	Lit.	Rel.	Pol.	Myth	Soc.	Ads	Skits
Sanskrit	x		x					
"Literary" Tamil		x		x	x		x	
"Colloquial" Tamil						x		x

COMPILED FROM AROKIANATHAN 1982:45–50.

the first three centuries of the Common Era, followed by a vast explosion of literary activity associated with the Cola Empire, ninth–twelfth centuries C.E While the major diglossia theorists explicitly discuss historical change, their focus on the stability of the opposition between H and L enables a kind of projection of the current sociosemeiotic of linguistic difference onto the remote past. True, Tamils have long recognized some kind of "proper" or privileged register called *centamil* (Britto 1986:54–106): the term *centamil* is being used to mark off the language of persons of learning as early as fifth- or sixth-century Jain epics like the *Silappathikaram* and *Manimekalai.* But based on the early eighteenth-century observations in Jesuit Constantine Beschi's dual grammars of "Kodun-Tamil" (1831 [1728]) and "Shen-Tamil" (1822 [1730]), the formal characteristics of what was called *centamil* in previous generations changed markedly over the centuries. And, one imagines, so too have the social imaginaries indexed by those characteristics.

In particular, the transformation of political Tamil was linked to the emergence of a movement that projected the antiquity and indeed the beauty of the Tamil literary canon onto the Tamil people as embodied in the leadership of the DMK. The transformation, in other words, was linked to a new nationalism. In this respect, the production of a phenomenological opposition between "pure" and "folk" varieties has its parallels all over the world, from the emergence of the H *Schriftsprache* in German (Ferguson [1959]:327) and even standard (H) French vis-à-vis the patois that characterized the vast majority of spoken practice in France well into the twentieth century (E. Weber 1976:67–94; cf. Errington 2007). Ferguson himself noted that the concept of the H *katharevousa* (vs. the L *demotiki*) in Greece was produced as a superposed "classical" language during the early nineteenth century, a period of cultural renaissance involving the creation of a classical heritage upon which a new Greek nation-state would be produced (Ferguson [1959]:327; Herzfeld 1992, 1996, 1997). In that respect the Greek situation is very much like the Tamil one, in which the ideological and aesthetic superposition of a classical and archaic form onto a wide array of dialectal and register variations serves to emblematize a link to an unbroken chain of cultural and literary continuity. Ferguson's H examples in general were associated with newspapers, universities, parliaments, and political meetings—all fairly recent institutions in Tamil society, indeed, institutions linked to the large-scale transformations we associate with modernity. And as Fishman observed (1967:32–33), whatever else it may have been in the past, the kind of diglossia that we encounter in Tamilnadu is likely to be a function of modern forms of political and national subjectivity in which elements of the language are mapped onto social and situational contexts and also onto new histories.

Finally, the concept of diglossia, especially when compared with bilingualism, as Fishman does, hides the fact that what constitutes a "language" is not only an empirical but also a phenomenological problem. Ferguson intentionally leaves the terms *language*, *dialect*, and *variety* vague and "without precise definition" as he hopes that "they occur sufficiently in accordance with established usage to be unambiguous for the present purpose" ([1959]:325, n. 2). Established usage holds that "dialects" are mutually intelligible varieties of a single language, whereas two varieties are "languages" when they are not mutually intelligible without training—fair enough for an empirical definition. However, two named "languages"—say, Hindi and Urdu—may be mutually intelligible in the oral/aural channel—indeed the same language for the vast majority of speakers—but be written in two different scripts, have different literary traditions, and—critically—be the official languages of two different (and often antagonistic) nation-states, India and Pakistan.[13] Similar relationships hold between Serbian, Croatian, Bosnian, and Montenegrin—a group of mutually intelligible "languages" known (controversially and offensively, for some) as Serbo-Croatian. Such examples give rise to the old linguists' saw that a language is nothing other than a dialect with an army.

Of course the complementary case also troubles the empirical definition of a language. On the one hand, the classically diglossic Arabic contains the pan-Arabian written standard (*al-fusha*), which is intelligible to anyone from Morocco to Baghdad (and on into the rest of the Islamic world literate in Arabic). On the other hand, multiple mutually unintelligible spoken varieties of Arabic (*al-'ammiyya*) are all called "dialects": without training, the vernacular spoken language of the Levant (Syria, Jordan, Israel/Palestine) is mutually unintelligible with Maghrebi, that form spoken in northwest African countries such as Morocco, Algeria, and Tunisia. Furthermore, the degree of intelligibility between *al-fusha* and most Arabic vernaculars—what diglossia theory would call H and L respectively—is similar to that between Latin and contemporary Romance languages such as French or Spanish (which were long ago, along with other Romance localisms, actually diglossic counterparts to the superposed Latin).

Why are *al-fusha* and *al-'ammiyya* a diglossic pair of one language, and Latin and French two different languages? What are two "varieties" of the same language and what are two different languages is not a matter of armies and formal politics anymore; it is linked to a far wider phenomenology of linguacultural worlds, of ethnicities, religions, nations, and the larger temporalities that include the pasts, presents, and futures of a "people" tied to a language.

Heteroglossia

Let us now shift paradigms in our understanding of *centamil* and *kochaitamil*. In the broadest sense we are speaking here about what M. M. Bakhtin (1981, 1986) and M. L. Volosinov (1973) call heteroglossia (*raznorechia*), "the social diversity of speech types" (Bakhtin 1986:263). When viewed from the perspective of heteroglossia, diglossia becomes a fairly limited way of understanding linguacultural difference that elevates the phenomenology of the "proper" to the status of universal theory.[14] Ironically enough for a concept developed for theorizing linguistic difference, diglossia was built upon a fiction of a unitary language containing two forms, written and spoken H and L, with everything else being relegated to the status of dialect. The opposition between the "pure" *centamil* and the "bent" or "vulgar" *kochaitamil* is not so much an empirically describable "superposed" variety as a phenomenological mapping of differently valued registers onto the wide range of differences among people and their associated projects within any society (especially massively complex ones such as that of India). Bakhtin and Volosinov called these varieties *speech genres*:

> Language is realized in the form of individual concrete utterances (oral and written) by participants in the various areas of human activity. These utterances reflect the specific conditions and goals of each such area not only through their content (thematic) and linguistic style, that is the selection of the lexical, phraseological, and grammatical resources of the language, but above all, through their compositional structure. All three of these aspects—thematic content, style and compositional structure—are

> inseparably linked to the whole of the utterance and are equally determined by the specific nature of the particular sphere of communication. Each separate utterance is individual, of course, but each sphere in which language is used develops its own relatively stable types of these utterances. These we may call speech genres.(Bakhtin 1986:60)

The totality of speech genres, writes Bakhtin, represents the living social diversity of any language, that is, heteroglossia.

> At any given moment of its historical existence, language is heteroglot from top to bottom: it represents the co-existence of socio-ideological contradictions between the present and the past, between differing epochs of the past, between different socio-ideological groups in the present, between tendencies, schools, circles, and so forth, all given a bodily form. These "languages" of heteroglossia intersect each other in a variety of ways, forming new socially typifying "languages."(Bakthin 1981:291)

All forms of any particular language, what we call registers or dialects, are each "socially typifying" genres tied to their own specific spheres of production, what Volosinov calls their own socio-ideological worlds—and what we might expand to call socio-*phenomenological* worlds. Each form of language, each genre, is intimately tied to specific kinds of people and arenas (or contexts) of practice, which are themselves indexed and (re-) produced by the deployment of those genres of language. And speech genres are stratified, hierarchically arranged, marked in social life—from oratorical, publicistic, newspaper, and journalistic genres, on the one hand, to the various genres of high literature and poetry on the other.[15]

What we imagine as a unitary language is the phenomenological and practical product of what Bakhtin calls *centripetal* (inward-moving, centralizing) forces by such privileged institutions as the state, the church, schools, the bureaucracy, and universities that freeze the historical *becoming* of a language and create proper modes of speaking and writing. We think of such proper languages of the center as accentless (Volosinov 1973:23–24). In reality, though, accentless language—a standard, as it is called by some—is accentless only by virtue of the establishment of some doxic proper produced by the proprietors of particular, privileged institutional positions in which that form of speech appears unmarked, given, "natural."[16] A genre may be considered accentless only to the degree to which a particular group or class has established itself as the hegemonic group within a particular society. This in fact is the essence of proper language. But at the same time, a language is being churned from the outside-in by *centrifugal* (outward-moving, diversifying) forces that are either antagonistic to the center or blithely indifferent to it as people form new terms, accents, dialects, registers, and even whole new languages. Such heteroglossic contradictions of centripetal and centrifugal forces characterize the natural life of language.

As socially typifying genres, the hierarchical arrangement of speech genres corresponds to definite and hierarchically ordered categories of people. The transformation of our thinking from diglossia to heteroglossia is one that moves from a binary opposition between H and L varieties in some languages to an understanding of linguistic difference that characterizes the natural life of all languages, from "top to bottom," and ties these differences to the socio-phenomenological worlds in which people live. The difference between *cemmai* and *kochai*, then, constitutes a phenomenological distinction of people, of epochs, of national space, and social processes within a massively heteroglossic situation. The Dravidianists' *centamil* revolution embodied *a proper distinction* insofar as the register difference between *cemmai* and *kochai* iconically modeled a distinction between leaders and the people; it embodied *a civilizational distinction* insofar as the purity of the Tamil iconically modeled a distinction between Dravidian and Aryan civilizations; it embodied *an epochal distinction* as *centamil* indexed a time-before, an antiquity to which the current Dravidian nationalism would be tied; and it embodied *a political distinction* as *cemmai* and *kochai* were mapped onto the Dravidianist (e.g., DMK) and nationalist (Congress) political organizations, valorizing the former as autochthonous and stigmatizing the later as alien in a new political field of vernacular democratic practice.

[1]

THE DRAVIDIAN PROPER

ANTHROPOLOGYLAND

On almost any night during my stays in Madurai (a city of approximately 1.2 million souls in the mid-1990s state of Tamilnadu) the sounds of "public" speaking could be heard; someone walking through the streets in the evenings invariably came across several platforms set up, or being set up, for speakers of one kind or another, political, literary, or religious. And there were times, during the election season of 1989, for instance, or during the series of three large political conferences that took place from August to October in 1994 (which will be described in chapter 4), when the cityscape was transformed by political workers into a distinctly nonordinary place, a place organizers attempted to infuse with very particular meanings by use of posters, flags, hoardings (billboards), sixty-foot-tall images of political leaders and ancestors called "cutouts," by tens of thousands—or hundreds of thousands—of celebrating marchers, and—most important for the purposes here—by the saturation of the city's air with the spoken word. That these practices are as prominent as they are in the ordinary life of Madurai, that these meetings appeared to involve not only some vast resources but also deep passions, and that so little had been written in the anthropological (or other scholarly) literature about them despite their importance in everyday life[1] made the prospect of studying political speech, and the communicative practices accompanying that speech, all the more compelling to me.

In October 1992 I began by attending as wide a range of meetings as I could, literary, religious, and political, to begin to get a sense of the genre and formulate a series of specific questions. My days frequently began with a drive around the city looking for and photographing wall posters advertising events. They often ended in late nights attending the events advertised. As so frequently happens in research, the very media in which we attempt to glean information regarding something else—in this case public events—also become our object of study: many of the posters were dazzling pieces of art employing unusual lithographs or letter styles; sometimes multipiece posters of 10 by 20 feet covered advertising hoardings. The very placement of the posters, it turns out, could be a highly political act; and as we see in chapter 5, I found that the semeiotic underlying posters resonated with a wide range of other activities and modes of expressing political life in Madurai.

But in my initial explorations of public speaking I found that the primary speech genre of oratory (*medaitamil,* literally "stage Tamil") varied dramatically depending upon the kind of meeting, the speaker, and the moment within the speech. My reception at the various literary, religious, and political meetings by organizers and other participants was also quite varied in nature. Literary meetings were no problem whatsoever—indeed, most folks were more than welcoming of my interest. One group of teachers and professors associated with a Tamil professor at Thyagarajar College, G. Gnanasambandan, warmly welcomed me into their fold, and I spent many nights accompanying them to the literary debates called *pattimandram* or *pattimandabam.* In these debates on topics of everyday life or literature, two opposing sides argue several rounds, all the while making comic asides and jabs at the expense of their opponents. The "judge" (*neethipathi*) or "mediator" (*naduvar*) of the proceedings finally resolves the debate in a long (one–two hour) summation of the arguments and problems. Gnanasambandan, a master orator and gifted comedian, was famous as a *naduvar* throughout the state and was much sought after for his services in villages and towns celebrating temple festivals, for which the literary debate, along with plays, musical performances of various styles, and religious discourses, also of various genres, had become regular "entertainments" during the proceedings.

It was during these many nights of travel and recording that I came to gain some sense (and understanding) of stage Tamil, some understanding of the structure of an oration, and the first inklings of the status and respect offered to the orator, the man of letters, the speaker of literary Tamil.[2] Gnanasambandan and his core debate team—two Madurai schoolteachers, A. Ganesan and S. Senduran, of the prestigious and historically important Labour and Sethupathi Schools, respectively—served frequently as judges of speaking competitions held among primary and secondary school children in Madurai. During these events, usually held in a schoolroom or auditorium, sometimes in the hall of a bank or on the roof of Madurai's New Century Bookhouse, which sponsored them, children competed with one another in delivering original speeches on given topics.

I found myself warmly welcomed, too, at religious discourses, usually at the Meenakshiyamman Temple, the city's largest and most famous temple. There I attended some dozen or so orations given by local and state-level speakers associated with Saiva Siddhantham, the literary and philosophically oriented organization of Tamil Saivism. On several occasions I attended *katha kalakshepams*, discourses on ethical and religious themes mixed with song and music.

Of the three types of oration mentioned, literary, religious and political, the last, the "public meeting," the *pothukuttam*, proved most problematic from the point of view of an outside observer. Despite the nominal "publicness" of these events, I suddenly came upon a situation in which I was not warmly welcomed; indeed, my presence appeared sometimes to be barely tolerated, and at best ignored. I began by attending a few meetings of the major parties: the Dravida Munnetra Kazhagham, the Dravidian Progress Association (DMK), the All-India Annadurai Dravida Munnetra Kazhagham (AIADMK), the Communist Party of India-Marxist (CPM), and Congress-I. At first I would approach the platform, determine who was organizing the event, request permission to attend and record, and then settle myself next to a loudspeaker for the proceedings, which frequently lasted some six to eight hours. Most meetings began at approximately 8 PM and frequently did not end till 2 AM or later. By the time I left Tamilnadu in 1995, I had attended some 40–50 public meetings.

My troubles began when I attempted to plug directly into the amplification system, called a mic-set, in order to get cleaner audio copies. In the first place, I was in direct competition for outlets on the mic-sets from police and journalists, each of whom were engaging in speech collection, like me, but for various other reasons. In the second place, my request for a "clean" recording of speeches made my activity suspect, "official" in some way (like the police); words recorded for posterity had a way of coming back to people in ways they could not control (as in a newspaper). And finally, what was this white guy doing recording political meetings? Was he a spy? Many people felt that way.[3] My use of recording technology and my habit of writing things down in a little book were unsettling to some, such things and practices being associated with various official kinds of people engaged in the production of records that might, in some unknown way, impact their lives at a later time.

But the concern also had to do with the nature of the "public meeting" itself. As I will discuss in chapter 4 in a description of these events, the term *pothu*, which is translated here as "public," might just as easily be translated as "general," i.e., as a "general meeting" of the party members. The location of the meeting in—and in opposition to—"public" space, its overall spatial structure and orientation, and some of the suspicions my and others' presence evoked, convinced me quite quickly that these meetings were anything but "public" in the common, and Western, sense of the term.[4] Indeed, the very first time I tried to hook into a system for a meeting of (then) DMK speaker Vai. Gopalswamy (Vaiko, of whom I will have much more to say in later chapters, particularly chapter 2), I was politely denied permission and all but asked to leave. I went home with a feeling of failure and a sense that I would be shut out of some of the most prominent events in the city.[5]

This was mid-December 1992. It was clear that political meetings were the most exciting things going on in terms of oratory, but my approach to them was awkward, half-baked. In the meantime, politics had become quite hot all over the country and in Tamilnadu following the 6 December destruction of the Babri Masjid in Ayodhya, U.P., by a mob of thousands of Hindu right-wingers under the unofficial umbrella of the Bharathiya Janatha Party (BJP). The DMK government that had been elected in 1989 was dissolved in January 1991, and in May of that same year Prime Minister Rajiv Gandhi was assassinated in Tamilnadu, allegedly by members of the Liberation Tigers of Tamil Eelam (LTTE), a group at war with the government in neighboring Sri Lanka. Finally, the AIADMK, headed by the former actress J. Jayalalitha and loosely allied (at the time) with the BJP (though formally allied with Congress-I), had come to power in the wake of the DMK's dismissal. Jayalalitha's rule was widely perceived to be as corrupt as that of any administration thus far in Tamilnadu, and the stage had been set for a bitter contest primarily between these two "Dravidian" parties. Ward- and city-level meetings were being held virtually every night on every conceivable topic, from Hindu/Muslim communalism, to an unending series of corruption charges, and to the quickly escalating prices of food staples under the economic liberalization and global policies of the Congress administration in Delhi.

My initial foray into the world of political speaking was shot through with anxiety. These meetings were clearly serious business conducted by some tough men engaged in the production of political power; they were not the same as "religious" or "literary" gatherings, which were phenomenologically cordoned off from the hard reality of a fist-and-knife struggle for advantage. They also involved the collection and distribution of vast sums of money, some of this not entirely legitimate. Considering the proprietary fashion in which political meetings were held and the emotional tensions that infused the air in them, I began to avoid going to them, and I started to internalize what I believed others might be thinking of me. Other than attending a number of literary meetings with my new friends, I spent some weeks loitering with neighborhood acquaintances in teashops, playing board games, and cultivating relationships outside the sphere of my research responsibilities. I knew I could not simply just show up at one of these meetings; I needed to know people who would invite me to their events. But I resisted going to party offices and introducing myself for a number of reasons, not the least of which was that I did not have official permission to study "politics" per se, and I was already aware that my activities were being monitored by the authorities (see note 5). I, too, began to feel anxiety over having my actions recorded by various "official" kinds of people engaged in the production of records that might, in some unknown way, affect my own life at a later time! At some level I enjoyed the irony. But how, then, was I to study political speech without studying politics?[6]

Many accounts of ethnographic research include the kind of anxieties I've described here. But they are usually followed by the "breakthrough experience," the moment in which the intrepid ethnographer overcomes cultural boundaries, develops a deep rapport with his subjects, and finally gets to the heart of the mystery that had alluded him. As far as studying formal democratic politics is concerned, I cannot claim that the problems I outlined above were ever solved. I never broke through into that storied anthropologyland (Cohn 1987:18–49) where I ask, people tell, and, in the end, I thank some of the many people without whose help I would never be able to have gained the insight I did. In my own private anthropologyland, to one extent or another, the anxiety that characterized those weeks in December 1992 was an almost constant companion throughout my time there, most especially when dealing with politicians.

THE KING, DURAI, VATTAM

But I did manage to move forward eventually. A longtime family friend, S. Shaik Samsudeen, asked if I would care to meet a friend of his in the DMK who was making a name for himself in the party and in Madurai. We will call him the King. The King and his comrade, more than any others, gave me at least some access into the world of public meeting organization and a glimpse of the backstage of such events. I hasten to note that they never violated strict party rules regarding the discussion of aspects of party functioning with outsiders, especially in regard to financial matters (e.g., how much was collected from whom for the staging of a public meeting and the dispersal of such funds)—that information was always announced in due time under official auspices. They were more than willing for me to make tapes of their meetings and have me provide them with copies. They even invited me as a guest to a major party conference in Madurai in which I was allowed into the backstage area reserved for city- and state-level party officers. But there were several situations early on in which one or the other of them would object when I attempted to write something down and then insist that I put my pen and notebook away. So, though I learned a great deal from them, "breakthrough" is hardly the word to characterize any moment in our relationship.

But my association with them was fruitful nevertheless. During the time I moved with the King and his associates, I watched as their names became larger and larger on the posters advertising political events in the DMK, iconically indexing the "greatness" (*perumai*) they were gradually achieving in Madurai as organizers of "big" (*periya*) meetings. By the time I left in 1995 the King had established himself as one of the DMK's most successful and prominent organizers of political events in the city.

The King of Madurai was by day a driver for the state-owned bus corporation (a very good job at the time), and by night a Madurai city- and district-level youth leader within the DMK. He was a beautiful man with a deep, dark, clear complexion, a slim but admirable build, and a winning smile. He was personable, with a commanding gait, and it was easy to understand how he enjoyed the central position he did among so many loyal lieutenants throughout Madurai.

His political partner and friend—whom we will call Durai—had other sources of income about which I was never clear—an omission intentionally cultivated on his part, I believe. It was widely whispered by many that some money lending was going on, but I never really pursued it, partly because of my fear of him. When I spoke with him, often as the butt of his constant joking, Durai—whose physical presence was far less impressive than the King's—always appeared to be scanning his surroundings with that deceptively vacant gaze that is in reality a heightened and acute awareness of the details of the people in his immediate space; it was a look I came to associate with powerful men who took pains to be aware of who was where doing what without making eye contact.

He called me *durai*, "Lord," the Tamil equivalent of *sahib*, which was employed to refer to the white men who formed an upper caste in those parts for a time. But nowadays the word is used sarcastically—a literary trope the ancients called *angatham* (satire), *puhazha puhazh* (the praise that is no praise), *vanja puhazhchi* (the praise that blames). The one time I ever saw Durai startled, in less than complete command of his immediate environment, was when I came back at him with a counter jibe. After he called me *durai* one morning, I asserted that it was not I to whom all the supplicants came, but to him. As I stepped in to jokingly go face-to-face with him, his expression of ridicule and disinterested contempt subtly shifted to vague alarm, and he took a small step backward in order to maintain the same distance between us. His entourage also took a keener interest in our repartee at that moment.

At the time I attributed this sensitivity to matters of personal space to an incident in which Durai had been badly injured some months before, an incident that had greatly increased his name recognition in the party and the city generally. It was said, and newspapers reported (e.g., *Tharasu* 5.4.94), that Durai had been injured in a clash between DMK party men and former but now estranged allies of a breakaway party, the Marumalarchi Dravida Munnetra Kazhagham (MDMK), the Renaissance Dravidian Progress Association. The altercation turned potentially deadly when an *arival*, a heavy sickle used for a variety of agricultural purposes, was allegedly brandished by one of the MDMK men. Durai held up his hands in a defensive posture and received two horrible wounds, with both his thumbs split to the knuckles. His picture appeared in the paper when DMK leader Mu. Karunanidhi—Kalaiñar himself—visited him in the hospital to offer his good wishes for a speedy recovery to one of his wounded soldiers.

Over the remainder of that year and during the next, in 1994–95, I met more of their associates, who also gave me insight into and access to the local political concerns and the staging of street-level events. But it was during my second year of work, after a move to a mixed class/community neighborhood in Madurai we will call Abdulahpuram, that I came in contact with another member of the DMK who helped me understand his world. I call him Vattam, as many people called him and other party secretaries in the 73 wards (*vattam*) of Madurai.[7] Like Durai, Vattam emerged as a leader in his realm through a willingness to commit, and a reputation for, violence. But unlike Durai or even the King, Vattam was a gifted orator, a man seemingly born to engage in politics. Like his leader Kalaiñar, Vattam made a name for himself early on in life, while still a schoolboy, by virtue of his "rowdy" (*raudi*) nature, his verbal beauty, and his organizational skills. Vattam was also a gifted visual and graphic artist, a man who painted banners and hoardings, who designed serial-light boards for the decoration of political events and temple festivals, and who was, or at least had been, a master in the staging of events. In earlier days he was sought out by DMK elders in the city for his skills in all these areas. But when I came to know him in 1994 his light had dimmed.

Vattam's political apogee was during the second DMK administration of Tamilnadu, in 1989–1991. In those days as a ruling party ward secretary, he told me, he would find twenty men waiting for him outside his home in Abdulahpuram every morning, seeking to ask his favor or receive his instructions. Organizers of city-wide events regularly invited him to speak at their meetings, and he was gaining a name for himself as an organizer. His prowess was even indexed by a second wife and family, a sign of his potency and virility (*veeram*) in all matters, and a not uncommon strategy/opportunity for men of power.

But Vattam's meteoric rise may have taken him to greater heights were it not for a crippling alcoholism that had left him senseless and incapable of reasoned judgment or action on too many nights. Though his reputation as a rowdy served him well enough as a functioning ward politician (as it served Durai and many others) it now eclipsed any other name he may have had. Despite this, Vattam had, in my eyes, a formidable natural intellect, a true belief in the rightness of his party, and a love for and loyalty to his leader, Kalaiñar. At his best, when he moved through Abdulahpuram with that same commanding gait that marked the King, when he wore the clean white shirt and *veshti* (*dhoti*) that is the standard uniform of the Tamil politician, and when I heard him speak on stage, I was frequently struck with the thought that Kalaiñar, in his youth, must have looked something like Vattam.

Vattam's Abdulahpuram, too, provided me with a highly complex neighborhood in which Hindus, Muslims, and some Christians lived side by side on the banks of the Vaigai. For my second year of work I had wanted to find a place where I could get to know a wide range of people and observe on a smaller scale the kinds of meetings and other "public" functions I had been attending on a city-wide basis during the first year. Abdulahpuram was perfect. In some of its lanes it looked like a suburban dream. Turn a corner, it was an urban nightmare. Turn again, it looked like a village. Abdulahpuram ranged from solidly middle-class families with multistory homes and rental shops to makeshift mud and thatch houses (*kudicai*) built illegally on the banks of a storm canal. It was an area of recycling and repair, of mounds of paper trucked in to be sorted and bailed, of workshops and sex workers for the lorry drivers passing through. A place of blacksmiths, "eversilver" forges, and weavers. It was also a place of actors and dancers, playwrights and dreamers, transvestites and poets who did not necessarily accept the rules of Tamil *panbadu*, "Tamil culture," unchallenged or at face value. Among these I found companionship and likemindedness. Some of my friends were living on the edge of things. Many had fallen on hard times. My middle-class friends were somewhat horrified by my move to this part of town, but after a few visits and after getting to know some of my new friends, most of them came to see Abdulahpuram differently from how they had believed it to be growing up.

Living there among recycled things and people I took up two other approaches to the study of speech and life in Tamil society: reading newspapers and conducting general interviews. Like anywhere else in the city of Madurai and all over Tamilnadu, men (particularly men) in Abdulahpuram gather at tea stalls early in the morning to smoke, drink tea or coffee, and read the newspaper or listen to a reading of it. The tea-stall owners keep a few papers around that are taken apart page by page, each leaf passed around so one paper can be read simultaneously by a number of people. Frequently, someone will read an article out loud, his recitation sharply marked as the written form of the language—indeed, his language is even marked as "journalese," that form of written Tamil massively influenced by the grammar of English newspapers. There is no mistaking the sound of a newspaper recitation, even by foreign ears like mine. The ritual of early morning reading is often repeated after 6 PM when the evening papers are delivered. In this way, I found, newspapers were a part of the daily rhythm of life in Madurai, like meals, prayers, going to work or temple, or taking an afternoon siesta, activities that vast numbers of people regard as integral, essential aspects of their days.[8] I wanted to know what people were reading, what the sources of their knowledge about the world might be; and so I took to reading and clipping three morning papers (*Dinathandi, Dinamalar, Dinakaran*) and two evening papers (*Malai Malar, Malai Murasu*) every day. The newspaper, of course, also gave me another take on political action in Madurai, one which informs much of what I have to say in general in this work and is discussed in some detail in chapter 5.

I also conducted some fifty in-depth open-ended interviews with people from the neighborhood regarding their sources of knowledge in newspaper and other forms of media (TV, radio, public address systems) and their experiences with and attitudes toward meetings and speaking. These wide-ranging discussions provided insight into the attitudes of people who take part in the meetings as members of their audiences sometimes, but mostly as outsiders who regard large "public" meetings in the middle of busy thoroughfares as nuisances that must be endured, avoided, and/or gone around in their workaday lives. They spoke of noise from loudspeakers, and listening to far-off meetings from their homes by virtue of strings of loudspeaker "horns" strung down their streets and lanes. I found a person who told me about a moment relished when flowers fell and covered the feet of the leader he had just garlanded. And I found another who had given a more durable gift, with his name on it, which, he imagined, adorned his leader's office, where the powerful man could from time to time look upon the gift and remember his loyal supporter. I met a woman who told me she could not speak on stages because she was not educated, could not read, and therefore could not "speak." One man spent an hour passionately discussing how hateful and "vulgar" literary *centamil* was when deployed on the political stage, and another spoke one line in praise of a "vulgar" speaker that clarified a point that had eluded me for two years. In short, my discussions with the people of Abdulahpuram gave me insights into the phenomenology of political practice that I found nowhere else.

THE DRAVIDIAN PROPER

Throughout all of my inquiries, primarily in the literary and political meetings, in discussions with people in Abdulahpuram, and in association with orators, I began to see that the speaker of the kind of Tamil identified as proper oratory (*medaitamil*) ritually embodied a status above that of the nonspeaker. The refinement of his Tamil, his *centamil*, was the primary diagnostic and iconicity of that status.

This was driven home to me one night toward the end of my first year when I attended the annual festival of my neighborhood's Rickshaw Drivers' Workers' Improvement Society, a festival that I attended two more times before leaving for Chicago. In a three-day celebration in which they raised a flag at the corner where they park their vehicles and boiled the sweet, sticky rice called *pongal* to pray for bounty and held a public debate (*pattimandram*) and discussion (*karutharangam*), the relative status of the stage speaker was made crystal clear in a way I had never seen before. Ward secretaries, including Vattam, from all the parties spoke; one of the local doctors even rose up on the stage to speak. And the crowning event was a *pattimandram* by the most famous of all debate speakers, Solomon Poppaiyah. But in three days of events, in perhaps thirty different speeches, not a single rickshaw driver rose to the mic to utter anything to the crowd but a few simple words of thanks to his guests. It was at this event that the "proper" of Tamil oratory was starkly forefronted, how the refinement (*cemmai*) of the language was a massive barrier to voicing one's concerns to a public. The fact of it was that if you could not read you could not speak. And literacy was probably the first of many barriers to speaking.

The use of *centamil* in political oratory is new, though by its very nature it embodies antiquity. In a world in which the concept of the "public" was emerging, Dravidianist politicians in the 1940s and '50s responded to the new situation of independent, democratic India by producing public language on the model of the written word. In doing so, they performed what we might call a "spectacular literacy." It was spectacular in two respects: first, it was a truly spectacular performance meant for a largely agrarian and illiterate population that would have heard the language as coming from a very different world; second, and by virtue of its literary qualities, it embodied a past, a specter of Tamil civilization itself. The people who spoke this new genre embodied that specter. They became Tamil civilization—with all its purity and antiquity intact.

The Dravidianist move was a radical one. Public speech during the independence movement and the Congress period in Tamilnadu had not been substantially different from the speech of everyday life in homes or streets. Pre-1940s political speech was an elite activity but it was not a literary one. Elites spoke to each other, and to their emerging "public" audiences in the independence movement, at first in English and later in dialects of the common register (*kochaitamil*). Older folks and scholars who lived through that period confirmed that orators speaking through conical megaphones basically "shouted" (*kattuthal*) their speeches; they claimed that speech through megaphones was like ordinary Tamil, not marked in any way, certainly not as literary speech.

Three such accounts by privileged respondents here suffice to illustrate this transformation.

Cinna Kuttoosi

Cinna Kuttoosi, an independent journalist and activist associated with Dravidianist politics, spent an hour or so at his room in Triplicane, Madras, describing for me what pre-Dravidian party political meetings were like (22 October 1994). Recalling the meetings of the mid-thirties, he said, "They would make a thing out of tin, like this [*indicates with his hands a conical shape*]. It was called a megaphone. No electricity. They'd hold it up to their mouths, and they'd speak loudly through it":

inru malai
"this evening"
inidattile
"at this spot"
innar peca poranga
"So-and-so is going to speak"

"That's the way they spoke," he said. "Another thing they would do is beat a drum. They would beat a drum called *tappu*; it was called *tappattai*. They would beat the thing along with a megaphone to advertise the meetings that were to occur at a particular place at a particular time. *Dandora pottu* was what this was called."

BB: *ninga cinna payan irukkum pothu megaphone pechchu kettiruppinga, illaiya?*
You would have heard them speaking through the megaphones when you were a little boy, right?

KUTTOOSI: *a*
Yes.

BB: *innikki medaippechchukkum eppadi vittiyasama irukkum?*
How was it different from today's speech?

KUTTOOSI: *athavathu vanthu, oru ragam pottu colvanga*
Well, they'd put their speech to a kind of tune
> *Ithanal cakalamanavankalukku teriyapada num enra:::*
> If all the general public wishes to know about this

appadi nu collittu,
they'd say it like that,
> *innikki malai aru manikki:::*
> This evening at six o'clock
> *tiruvalikkeniyile innar pecurango:::*
> So-and-so will speak at Tiruvalikeni
> *ella varatu:::*

Come one and all.
appadi nu dandora pottu pecuvanga

that's the way they'd speak, beating the drum [*dandora*]
ragam pottu colvanga
they'd say it musically.

Cinna Kuttoosi remembers this speech as *nadaimuraitamil*, morphophonologically and lexically "ordinary" (with some interesting prosodic features). The word for "want/should" in the written form, *vendum*, is shortened to *num* following an infinitive verb (as in *teriyapada num*, "want to know"); the term for "speak" (3 plural, present tense) is *pecukirarkal* in written, and *pecurango* in one variety of spoken, Tamil. The reported speech is even more unusual, though, as each breath group ends with an elongated—and lengthened—vowel, as one would when shouting: the spoken standard for "one o'clock," *oru manikki*, becomes *aru manikki:::*, *innar pecurango*, "So-and-so will speak," becomes *innar pecurango:::*, and *ellam varathu*, "come one and all," becomes the truly odd *ella varathu:::*.

Cinna Kuttoosi claimed that the public address system, the mic-set, which started to become more prevalent in the late '40s, did not change "the speaking arts" (*pechchu kalai*) at all; but it did allow for much larger meetings. Before the mic-set three hundred people at most could attend a meeting and clearly hear what the speakers were saying. After the mic-set, though, speaking became a much more invasive part of urban life. "Before, if you didn't like my speech you could avoid it; now you can't. Now the speech will 'hit' [*mothuthal*] the ears of anyone passing by, of anyone who just happens to be there whether they like it or not. The speakers would say, 'You have to hear what I have to say! Just listen to my words.'"

But there were differences, he admitted: "These days," he said, "people speak without straining. Before they had to shout [*kattuthal*]; only if they shouted loudly could people hear it. They had to strain in order for the people in a larger crowd to hear them, people sitting even a furlong away. . . . They would have to drink soda and speak; drink milk and speak loudly. After the mic-sets came, they began to speak 'technically.' In places where one should speak softly they would speak softly, in places where they should speak loudly they'd speak loudly. Then there came differences among the speakers. He speaks that way, that guy speaks this way. Before everyone spoke only one way, shouting."

S. V. Bhoominathan

A man of approximately forty years experience in various media businesses, from cinema to sound and light work for festivals and political meetings, S. V. Bhoominathan also claimed that the speakers had once "shouted" their words loudly (26 April 1995). He also claimed that there was very little difference between the ordinary speech between two people and the speech of politicians in a street-level meeting. He even more pointedly claimed that prior to the rise of the DMK there was nothing that resembled *medaitamil* at all.

BB: Was there a difference in the speech of those using the megaphone?

SVB: There was no difference. Look at our speech: just a bit louder, that's all . . . just a bit louder . . .

BB: Was it like *medaitamil*?

SVB: Uh-uh—it wasn't *medaitamil*. The coming of *medaitamil*, only after the DMK. After '58 or '59 *medaitamil* came. DMK guys came, see; only after they came did *medaitamil* come. After them—before that no one spoke.

Tho. Paramasivan

Both Cinna Kuttoosi and S. V. Bhoominathan confirmed that whatever was spoken prior to the DMK, it was more-or-less akin to what they called "ordinary speech" (*nadaimuraitamil*); Bhoominathan even claimed that one couldn't call it *medaitamil*, at least not the *medaitamil* heard on stages today. Dr. Tho. Paramasivan claimed that the ordinary Tamil of the first stage speakers—such as Congress leader Perunthalaivar K. Kamaraj (1903–1975) and the founder of the Dravidian movement E. V. Ramaswamy (1879–1973), a.k.a. Periyar ("The Great One")—indexed the speakers' solidarity with their audiences, as Indians as opposed to British. Periyar, the founder of the Dravidian Association (*Dravida Kazhagham*, or DK) and universally recognized intellectual leader of the Dravidian movement generally, was widely described as speaking "vulgarly," his speech marked by the quality of *kochai*-ness. In his rationalist (*pahutharivu*) movement, he stood against the old ways, against caste and gender discrimination, which he attributed to Brahminism and religion in general. And in line with his egalitarianism his speaking voice did not mark him off as someone different *in kind* from his audience, just in age, wisdom, and experience.

According to Dr. Tho. Paramasivan (22 March 1995), public speech of the pre-independence era was like that of a community elder dealing with a problem among younger members of that community:

THO. PA.: The Dravidian movement . . . ah, the Congress movement
was a movement of people from the upper classes.
The speech style of the upper caste is what style, do you know?
A big man
in a *panchayat*—there's the *jati panchayat*, right?

BB: Right, like a *jati panchaya*t.

THO. PA.: When the boys in a town [have gotten into trouble]
okkaranga da, okkaranga da
"Sit down! Sit down!
na colren da
I'm gonna speak."
that kind of a . . .
pacifying kind of speech, right?
It'll be in this kind of style.
nama desa ivvalavu kashtamana idattile irukku
"Our country is in difficult straits;
namella enna ceyya num na . . .
If you want to know what we should do . . ."
it'll be in this style.
Well, the speech of a big man in a *jati panchayat* is like,
enakku ellam teriyum
"I know everything
na colren
I'll tell [you what to do].
ninga ella kobapadathinga
Please don't get angry, everyone.
ippadi ta parkkathinga
Don't just look at it like that.
na collute kelunga
Listen to what I say."
It'll be in that kind of style,
it'll be with the bearing of a big man.

Tho. Paramasivan's sense of how the DK's Periyar and his contemporaries in the Congress Party spoke was similar to Cinna Kuttoosi's: the reported speech in the above segment is remembered as "ordinary," not "written" or "proper." Among many transformations, they nasalize vowels that precede a word-final nasal consonant and drop word-final consonants in general; or they simplify consonant clusters (e.g., *enna* vs. *enral*).

The people of the Dravidian movement, however, with the exception of Periyar, developed a new form of political discourse, and consequently a new relationship of speaker to audience, that would help them to capture power in the mid 1960s; descendants, of sorts, have ruled ever since.

What has been called the Dravidian Movement of Tamilnadu emerged in the beginning of the twentieth century on the basis of a racialist understanding of a millennia-long civilizational complex considered to be independent from the Sanskritic/Brahminical ("Aryan") civilization of North India (a civilization, note, that the British and Indian educated elite considered synonymous with India itself). In the second and third decades of the twentieth century politically active members of non-Brahmin upper castes and classes opposed themselves to what they considered the disproportionate representation of Brahmins in the upper and landowning classes, in the leadership of the Indian National Congress Party, and in government bureaucracy and educational institutions.

While this book is not directed to a detailed accounting of the movement, it is important to note here that the notion of "Dravidian" itself was originally a *linguistic* distinction, a philological discovery first made widely known in the 1856 publication of Robert Caldwell's *A Comparative Grammar of the Dravidian, or South Indian, Family of Languages.*[9] Over the next half-century, the vast ocean of Tamil literary work, continuous from the Sangam age (ca. first–third centuries centuries C.E.), began to be transcribed from palm-leaf manuscripts (which had been passed down from scholar to scholar as family property) into volume after volume of scholarly publication (Venkatachalapathy 2006; Cutler 2003; Sivathamby 1995).[10] The resulting body of texts was gradually transformed into a civilizational canon and became a central sign of an independent ethical universe for the new politicians of the Dravidian South (Ramaswamy 1993, 1997; Venkatachalapathy 2006).[11] As Sivathamby writes of the evolution of the term *Dravidian,*

> A semantic extension (the ethnological connotation) that had come about in the beginning of the twentieth century to a term that had been in existence for only a few decades at that time to denote the linguistic collectivity of South, had enveloped the social and the political consciousness of the Tamils within the next fifty years so much that it becomes the dominant political "ideology" of the region. (1995:14)

The Dravidian canon as such first develops in association with the establishment and production of the neo-Hindu Saiva Siddhantham movement. Modeling the movement on Christianity, as a discrete "religion" complete with established texts, modes of propagation, theology, and ethical *cum* scholarly instruction (Bate 2005), the scholars of Saiva Siddhantham were probably the first to begin using an oral language modeled on the written word. This shift represented a profound transformation in Tamil understandings of textuality, considering that despite having a nearly two-thousand-year-old tradition of textual production, the Tamil notion of the "text" (*nul*) was oral. The relationship of any particular textual artifact (the palm-leaf manuscript, for instance) to the "text" is akin to the relationship Westerners recognize between the musical score and the music; the artifact is merely a residuum of the original phenomenological object, whose reality (for most people) exists largely in performance (Kersenboom 1995; Zvelebil 1992). These new scholars in many ways set the precedent of considering the written as opposed to the spoken word as the basis of their authority. Arumuga Navalar (1822–1876), a Saiva Siddhantham scholar and Hindu activist born in Jaffna, Ceylon, and a monumental figure of the Tamil Renaissance, is considered to be the first practitioner of a new form of public discourse employing elements of *centamil* on stages for his audiences, i.e., *medaitamil* (Bate 2005; Kailasapathy 1986:13; Kailasa Pillai 1955 [1918]; Hudson 1992a, 1992b, 1994; Young and Jebanesan 1995). His impact on intellectual life in the Tamil lands was so great that the decade in which he resided in Madras became known as the Jaffna period of scholarship. By the 1920s this same ideology of language had broadly diffused to the worlds of university and secular literary discourse and criticism (Arooran 1980).

The fateful move the Dravidian speakers made was to transform literary discourse into political propaganda; or, to use Jay Fliegelman's terminology, the model of the spoken word was supplanted by one of the written word (Fliegelman 1993). A journalist and early leader of the Dravidian movement, Thiru. Vi. Kalyanasundaram (1883–1953, hereafter Thiru. Vi. Ka.) was probably among the first to employ this form of Tamil in political discourse in elite political meetings. A pioneer of journalistic writing, he was said to be a master of the short sentence (Meenakshisundaram 1958:19). Frequently cited among a generation of literary thinkers who called for authors to "write as they speak" (Meenakshisundaram 1958:17; Kailasapathy 1986:20), Thiru. Vi. Ka., like other Saivite intellectuals of the day, spoke as he wrote with a lexical and morphophonological style marked specifically as written—a written style that marked his being and thought as ancient. According to an author who knew him personally and heard him speak many times, his speech and person bore an iconic relationship to each other: he spoke as one might imagine the great kings of old to speak, and his being was as noble.

> Thiru. Vi. Ka., with a unique style, was a great master of speech overflowing with beautified emotion. He had the style of monarchy which embraced the ancient Tamil people, a broad and open mind that said "Everywhere is Home, All are Kin," elevated thought with no meanness—puns and verbal tricks danced in his speech. . . . His speech did not exceed the bounds of grammar. . . . Thiru. Vi. Ka.'s speech, writing, appearance, and shadow were all alike.(Sambandan 1997:10)

But though Thiru. Vi. Ka. began speaking this way to public audiences, Ariñar ("The Learned") C. N. Annadurai (affectionately known as Anna, or "Elder Brother"), the first Dravidian chief minister of Tamilnadu, and his successor, Kalaiñar ("The Artist") Mu. Karunanidhi, were the first general practitioners of the new mode within mass politics in the early 1950s. Considered today one of the great political and cultural intellectuals of twentieth-century Tamilnadu, Annadurai gave the appearance of a common man; he frequently spoke on stage dressed in a rumpled shirt and *dhoti*. But though his physical appearance was relatively unimpressive, his speech was revolutionary in its use of the "fine," refined, or "beautiful" register of Tamil, *centamil.*

> Among those marked by a verbal eloquence [*navanmai*] that steals the hearts of the Tamil people, "Anna" was the one who had the greatest impact. Anna utilized the true Tamil Renaissance in his Tamil speaking style. . . . A sweet voice that was never cloying even after listening for a long time; a modest appearance for a genius; an ability to evoke deep ideas with beautiful citations—Anna possessed a quality of annealed ores [*urukki varkkappatta panbu*].(Sambandan 1997:55)

Annadurai's unique "articulation of Tamil nationalism" emphasized "the antiquity of the Tamil language; the antiquity of its kingdoms, the richness and uniqueness of its literature" (Sivathamby 1995:55).

The DMK response to the universal enfranchisement of a public electorate was to develop a form of campaigning—called "propaganda" in English and *pirachcharam* in Tamil—that iconically instantiated this antiquity in decisively modernist terms: DMK public meetings were modeled partly on parliamentary practices and partly on temple festivals. As will be discussed at length in chapter 4, the resulting public meeting was a spectacular bricolage of styles and practices—from loud, colorful, energetic, and ostentatious decorations and musical or dramatic performances, to chief guests who occupied the same spatial and interactional position in these events as deities do in festivals, and, most important, to the literary discourses suggestive of a lecture in a schoool, temple, or university. And the new oratory was no less spectacular: it instantiated the division between the Tamil of literature and the Tamil of the streets, *kochaitamil*, by actually speaking as one would write; the phonology, syntax, and lexicon and poesy of *centamil*, as a radically different speech genre associated with discussing aspects of poetic convention, linguistics, the glorious history of the Tamil language and people, etc., distinguished the speaker of *centamil* as a man of learning, of letters, of intelligence. Now, instead of presenting oneself as an elder in an undifferentiated community of common interest—as Periyar as well as the Congressmen of the independence movement had done—Annadurai and his colleagues in the DMK presented themselves as persons of a different kind, masters of literature, and therefore, masters of a knowledge quite alien from that of the farmers and laborers in a state where few knew how to read or write. Again, as Sivathamby notes regarding these transformations under the leadership of Annadurai:

> In the eyes of the average DMK follower, Annadurai is associated with learning. Most of the statues erected in his honour in the various villages and towns of Tamilnadu show him engrossed in reading a book, presumably "Thirukkural."(1995:59)[12]

Annadurai, in many respects, inaugurates and becomes the embodiment of the democratization of the Dravidianist paradigm. His rumpled appearance and spectacular literacy emblematized a new kind of political being, a common man, in particular a non-Brahmin—the most marked of nonordinary men—a man of the people, an emblem of the people, albeit one who spoke in anything but the *vox populi*.[13] This is the genius of the Dravidian proper, as it instantiated a new and highly elaborate speaking style that simultaneously excluded Congressmen who had cultivated the habitus of big men and community leaders, as Tho. Paramasivan observed: during the period of elite politics in Tamilnadu (ca. 1880s–1940s) educated politicians spoke to each other first in English and then in a common register, in *kochaitamil*; but as soon as the politicians started to move out into the wider electorate they began to employ a speech genre marking them as different kinds of persons by using a language that no one but themselves could speak, *centamil.* Ironically enough for a democratic moment, it also established the Dravidianists as beings of an entirely different kind from the ordinary men and women of the Tamil-speaking lands. Despite deploying a semeiotic of revolution and the uplift of the "backward" castes, the new Dravidianist style of political propaganda actually served to protect the position of (non-Brahmin) privileged castes and classes. It was not merely the ability to read, but literariness in speech, the written model of oral discourse, that became the gatekeeper in Tamil politics, ensuring that no one without the necessary class position and training could participate.

A new "proper" Tamil had been established for the speaking stage.

[2]

THE KING'S RED TONGUE

WE BEGIN this chapter the Tamil way: with poetry. The following poem was written during the Sangam period of the Tamil academies (*sangam*), ca. first–third centuries C.E.:

> Pari! Pari! so many
> red-tongued poets praise
> this king of singular excellence
>
> But not just Pari:
>
> Don't the rains, too,
> play some part
> in protecting the world around here?
>
> (KAPILAR, PURANANURU 107)

The word for "red" (*cen*) in "red-tongued poets" (*cennapulavar*) could just as easily be translated as "fine," "cultivated," "good," "skillful," "beautiful," or even, as George Hart and Hank Heifetz have translated it (2000:73), "eloquent." It is the same root as in *centamil*, "beautiful Tamil." A. K. Ramanujan, in another translation of this poem (1985:125), rendered it as "good red."[1] Perhaps, as a poet himself, he enjoyed the evocation of color in the poem; perhaps he wanted us to think of courtiers whose betel-stained mouths were at once marks of excellence and privilege. Ramanujan's translation is good not only because it delights (a good in itself), but because that flash of red draws our eye to the poets in the court and helps us to visualize them two thousand years ago. Kapilar, the poet, mocks them gently, and mocks the king, too, gently, by focusing on what was probably one of the dominant practices of political communicative behavior in the ancient court, praising the king. We have, in fact, evidence of nothing else: no kings addressing their ministers in the plural. Perhaps the king did that, but we don't know; he is never depicted as such. From the historical *cum* literary record, it is the poets' speech, specifically the poets' songs of praise, that gives us any clue as to the nature of formal political discursive interaction in the Tamil-speaking lands from the Sangam age till just into the British period, when all such things were lost forever and a new beauty was born.

That new beauty is evident in the following poem, in which the king finally speaks. This was written almost two thousand years after the time of Kapilar and King Pari by Sundaram Pillai in the first play of the modern period to be written in Tamil, *Manonmaniyam* (1891). Jeevagan, the king, sings these lines in a coda to a "heroic oration" (*veeravasanam*) he gives to his troops massed before his fortress walls upon the field of muster:

To our mothers, our kin whom well we love,
and good folk of faultless ways,
and to our country have soldiers come;
bringing affliction on us;
he will not stand his scandalous ways,
in line upon line he will scatter and fall,
we will smash him and destroy his honor;
his face will we hit, his guts will we rip,
his waist we break, his head we crack, to dust
and pieces we render him, cleanse his faults
and drink his life, block his way, we wreak
revenge; and now we walk
saying Come!
the drums clamor loudly, Away!
they roar like thunder-black clouds.

MANONMANIYAM (PILLAI 1968:186)

His troops cheer and sing and pound on drums. When Tho. Paramasivan first pointed this play out to me and recited a few lines, he held his arm up in the air in an oratorical gesture, like an orator of Athens or Rome or present-day Madurai:

porkurikkayamey pukalin kayam
The wound of war is a wound of fame!

punnakum pukalin kanney
your wounds will be the Eyes of Praise!

The song, written in an archaic language resembling that of the Sangam age, is sung in a meter called *kuraladi vanjippa*, a folksy, quite common rhythm in the ordinary songs of ordinary people throughout Tamil lands and Tamil time. With a five-syllable foot composed of two short metremes (*nirai*) and one long metreme (*ner*) repeated over and over again, it sounds like a drum beating for marching soldiers. Note in particular the use of the I-person plural ending /*-om*/ in combination with "strong" (effective) verbs whose future stem /*-pp-*/ results in the down-beat /*-pom*/. Tamil scansion uses the names for long and short metremes—which are iconic of the long and short syllables to which they refer—to provide a sense of the rhythm: *nirai* NER *nirai nirai* NER *nirai / nirai* NER *nirai nirai* NER, etc. (lines 7–13):

nirai ner nirai nirai ner nirai
adi -ppom adal kedu -ppom muka
hit$^{\text{-I-pl fut}}$ honor ruin$^{\text{-I-pl fut}}$ face

nirai ner nirai nirai ner nirai
idi -ppom kudal edu -ppom idupp
smash$^{\text{-I-pl fut}}$ guts take$^{\text{-I-pl fut}}$ waist

nirai ner nirai nirai ner nirai
odi -ppom ciram udai -ppom podi
break$^{\text{-I-pl fut}}$ head crack$^{\text{-I-pl fut}}$ dust

nirai ner nirai nirai ner nirai
podi -ppom vasai tudai -ppom uyir
pulverize$^{\text{-I-pl fut}}$ fault clean$^{\text{-I-pl fut}}$ life

nirai ner nirai nirai ner nirai
kudi -ppom vali tadu -ppom pali
drink$^{\text{-I-pl fut}}$ way block$^{\text{-I-pl fut}}$ revenge

nirai ner nirai nirai ner nirai
mudi -ppom ini nada- ppom nodi
finish$^{\text{-I-pl fut}}$ henceforth walk$^{\text{-Ipl fut}}$ turn toward$^{\text{-AvP}}$

nirai ner ner
ena vangu
quote$^{\text{-INF}}$ come$^{\text{-pl IMP}}$

But it is in this speech—at this moment he is actually singing—that the Tamil king, relatively silent for two thousand years, suddenly awakens to find his voice. Think of it: the king is singing to his troops. A high-status being does not address an audience this way, let along sing. It is not done. And to address an audience at all is very rare in premodern Tamil letters. When it happens it is generally done by lower-status beings, frequently women. The classic example of this is Kannaki's appeal to the people of Madurai in the sixth-century epic *Silappathikaram* as she decries the injustice done to her when the king wrongly killed her husband:

Virtuous women who live in this city
Ruled by an unjust king! Listen to this!

(CANTO 19:4–5; PARTHASARATHY 1992:182)

And, shortly thereafter:

Men and Women
Of Madurai of the four temples! O Gods in heaven
And Ascetics, listen! I curse this city. Its king erred
In killing the man I loved. Blameless am I!

(CANTO 21:56–59; PARTHASARATHY 1992:193)

Something has dramatically shifted here, for in *Manonmaniyam* the king's tongue too is now red.

THE NEW RHETORIC

It comes as something of a shock to the Western-educated Indian and Euro-American to realize that nothing like a Ciceronian style of political discursive interaction was ever depicted in Tamil letters until very late in the nineteenth century. The 1891 publication of Sundaram Pillai's *Manonmaniyam* marked the very first time in some two thousand years of continuous literary production that this model of discursive interaction was represented in Tamil. Based on an English epic poem written by Sir Edward Bulwar-Lytton called "The Secret Way" (1866), *Manonmaniyam* was written with the explicit intention of creating a Shakespeare-like play for an educated Tamil audience.[2] Sundaram Pillai explains in his English preface to the first edition that the play "is meant for the study room and not the stage, and it is therefore written in the literary and not altogether colloquial dialect" (1968:17). Perhaps Sundaram Pillai wished to replicate for the Tamil intelligentsia the experience of an English gentleman *silently reading* a Shakespeare play. Such a model of reading was relatively new in 1891 (Venkatachalapathy 1994:278; 2006); and certainly the models of interaction depicted therein were completely unprecedented. And that this text was written for not only a literate but an *elite* audience is suggested when he writes, "Every endeavour has been made so as to regulate the style, as to enable an average Matriculate, not guilty of having altogether neglected his Tamil, to follow the work with ease and interest, *provided he has a good Tamil Dictionary*" (1968:18, emphasis added).

No Marc Antonies. No Ciceros. Nor anything resembling Aristotle's *Rhetoric*—no treatise outlining the "arts of persuasion" was written in all those millennia, until 1949 and the publication of Devasigamani Achariya's treatise entitled simply *Medaitamil,* "stage Tamil" (1987 [1949]:19). Such manuals have been published thick and fast since then, however, including Kovai Kaliyappa's *How to Speak on Stage* (1955), Kumari Anandan's *You Too Can Become a Speaker* (1977), Thamizhvanan's *How to Become an Orator* (1978), Mu. Karunanidhi's *We Will Cultivate the Speaking Arts* (1981), another book with the title *You Too Can Become an Orator* by P. C. Ganesan (1981) along with his *Orate and Achieve Success* (1992), Vi. Ma. Dasan's *Speech: The Bases of Stage Speaking* (1984), A. Ki. Parandhamanar's *To Become a Speaker* (1989), and Arandhai Narayanan's *Come, We Shall Speak on the Stage* (1994). Though they are legion now, no one had ever thought it necessary before recent decades to write such books.

Discussing and comparing a Sangam period poem with *Manonmaniyam* is not to imply that some essential cultural model froze from the first to the nineteenth centuries; indeed there were most likely massive changes during the rise and fall of several important imperial formations in Tamil-speaking lands. But considering the work of scholars describing courtly practice in the Cola courts (ninth–eleventh centuries C.E.) and in those of the Nayakar kings of Madurai (fifteenth–seventeenth centuries C.E.), precolonial models of formal discursive interaction probably more resembled the devotional model of the Sangam age than the model represented here by King Jeevagan's oration (despite the fact that Jeevagan's speech is modeled largely on Sangam age Tamil!). We can quickly cite supporting examples from the Cola period (ninth–twelfth centuries C.E.) *meykeerthi* inscriptions, akin to the Sanskrit *prashasti,* which, as Richard Davis (1985) has described, contrast the king's achievements in violence on the charred battlefield with those of love and just rule in the fertile "parasol landscape" of the homeland. Or consider Daud Ali's (1996, 2004) description of the *ula* genre of Cola courtly discourse, which depicts the king in procession as well as his prodigious erotic "sports" (*lilas*). A kind of "hypertrophied eroticism," in the words of Narayana Rao et al., was in fact the "diagnostic feature" of the praise of kings by Nayakar period poets (1992:62). These examples can be vastly multiplied from the late Sangam into the British periods.

What should be noted here is the implicit model of discursive interaction that is presupposed in courtly praise, a model of interaction involving verbally active poets who proclaim for all to hear their worshipful praise of a relatively silent king. And while the king is represented in various dialogues with others, nowhere does he engage in anything resembling oration, certainly nothing resembling the classical "rhetorical" model of discursive interaction: the single rhetor and the multitude. Indeed, until *Manonmaniyam* the multitude addressed the king.

Why? This is a land with grammar and poetics, and this a land with a well-developed martial tradition. Why had no rhetorics been written? Aren't the "arts of persuasion" and public speaking integral to political action? Ancient and medieval Tamil scholars were among the world's most sophisticated linguists, unrivaled, in fact, until the rise of Western linguistics in the nineteenth and twentieth centuries. In addition to the Sangam period *Tolkappiyam* and the fourteenth-century *Nannul*, they produced a wide range of treatises on poetics and metre (*yappu ilakkanam*), in particular the *Yapparungarakkarikai*, the masterpiece of Tamil prosody (*yappu*), which features hundreds of different named metres. Why one form of virtuosity, in poetics, and not another, in oratorical rhetoric?

In this chapter I demonstrate some of the bases upon which a new model of discursive interaction developed in twentieth-century Tamilnadu and illustrate its production. There were at least two major models of political discursive interaction from which the new ideology emerged. The first, what I here call the "devotional" model, is illustrated by Kapilar's understated comparison between the beneficial effects of the rain and the greatness of the King Pari. Why does he poke fun at poets praising kings and kings being praised? Precisely because it was very serious business. Treatises on poetics and grammar perhaps filled the role of what would otherwise have been a "rhetoric" because the production of verbal arts, not by the leader but by his subordinates, was *the* mode of political verbal interaction throughout Tamil history: to praise well the king with beautiful words (and beautiful music) was the manner in which people participated in the power of the king and thereby gained benefits.

But not just the king—"not just Pari"—poets also praised gods. In both cases the praise is hypertrophied, hyperbolic (cf. Appadurai 1990). It focuses on the superiority of the king or the god, it marks out for special attention the good and powerful deeds done by the powerful entity, and, most important, it expresses a desire on the part of the poet—a fervent desire—to be close to the entity, to participate in his realm of power, and to enjoy its benefits. This tripartite definition of praise—recognition of superiority, praise of actions, and desire to participate in the god/king's realm—is how Richard Davis (1991:7) describes *bhakti*, that form of devotional worship to personal deities that burned across India during different periods in its history (Ali 1996, 2004; Appadurai 1990; Cutler 1987; Davis 1991; Kelly 1988; Peterson 1989; Ramanujan 1992 [1981]; Singer 1972). It can also be translated as "love."

The second source for this new style of discursive interaction is the rhetorical model, which emerges in the late nineteenth and early twentieth centuries and has leaders speak to audiences; it is clearly based on British and American parliamentary discourse, Christian sermons, and English literature. This model can find no more perfect illustration than that provided by Jeevagan in *Manonmaniyam*. We find a discussion of it in Devasigamani Achariya's *Medaitamil* (1949), wherein the "rhetorical" model is first systematically articulated in Tamil (fig. 3). As we will see below in Achariya's and others' treatises on the "arts of persuasion," the model of discursive interaction was explicitly borrowed from orators such as Gorgias and Cicero (as well as Jesus, Abraham Lincoln, Ingersoll, Churchill et al.).

A good illustration of how Achariya developed a Tamil "rhetoric" can be found in his long set of appendices, in which he provides model speeches from the ancients (Cicero, Cato, Socrates, Jesus), the greats of British and American oratory (Benjamin Disraeli, William Ewart Gladstone, Abraham Lincoln), and literature (Shakespeare's Marc Antony)—models you might expect in any rhetoric practorium in the Anglophone world. He also produces translations of Indian speeches in English from the time (prior to ca. 1920) when that was the public language even among independence-seeking Congressmen; and great speeches in Tamil—*none* before 1935—of the first Tamil orators.

As one might expect, the treatise is composed of chapters dealing with such practical issues as how to begin, build, and conclude an argument, how to prepare for a speech, tailoring a speech to one's audience, parliamentary rules of order, using a microphone, and how to avoid disasters to one's honor and name in a public forum. Achariya even specifies the minutia of tongue movements and breathing in his presentation of the familiar "midsagittal view" of the upper vocal tract (fig. 4), a chart several

FIGURE 3 "The author shown finishing a speech." Achariya 1949:96–97.

generations of linguists around the world have memorized and can reproduce on blackboards.

But quickly note what the midsagittal man is saying here: the syllables—*sa, ri, ka, ma, pa, da, ni, ca*—the *do-re-mi*'s of Indian classical singing. Achariya's discussion of breathing here is a long discourse of the *kiramams*

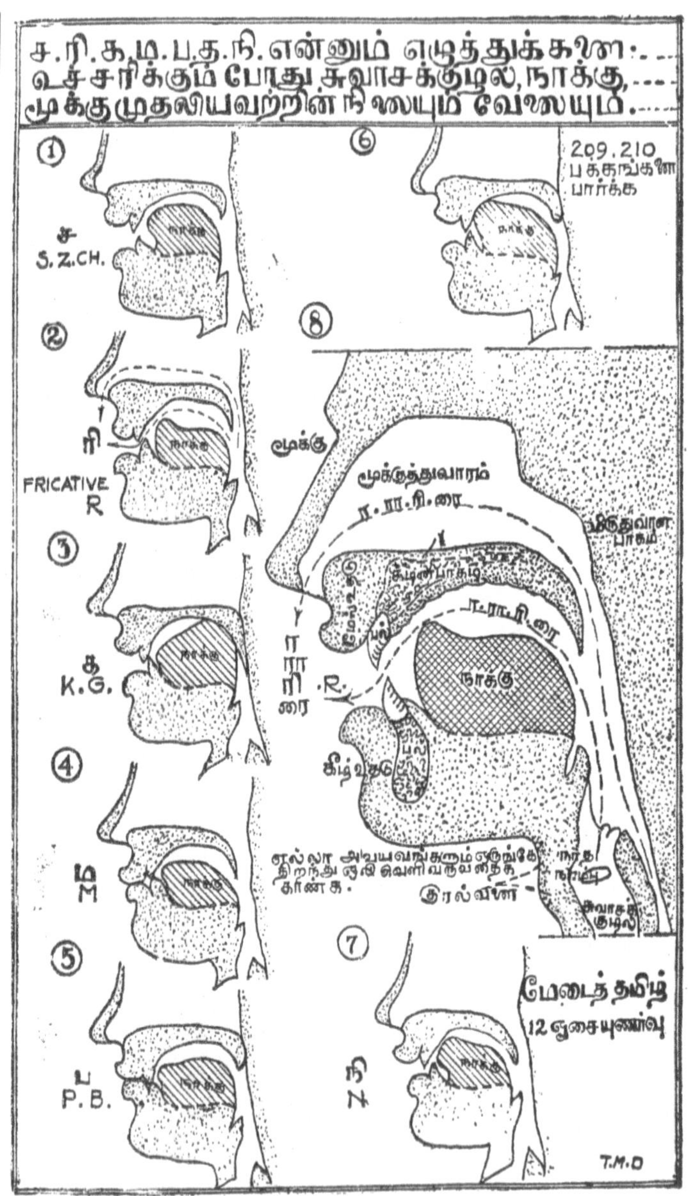

FIGURE 4 Achariya's illustration of the classic midsagittal view of the upper vocal tract. "The state and movement of the windpipe, tongue, and nose when pronouncing *sa, ri, ka, ma, pa, da, ni, ca*." Achariya 1949:209.

TABLE 2 Thiru. Vi. Ka.'s Epistemological Hierarchy

Level of Reality Phenomenology of Mind I	Phenomenology of Mind II	Mode of Truth	Locus of Activity
akam (interior)	*adi* (base)	*unmai* (inner)	*ullam* (heart/mind)
	nadu (center)	*vaymai* (verbal)	*vay* (mouth)
puram (exterior)	*mel* (top)	*meymai* (physical)	*mey* (body)

FROM ACHARIYA 1949:4–5.

of yoga, the right methods of inhaling, holding, and exhaling to yield total physical *cum* spiritual health. And in the introduction, written by the journalist and activist Thiru. Vi. Kalyanasundaram (discussed above in chapter 1), the discussion of public speech begins with an assertion that public speaking is a new art that is necessary for the improvement of society. But shortly after praising the practical aspects of Achariya's treatise, Thiru. Vi. Ka. launches into a long epistemological essay that locates the truth (*vaymai*) of the mouth (*vay*) in an inclusive hierarchy midway between an inner truth (*unmai*) of the heart/mind (*ullam*) and an outer truth (*meymai*) of the body (*mey*), an epistemology found also in South Indian Saivite philosophy, as shown in table 2.

Thiru. Vi. Ka. mentions two different "traditions" (*marapu*) of understanding levels of the mind, called here phenomenologies, and weaves back and forth between them. The phenomenologies of mind listed as I and II represent two different spatial metaphors: "phenomenology of mind I" utilizes the ancient Tamil division between the "interior" (*akam*) and the "exterior" (*puram*) that is iterated in such oppositions as female: male:: essence:substance:: breath:body:: vowel:consonant:: moving:standing:: etc.—all of which can be visualized as concentric circles, one reality contained within the next (Egnor 1978; Daniel 1984; Ramanujan 1973). Phenomenology of mind II appears as a clear vertical hierarchy, base–center–top; but note that it is more an architectural image in which a superstructure is built upon a basic foundation—i.e., the heart/mind—than a hierarchy in which the top is "higher" than the base. Thiru. Vi. Ka. intriguingly blends these two images, placing the base (*adi*), i.e., the heart/mind (*ullam*) and at the inner core and the source of reality, and audible words (*vaymai*) and physical action (*meymai*) in a more derivative, outer, position. The dominant concentric model, in combination with the architectural metaphor, does not radically oppose some kind of semeiotic "meaning" vis-à-vis a physical world of action, i.e., sign vs. substance. Indeed, language finds itself in the center of a continuum of meaning, a place midway between thought and action and in a position to partake of characteristics of both.

The appearance of this epistemological discourse as an introduction to a manual of "rhetorical arts" demonstrates that the ancient Western practices of oratory will be cast anew in a Tamil treatise. Just as the classical Indian scale strikes the Western-trained ear as a haunting mixture of minor and major keys, Achariya-the-bricoleur blends in his treatise a Western model of discursive interaction with a decidedly Indian soul.

THE PROBLEM WITH RHETORIC

As Achariya and Thiru. Vi. Ka.'s discussions suggest, the new politicians did not adopt the Western phenomenology of rhetoric wholesale. Though the form of contemporary stage speech resembles the Aristotelian/Ciceronian style, the logic of the practice does not entirely replicate the logic of what we would call "rhetoric." As far as I know, no Tamil equivalent for "rhetoric" exists (with the exception of various neologisms with myriad possible senses).[3] Widely deployed in the scholarly and public cultural discourses of Western societies in the late twentieth century, but little reflected upon, in practice it is portrayed as self-evident, as if all people throughout all time recognize a function of language called "rhetorical" (cf. Gaonkar 1997).

Let us look carefully at the specific concepts of language function and the models of discursive interaction assumed to accompany "rhetoric." I will make a distinction between two senses of the term, here labeled rhetoric$_1$ and rhetoric$_2$. Rhetoric$_1$ denotes a universal aspect of the phenomenology of language, i.e., ideologies and aesthetics of how language *functions*. All human beings use language to do things in the world, and they all have more or less self-consciously conceptualized understandings of that functionality. Rhetoric$_2$, however, is something far more specific: the historically and culturally contingent understandings of language function that have been developed by Europeans.

Rhetoric$_1$ involves phenomenologies, ideologies, and aesthetics, of "strategic language use" (Silverstein 1979:204). The idea of rhetoric$_1$ as the analytical and prescriptive set of ideas and feelings regarding the effectiveness of language use in achieving social goals is, in one way or another, a universal aspect of language phenomenology. In other words, all human beings have ideologies and aesthetics of how to do things with language. As Kenneth Burke defines it, rhetoric$_1$ involves

> strategies for selecting enemies and allies, for socializing losses, for warding off evil eye, for purification, propitiation, and desanctification, consolidation and vengeance, admonition and exhortation, implicit commands or instruction of one sort or another. (1957 [1941]:262, cited in Crocker 1977:42)

Burke's definition could be expanded to include almost any communicative act whatsoever. In this it fits in with the "rhetorical turn" of our day, which is to expand the concept of $rhetoric_1$ into fields, such as architecture, clothing or industrial design, or science,[4] in which the concept previously had no relevance. But Burke's $rhetoric_1$ appears also to be limited to a conscious "strategy," what I would call the more ideological—rationalized, conscious, systematized—aspects of language phenomenology. And it is not only that—the definition given by Friedrich and Redfield perfectly captures the ideological and aesthetic dimensions of a universally applicable sense of the term:

> By "rhetoric" we mean simply those devices or strategies which, effectively employed, make a "good speech" and a "good speaker." . . . These devices may be acquired by systematic instruction, but more often are unconsidered by the speaker and organized at a subliminal level. Rhetoric impinges on argument since it involves the selection of relevant points, and orders them into a persuasive structured relation; rhetoric also impinges on style and syntax, since it involves the organization of linguistic elements into meaningful and pointed utterance. (1979:412)

$Rhetoric_1$ is here organized both at a conscious level (it "may be acquired by systematic instruction") as a rational ideology of strategic language use (as in the definition provided by Burke) and on a "subliminal level," as an aesthetic of language that we feel, that we know on a "gut" level is good or bad, beautiful or ugly, meaningful or empty.[5] It is clear from all of this that $rhetoric_1$ is about not only "strategies" of language use and criticism, but, more broadly, phenomenologies of language function in general.

This is where we frequently slip between $rhetoric_1$ and $rhetoric_2$. The description of $rhetoric_1$ as the most general conceptualization of "goal-directed and sometimes goal-achieving occasions of language use" (Silverstein 1979:204) in various historically and culturally contingent activities among various peoples in the world does not make any particular claim about what kinds of practices people may engage in and how they may understand their language to function in any of those practices. What kind, or model, of discursive interaction stipulated by any real-time communicative event is highly variable. Indeed, one of the dangers of the universalized concept of rhetoric$_1$ is that the dominant language ideology of Western rhetoric$_2$—a *culturally contingent* phenomenology of language and its *very specific models* of discursive interaction—takes over the work of a more generalized notion of rhetoric$_1$ and is misapplied to non-Western peoples. Through this sleight-of-mind (not generally recognized by the analyst) we misunderstand the actual phenomenologies of language that may be applicable to the particular practices we examine and so misunderstand what it is people believe they are actually doing.

Consider, for instance, Marc Antony's famous invocation of the people of Rome:

> Friends, Romans, countrymen, lend me your ears

His vocative phrase indexes (points to) the actual participants of a speaking event and strategically (rhetorically$_2$) ennobles them. But at the same time it does something so obvious that we frequently overlook it as an element of the meaningfulness of the phrase: the vocative case of the terms "friends, Romans, countrymen," in their interpellation, simultaneously instantiates the oratorical model of discursive interaction in which there is a "rhetor," a single apical figure addressing some multitude (sometimes called an "audience," "the people," "the masses," or "the public," depending upon the specific sociological imaginary). This particular model, the rhetor-multitude model, is not universal, though we tend to attribute it to any act of political language. This, as we shall see, is precisely where the concept of rhetoric$_1$ can be misleading as we conflate it with rhetoric$_2$.

The specific notions of Western folk rhetoric$_2$ can be placed in two broad categories: the *constructivist* and the *pejorative*. The constructivist sense of the term, as in "the rhetorical crafting of the argument," "a rhetorical position," "the speaker's rhetorical strategy," etc., involves a speaker building an argument by use of numerous tactics (including various tropes, metaphor, irony, analogy, etc.). The added information that the adjective "rhetorical" gives to each of those phrases suggests that the communicative act is constructed, crafted with the intention, the hope, that the speaker can calibrate the imaginations of his audience with his own particular take on the world. In other words, the rhetorician attempts to enact an identification of himself and his audience (Norman Cutler, personal communication). The "rhetorical" turn, then, involves an understanding of language in which signs may function in order to effect this mutual calibration between speaker and audience of a vision, of an imaginary, of some other, more "real," reality. When viewing rhetoric constructively, we may call this latter reality a "material reality" of persons, actions, and things that the speaker opposes to some purely ideal semeiotic reality, a world of illusion, an "empire of signs."

In the second view of the term, the "pejorative" sense, "rhetoric" is a lie. "Mere rhetoric," they say. *"He talks the talk, but does he walk the walk?"* The producer of this phrase is very clearly making the opposition between what, say, the president "says" and what he "does." Note that what people "do" in the world of government comprises various kinds of communicative acts—i.e., legislation—that will set up institutions or sanction particular practices that are, or that enable, other forms of communicative behavior. Such laws may be lies in the sense that they construct ideas that may be unrealized in behavior. Both categories, the material and the semeiotic, are equally abstract, equally contingent upon our folk-understandings of what constitutes action on the one hand and language and broader communicative practice on the other.

Both views of rhetoric$_2$—constructivist and pejorative—thus involve the familiar ideal/material dichotomy, the Cartesian division that seems to represent a dungeon, to the farthest walls of which the Western social philosopher has paced like a prisoner (to paraphrase Marshall Sahlins [1976:55]). Both views posit "the crucial nexus of representation in the relationship between reference and reality" (Hill 1992:264), between word and world, between speaking and doing. This dichotomy, it appears to me, is the defining characteristic of Western language ideology that recognizes reference as the sole function of language, which of course it is not (Friedrich 1979a:447–450, 1979b:18–25; Jakobson 1960; Silverstein 1979, 1993). This dichotomy, in other words, characterizes rhetoric$_2$.

The earlier Tamil models of discourses of/with power, such as Kapilar's representation of kingly praise, do not necessarily reference reality and thereby split the ideal from the material, the word from the deed. This is not to say that Tamils did not have a concept of "reference," but rather to claim that the devotional model of language functionality does not privilege the difference between speaking and doing; nor is there some other reality "out there" that the poet is attempting to persuade the king to understand. Praising kings and deities is itself an action that results in a relationship with that powerful entity. It is not "mere rhetoric" (i.e., rhetoric$_2$), in this understanding of language: to speak, in this model, is in and of itself real material action.

In the remainder of this chapter I explore several possible sources for the new model of political discursive interaction in the Dravidian style of democratic political action and demonstrate how it works in several swatches taken from two different speeches. I start with Tho. Paramasivan's theory of the transformation of models of discursive interaction in what he identified as an oratorical revolution that occurred in the transfer of power in Tamilnadu from the Congress to the Dravidian movements. Paramasivan suggested to me in a memorable meeting in March 1995 that Dravidian politicians of the post-independence period modeled their speech explicitly upon that of Jeevagan in *Manonmaniyam*. Following his lead, then, I look at Jeevagan's speech and a moment in a speech by Vai. Gopalswamy (Vaiko), who was then among the most powerful leaders in the DMK and widely thought to be among the best speakers of the land. I do so in order to demonstrate some of the features Paramasivan had in mind when he made that observation, as well as the broader implications such features instantiate in Tamil semeiosocial practice. After the fragment by Vaiko, I turn to look again at more of the speech by N. G. M. Kavitha, our workaday orator for the DMK introduced in the preface, to see how she shifts between Western oratory–inspired rhetoric$_2$ and longer-standing phenomenologies of communicative practice in Tamil.

WAR AND ORATION: *MANONMANIYAM*

Very excited earlier in the day, Tho. Paramasivan had insisted that I show up at his room that evening; he had something important to tell me for my research. I arrived at about 7 PM at the small room he used during the week while teaching in Madurai. His room is usually a center of action, with students and colleagues dropping by and talks of matters literary and political stretching well into the night. But only his student Tamil Kumaran was there this time, and he too gave voice to his literary memory in the conversation that followed.

THO. PA.: Generally, you've noticed the speech of people in the Dravidian movement?
What's it like?
Aaaaaa fortress

According to tradition, they wage war from atop [*unclear*] a fortress.
Right?
Before heading out to war he gives an oration, right?
veerarkaley!, nammudaiya taynattai kakka purapattu
O Heros! To protect our Motherland start out . . .
Notice how the style of this oration is in the speech of the Dravidian movement people.
Whenever you look . . . but you have to look very seriously.
Only then [can you see it]. Going off to the battlefield,
a hero will speak before all of the troops standing in their ranks.
Won't he speak?
Yep.
You can see this for the first time in *Manonmaniyam*.
Jeevagan, to the troops, before they go off to the battlefield . . .
This morning we said it, didn't we, that song?
porkurikkayamey pukalin kayam
"The wound of war is a wound of fame!
punnakum pukalin kanney
your wounds will be the Eyes of Praise!
yarkkithu vaykkum?
To whom is such fortune granted?"
This is not something granted to everyone, a war wound.
tay tirunattai takarttidum nilaiceru
"[One who does not kill] the one who destroys his sacred Motherland
mayittiru vilampan valvu oru valvukol?
Can his life be really called a life?"
A guy comes to destroy the Motherland.
If one doesn't kill him, can one's life be called a life?
This is a heroic oration.
Just like that, there's a speech to speak before death.
The Revolutionary Poet's . . . Bharatidasan's, that . . .
You know that speech?

TA. KU.: *Virukazhiyam.*

THO. PA.: *Virukazhiyam:*
peranbu konthorey! periyorey!
"O, Greatly Beloved Ones! O, Great Ones!
enpetra taymarey!

O, Mothers who bore me!
nallilan cingangal!
O, Good Young Lions!"
What I'm trying to tell you is:
These styles are like
when they're standing about to go off to the battlefield the speech that the leader speaks will mention all the names of the smaller leaders.
To get them excited
you have to say that.
That is the meaning of *avarkaley, avarkaley, avarkaley.*
They're waiting to go to the battlefield.
in order to get all the leaders excited.
avarkaley! avarkaley! avarkaley! avarkaley![6]
Decorations like a fortress;
gestures,
bodily movements;
They hold their hands up like this, Vaiko or Kalaiñar, they hold their hands like this [*gestures like Cicero*].
Ah?
Secondly, Jeevagan comes in *Manonmaniyam* saying "O, Heros!" right?
That very line,
porkurikkayamey pukalin kayam
"The wound of war is the wound of fame
punnakum pukalin kanney"—
your wounds will be the Eyes of Praise"—that line
Vaiko has quoted this line, and Kalaiñar has quoted it as well.
That is a battlefield heroic speech, this.
. . .
Now, what I'm saying, the thing I really want to say is there's these styles, right? These styles
before going off to the battlefield [*unclear*] they deliver a heroic oration
adalerey!
O, Strong Warriors!
purappattu va! [*unclear*] *va!*
Go and come! [*unclear*] and come!

> and all that, when do they speak that speech?
> Halting them in front of the battlefield, stopping them before they die,
> to raise the blood!
> This style is the stage style itself!
> Specifically, the people of the Dravidian movement.

Excited by this breakthrough, Tho. Pa. laughed and clapped his hands: "That's it, Barney, that's it!" In his lesson that night he put together for me a number of things I had been noticing over the some two years of research but had not yet conceptualized that way: the paper and painted wood battlements that frequently deck out the Dravidian party meetings; the names applied to leaders and prominent partymen, such as *Kazhaghattin Porvaal Vaiko* ("Vaiko, The War Sword of the Party"), *Eettimunai Ilamaran* ("Spear-point Ilamaran"), *Theepori Arumugam* ("Roman Candle Arumugam"); the swords and knives occasionally brandished at meetings; the processions, the most organized aspects of which were arranged as military parades; the sometimes warriorlike postures of some of the more prominent local leaders. It all shifted into new focus.

MANONMANIYAM AND VAIKO

When I first heard Vaiko's voice rumble from the loudspeakers after many other very competent orators had finished that night, I wondered if perhaps the public address system operators had surreptitiously turned up the volume; his deep, resonant voice visibly shook the surroundings, saturating the air of the neighborhood. Organizers had set up a bifurcated audience space, with loudspeaker boxes and "horns" strung away from the stage perpendicular to each other along the two branches of Masi Street (west and south) that meet at the corner popularly known for the old (now no more) Madras Hotel. As there had been rumors of Vaiko's imminent defection from the DMK to form a new party, all of Madurai, it seemed, had shown up to witness a historic moment for a historic organization. The crowd that night was astonishingly large, the biggest political congregation Madurai had seen since 1988, when Kalaiñar Mu. Karunanidhi himself—the DMK leader and C. N. Annadurai's political, literary, and oratorical heir—had spoken at that very spot. It rivaled, and perhaps exceeded, the crowd that gathers to witness the annual wedding of Madurai's Goddess Meenakshi to the Lord Sundaresvarar. The stage was decorated to resemble a fortress or royal court of the Nayakar kings (ca. fifteenth–seventeenth centuries C.E.)—in other words, the usual trappings of a Vaiko meeting.

As Vaiko spoke to his audience at the Madras Hotel corner that night, it required only the slightest leap of imagination to see and hear him in some epic time and place, arrayed as a king, addressing the troops massed for battle below his ramparts.

> Like the promise of blessings
> When lightning flashes, when the sky thunders;
>
> like the rising sound
> of ten-thousand birds taking to wing;
>
> with the overwhelming sensation,
> like the rejoicing sea;
>
> with the power of the mighty sword
> which gashes the heart of betrayal;
>
> a crowd swelling unfettered to the horizon and beyond,
> as if to proclaim the ascendancy of the Dravidian Progress Party.

The poesy of this passage is politically potent and worth a close reading:

> *ubagaram ceyvathai* pola
> blessing do$^{\text{-VNacc}}$ *like*
>
> *minnal payum pothu meka mandalam kumuravathai* pola
> lightning leap$^{\text{-FAjp}}$ when cloud system thunder$^{\text{-VNacc}}$ *like*
>
> *paravaikal pattayiram seeradikkum* pothu
> bird$^{\text{-p}}$ ten-thousand wing-beat$^{\text{-FAjp}}$ *when*
>
> *elukinra oliyai* pola
> rising sound *like*
>
> *arpparikkum alai kadalay*
> rejoice$^{\text{-FAjp}}$ wave ocean$^{\text{-adv}}$
>
> *kondalikkum unarvukal*-odu
> swell$^{\text{-FAjp}}$ feeling-*as*
>
> *vanjattin nenjattai keerukinra val veeram kattukinra veerattodu*
> betrayal-^{gen} heart$^{\text{-acc}}$ gash$^{\text{-Ajp}}$ sword virility show$^{\text{-Ajp}}$ virility-$^{\textit{as}}$

tirumpukinra pakkamellam diravida munnetra kazhaghattin
turn$^{\text{-PrAjp}}$ side/all Dravidian Progress Party$^{\text{-gen}}$

eluchchiyai paraisatrukinra vakaiyiley thirandu irukkinra
rising$^{\text{-acc}}$ proclaim$^{\text{-PAjp}}$ manner$^{\text{-loc-emp}}$ crowd/roll$^{\text{-PAjp}}$

Kannu kettiya durattirkku appalum kattukkadankamal 9
eye$^{\text{-dat}}$ go bad$^{\text{-PAjp}}$ distance$^{\text{-dat}}$ beyond/even contain$^{\text{-neg-Avp}}$

As he opens his oration Vaiko describes the sound and sight of the crowd massed below him to begin the first salutation to the leader (*talaivar*) of the meeting—over the next few minutes in the speech he will hail 46 of the individuals and groups assembled that night; each person will be addressed with his name and the III-person plural demonstrative pronoun inflected with a vocative ending, [Name] *avarkaley*! literally, "O, He who is [Name]!" The "introductory salutations" (*munnilai vizhikal*) are perhaps the emotional highlight of any speech, the part about which many will speak for days to come, the moment all who were mentioned will remember their entire lives.

His description of the sights and sounds of the crowd strongly echoes with the opening lines of *Manonmaniyam*, in which four servants are preparing for the arrival of King Jeevagan's family guru, Sundara Munivar, who is coming from Madurai to the new Pandian capital city in Tirunelveli. The fourth servant asks the third what is happening:

III SERV: like the sound of thunder on a street of endless festival
a great sound from the trumpeting of elephants chewing on sugarcane
and the sound of the hooves of horses whose manes have been trimmed
are the strong beats of the drums, saying,
"O Sundara Munivar! Welcome! Welcome!"
Hear the rising sound!
II SERV: The Munivar is said to turn stones into fruits!
IV SERV: What *bhakti*! What a crowd!
Not room for even a sesame seed to fall. I went and saw!

But it is in the salutation to the first addressee this night, to the relatively low-ranking city ward leader and party servant, Mr. Nachiyappan,[7] in which Vaiko makes clear his political intentions. Note well in the following segment the repetition of the word *talaivar*, "leader," for this repetition itself is a demonstration of his humble service to his leader, Kalaiñar:

to the *leader*
of this teeming,
immense conference meeting

—for the *leader* I hold higher than even my life,
the *leader* who directs me, whom I would never forsake
  for even the wink of an eye,
  my precious elder brother, Dr. Kalaiñar—

to the *leader* of this meeting in celebration of his seventieth birthday
  my greatly beloved brother,
  the 38th Ward Party Secretary,
  the esteemed Nachiyappan!

thirand- irukkinra
crowd/roll$^{\text{-PAjp}}$

manattin inta maperum kuttattinudaiya talaivar
conference$^{\text{-gen}}$ this great meeting$^{\text{-gen}}$ *leader*

enatu uyirinum melana talaivar
His$^{\text{-gen}}$ life/more/even high$^{\text{-Adj}}$ *leader*

imaip poluthum nenjil neengamal ennai iyakkikondirukkinra talaivar
eyelash time even heart rid$^{\text{-NegAjp}}$ I$^{\text{-acc}}$ control$^{\text{-Avp}}$ keep$^{\text{-PAjp}}$ *leader*

aruyir annan Doctor Kalaiñar avarkalin elupathavathu
precious-life elder brother Doctor Kalaiñar$^{\text{III-pl-gen}}$ seventieth

piranthanal vila kuttattinudaiya talaivar
birthday celebration meeting$^{\text{-gen}}$ *leader*

peranbukkuriya sakotharar
greatly/beloved/be$^{\text{-PAjp}}$ sibling

muppattiyettavathu vatta kazhagha seyalalar
thirty-eighth ward party secretary

Nachiyappan avarkal-ey!
Nachiyappan$^{\text{III-pl-voc}}$

Lines 1–18 are actually one long and complex syntactic unit, one phrase within a far more massively complex "sentence" that will end about two minutes later with a finite verb, only after he has greeted all of his comrades and the audience.

Vaiko begins with a series of parallel lines (1–6) describing the crowd, each ending with a phonic and metrical echo refracted from the previous line by use of the infinitive *pola* ("like"), the adverb *pothu* ("when"), and the associative ending *-odu* ("with"). He utters a number of isometric pairs, such as *paravaikal pattayiram* ("ten-thousand birds," line 3) and the critically important *vanjattin nenjattai* ("the heart of betrayal," line 7); at the mention of both these dyads the energy of the crowd swelled and the people cheered, for in his deployment of the metrical reduplication *vanjattin*, CVC–CV–CCC / *nenjattai*, CVC–CV–CCV, he "gashed the heart of betrayal" with "the mighty power of a virile sword" and demonstrated to the crowd his loyalty to Kalaiñar. His loyalty to Kalaiñar is reconfirmed in the second moment of the salutation (lines 11–18) by the refraction of the word *talaivar*. The *talaivar* of line 11, "the leader of this meeting," unambiguously refers to Nachiyappan, Madurai's 38th ward secretary for the DMK. But in line 12 *talaivar* subtly refracts to refer to Kalaiñar, *enatu uyirinum melana talaivar*, "the leader whom I hold higher than even my life." (This phrase explicitly resonates with Kalaiñar's trademark salutation to his audiences, *enatu uyirinum melana anbu udanpirappukkaley*, "O, My Siblings, whom I love more than life itself." In uttering the words of Kalaiñar, Vaiko is demonstrating that he resides in the same ethical universe.) Line 13's *talaivar—ennai iyakkikkondirukkinra talaivar*, "the leader who directs me"—again refers to Kalaiñar; but that of line 15—"the *talaivar* of the birthday celebration/meeting"—refracts back again to Nachiyappan, the DMK worker.

Those of us who separate the aesthetic from the political, the spirit from the body, might expect that in such a poetic moment nothing of weight occurred, such things being saved for more important moments later in the speech. But Vaiko achieved his primary objective of the speech that evening—declaring his allegiance to Kalaiñar—all within this first minute—indeed, he had done so by its seventh line. It is exactly in such a poetic moment that the Dravidianists set to work to meet the political demands of the day.

The man to whom Vaiko swore allegiance had been given the title Kalaiñar by C. N. Annadurai, the original Dravidianist orator, by virtue of his oratorical speaking abilities. At the time of this speech, Vaiko was the only person in the state whose name was uttered in the same breath as those of these other two men in terms of political oratory. Perhaps it is not surprising, then, that four months after this speech Vaiko split off from the DMK to form another party, the Marumalarchi Dravida Munnetra Kazhagham ("Renaissance Dravidian Progress Association," or MDMK), and took a large portion of the younger half of the DMK with him. Whereas his name had been seen in wall posters on a line below that of Kalaiñar's, we thereafter saw lithos of him alone on giant posters plastering the walls of Tamilnadu, standing atop paper fortresses of stone and brick, raising his hand to crowds off-picture, speaking into a microphone.

KAVITHA AND TWO MODELS OF DISCURSIVE INTERACTION

Hints of the devotional model appear in Vaiko's speech, but the dominant rhetorical model is clearly that of rhetoric$_2$. Vaiko's salutations presuppose and entail a rhetor–multitude model of discursive interaction in which the devotional theme has been strategically deployed in a highly ideological fashion. That is, he knows precisely what he is trying to communicate and, as a master orator, just how to do it. The cheers he receives from the crowd massed before him index a rather high degree of uptake in accordance with his strategic deployment of artful, red-tongued praise. In the following fragments from Kavitha's speech we see a more complex—in some ways starker—representation of how the two models operate in Tamil oratory. Let us now hear the voice of Kavitha.

The two segments of the speech I present here begin about 13.5 minutes into a twenty-minute oration in which she cycles between praise of her leader, Kalaiñar, the DMK supremo, invective against her political enemies, and criticism of misrule by the then–AIADMK chief minister, Jayalalitha. She takes particular aim at the escalating inflation of prices for basic necessities such as rice and kerosene and at a disturbing rise in reports of gross police misconduct. There are two unusual features of this speech: first, that it is delivered by a woman—a relatively marked category of person in late-night political meetings; second, Kavitha's speech is somewhat better crafted than most and is far more specific regarding the kinds of effects AIADMK government policy was having on the lives of ordinary people.

In the first segment her speech does not surprise us in any way, given that it is a political speech delivered in a DMK meeting in the mid-1990s in Tamilnadu:

[*ca. 13:37*]

In the administration of a woman chief minister, who should be able to

provide protection for women,
wherever one looks murder, robbery, rape, and highway robbery today occur on a regular basis.
What is the reason?
O, my dear gentlemen [*arumai periyorkaley*], laws dealing with the law-and-order problem have been destroyed.
No protection for an IAS woman officer, Chandralekha;
no protection for innocent poor women either.
Viduthalai Rathinam, who spoke before me, put it to you beautifully:
For seven-year-old girls
there is no protection;
neither is there protection for seventy-year-old women.
Wearing khaki shirts, members of the police department are raping women,
Wearing a saffron shirt, a priest is raping women during the administration of the former actress Jayalalitha.
Looking at the Maharani of Corruption, the Queen of Corruption Jayalalitha,
O, Kanji Kamachi! O, Madurai Meenakshi! O, Kashi Visalachi! Athiparasakti? Mother Kaveri? Amazon Warrior?
Just who is being praised?
Is it former actress and Queen of Corruption Jayalalitha who is being praised? A list of corruption charges are being placed before you in stacks and stacks.
Meanwhile
Congress corruption is occurring in the state!
Corruption is occurring. Because I do not have a long time to speak . . .

We will continue the speech in a moment. This segment, I would argue, is rhetorical in the classical sense of the term: note the vocative phrase in line 186, *arumai periyorkaley*, "O, my dear gentlemen," which in and of itself instantiates the oratorical/rhetorical model, the rhetor and the multitude. In this moment of the speech Kavitha makes an argument about realities outside of the immediate speaking environment; it is a rather bald-faced polemical attempt to calibrate the imaginations of members of her audience with her own through artful use of language, to evoke in the minds of her audience an image of misrule and the effects of that misrule on the lives of women. She refers to the widely publicized attack against Indian Administrative Service (IAS) officer Chandralekha, who had been horribly disfigured by AIADMK hired thugs who threw acid in her face;

she refers to the then-raging scandal of a pop-guru (Premananda Swami), with ties to Jayalalitha's lover, who was found to be taking obscene advantage of the young female devotees staying at his *ashram*; and she refers to the prominent rapes of a number of women and girls in police custody. She also attacks Jayalalitha's association with the police. Jayalalitha had spent the previous year and a half courting police departments around the state in grandly staged "awards ceremonies" that resembled the kinds of events we associate with national leaders reviewing their troops, state visits of foreign dignitaries, etc. (described more fully in chapters 4 and 5). In Kavitha's critique of the police she merely draws an opposing perspective on what Jayalalitha had in fact been doing. She uses classic rhetorical$_2$ tropes of irony—a woman leader but no protection for women—and several cycles of analogy between powerful and powerless women, young seven-year-old girls and old seventy-year-old ladies, police khaki and pseudo-religious saffron. Note, too, that Kavitha betrays the lie of rhetorical moves by ruling party AIADMK workers who hail Jayalalitha as a goddess: O, Kanji Kamachi! O, Madurai Meenakshi! O, Kashi Visalachi!

But let us continue with Kavitha's speech and examine to the second segment, which immediately follows the first. This segment complicates her critique of praise practices. We see in the second segment that Kavitha's objection to praising a leader as a deity is not so much about the form of that interaction, but about the particular content and the inappropriateness of praising Jayalalitha that way. At line 201 Kavitha has explicitly broken away from the interactional model in a pragmatic shift of footing by saying, "Because I do not have a long time to speak . . . "

[*ca. 14:55*]

I think I will praise the Golden Leader, the Leader of the Tamil Race, Dr. Kalaiñar, and then take my leave. 202

O, he who fills the hearts of the world's Tamilians, who thrills us with emotions, calling us, "O, My Siblings! O, My Party Siblings!" [*udan pirappey kazhagha udan pirappey*]

O, he whose heart beats to raise us up, who leaps up to run to the Tamil race which suffers here, having fallen into an abyss!

O, Lion of the South Pandi Land, born in the earth of Thiruvarur! 205

O, Sacred Lamp of self-respect, who has a heart that can bear anything! O, Holy Water of the Temple of Tamil!

O, Mast of the Dravidian Flag which no storm will fell! O, Only Earth that circles the Sun!

O, Lightning Light of the Sky that brightens with the colors of the eternal elements!
O, Auspicious Hero who brings life in songs of auspicious deeds!
O, Master, O, Sage of the Threefold Tamil who turned a Kalingapatti banana tree into a stone of teak, who turned valuelessness to value!
O, Creator of the skills of oration which break the backs of weaklings!
O, Leader of the Tamil Race who gives poems with words sweeter than rock candy!
[*ca.* 15:50]

While this segment certainly might be criticized as "mere rhetoric," rhetoric is not the model of discursive interaction that Kavitha inhabits in this moment. Rather it is closer to the devotional model of praise that I outlined above, in the first half of the chapter. Between the two sections Kavitha makes an explicit break in the pragmatic footing of her address—"Because I do not have a long time to speak . . . I think I will praise the Golden Leader"—and in so doing shifts between two different models of interaction. She recalibrates the discursive frame (Goffman 1974, 1983; Silverstein 1976, 1993) and in so doing transforms both her own role in the interaction and that of the addressee. In the first segment she addresses her audience, "O, my dear gentlemen," which instantiates the rhetorical$_2$ model; now her vocatives presuppose and entail a new model of interaction, that of praiser and praised (even though the latter is not actually present). Here Kavitha is not attempting to effect some mutual calibration of imaginations (as she was attempting in the first segment)—rather she is now enacting a particular relationship between herself and her leader, Kalaiñar, master of threefold Tamil, master of oratory, who is red-tongued king to her red-tongued poet. Here her oration is not "talking the talk," as opposed to some other reality of real action, "walking the walk"; rather it is walking the talk or talking the walk; her words are explicitly aestheticized as a form of social action itself that she hopes, as I know from a long interview with her, will result in raising her status in the party, drawing her closer to the source of power, Kalaiñar.

A FUSION OF MODELS

Kavitha's speech is the production of a bricoleur, a person mixing different models of political discursive interaction, the rhetorical and the devotional. She does not merely instantiate some ancient devotional model, some continuous transmission from antiquity in a static cultural universe.

And neither is her practice the result of a colonial imposition of a "rhetorical" model of "rational" political action or some a-cultural logical entailment of democracy. She is in fact an artist, a virtuosa, who creates something new out of available possibilities along with all the other artists of her time. I reiterate that her bricolage of the rhetorical and devotional models of political discursive interaction is very new, and that we would not have seen anything like this on the political stage prior to the 1940s and the rise of the DMK. Indeed, much of this transformation occurs far later than that.

To summarize and further flesh out the history of this transformation begun in the previous chapter, the deployment of "beautiful Tamil" (*centamil*) on the political stage begins with the DMK (founded by Annadurai and Kalaiñar in 1949). But the use of this genre becomes routinized during M. G. Ramachandran's rule (AIADMK) in the 1970s and '80s. MGR was the original cinema idol in every sense of the word (Dickey 1993a; Hardgrave 1975; Pandian 1992a). Suffice it to say here that political culture during the rise and rule of MGR became cinematic and distinctly devotional. Upon his death on 24 December 1987 some thirty-one people committed suicide (Pandian 1992a:17). The astonishing Jayalalitha continued the development of this culture of devotion. A leading lady in many of his films, a minister in his government, she artfully snatched the scepter from her dead lover's hand. During her rule, between 1991 and 1996, political devotion went "over the top." But it did not remain within the AIADMK. Other parties matched praise for praise, act of devotion for act of devotion, particularly the DMK and MDMK. The Dravidianist mode spread throughout the political landscape, beyond the DMK, MDMK, and AIADMK to Congress meetings and even to the CPM, the Communist Party (Marxist), though perhaps without the same intensity as in the Dravidianist parties.

The Dravidianist oratorical revolution was built upon a previous one, in which several politicians associated with the Congress and Home Rule movements had begun to speak in Tamil to audiences in ever larger public meetings during the second decade of the twentieth century. Thiru. Vi. Kalyanasundaram reports in his memoirs that he put forward a resolution during a Madras Presidency Association meeting on 21 April 1918, in Thanjavur, that henceforward all public meetings in Tamil lands must be conducted in Tamil (1982:212–26). On 23 August 1919 Somasundara Bharathi proposed and had passed a similar resolution that Tamil be used for Congress meetings instead of English (Irshick 1969:307). Elite politics in Tamilnadu had been conducted in English prior to that in English-style meetings, employing English styles of oratory. The Tamil of the first political orators, such as E. V. Ramaswamy (the "Great One," Periyar), and early Congress leaders, such as Rajaji or Kamaraj, was different from what we hear today. It was not modeled on the written word, and therefore it did not instantiate a division between the written and the spoken, the literate and the illiterate. And the first Tamil orators were probably far more rhetorical$_2$ than the later Dravidianists of the DMK, far closer to the English models that a previous generation of politicians had cultivated. That first rhetoric of Tamil, penned in 1949 by a Congressman, Devasigamani Achariya, clearly suggests the linkages to Western oratorical tradition.

The new orators of the Dravidianists, such as Kalaiñar and his elder contemporary, C. N. Annadurai, explicitly broke from their Congress predecessors sometime in the 1940s by modeling their speech on some ancient, "pure" written word. This transformation, this oratorical revolution, coincided with the establishment of mass suffrage, the emergence of a mass electorate, and the full-scale politicization of the Dravidianist historical and cultural paradigm. *Tamil is ancient, Tamil is pure, the Dravidians are a great independent civilization.* This paradigm is iconically indexed by the use of a "pure" Tamil on the speaking stage as well as the particular models of discursive interaction imagined to be associated with the speaking practices of that ancient civilization. Strikingly, at the very moment when Tamil purist politicians began to speak on the model of the written word, the vanguard of the Tamil literary movement, especially those writers associated with the publication *Manikkodi*, began to write on the model of the spoken word. Va. Ramaswamy, the editor of *Manikkodi*, stated, "One should write as one speaks," echoing the words of many of his contemporaries, including the short story writer Puthumaippithan as well as the great poet Bharatiyar, who had said the very same words a half-century earlier. "Most of these writers [of the *Manikkodi* group] were romantics, whose individualism, aesthetic commitment and creative zeal called for felicitous, sensitive and unrestricted language and style. To them, pure Tamil was intellectually abhorrent" (Kailasapathy 1986:20). That models of the written and spoken words were the objects of debate and criticism during this period further suggests how language was being functionalized and re-functionalized not only by the political elite but by the Tamil intelligentsia as a whole. Ideas of language itself were intimately involved in ideas about what people were doing politically.

This chapter began in parochializing rhetoric. I did so not to make some facile contrast between the "Western" and the "Eastern" but to clearly delineate the properties of a particular phenomenology of language (that we take too much for granted) so that we might contrast it with others that may be in play. By looking at the specifics of the phenomenology of public language production we get a glimpse of changing understandings not only of language but of new models of political discursive interaction in general. New models of language are, at the same time, new models of interaction, new kinds of political action instantiating new political problems. The Dravidianists borrowed aspects of the ruling phenomenologies of lingua-politics and merged them with ongoing practices, especially those relevant to the cultivation of power in what we might call the religious and political realms (not really separate at all, as we will demonstrate in the following chapters). There were specific bricoleurs who, in their own times and through their own politics, extracted new forms out of existing and emerging models.

We need a rhetoric of Tamil; but we need, too, to beware of the concept of rhetoric$_2$, the implicitly Western ideology and aesthetic of language that sneaks in behind what appears to be a universal rhetoric$_1$, that is, all notions of language functionality. Given that nothing resembling Aristotle's *Rhetoric* was ever written in Tamil until well into the twentieth century—and that heavily influenced by Western rhetorical traditions—and given that no king in over two thousand years of Tamil writing had ever been represented as addressing his troops or his court until the writing of a play in 1891—again based on a tale in an English book—we might beware of a term so powerful and so pervasive in Western thought as to be considered a universal aspect of linguistic practice. And even when Tamil-speaking Ciceros stand upon stages and address their audiences, there are other phenomenologies of language use in play.

This is not to claim that the devotional model of political discursive interaction was carried into the twentieth century by an unbroken chain of transmission from the Sangam period two thousand years ago, through various medieval polities, colonial period little kingdoms (Price 1996a, 1996b; Dickey 1993a, 1993b; Waghorne 1994) to the present. Neither am I claiming some kind of colonial rupture that utterly and fundamentally wiped out precolonial modes of social and political organization as some readings of Nicholas Dirks (1987, 1989, 2001) or Ronald Inden (1990) might argue (cf. Wagoner 2003). On the one hand, politicians of the Home Rule/Independence, Congress, and early non-Brahmin movements followed a model of political discursive interaction that was "rationalized," "Western," "rhetorical." In their shift from English to Tamil sometime in the latter part of the second decade of the twentieth century, early Congressmen and Dravidianists—such as Home Rule activist P. Varadarajulu Naidu, Congressman Kamaraj, and Periyar E. V. Ramaswamy—all responded to an early stage of mass politics by speaking in a common register of the language in political meetings, by speaking in the *vox populi* that emblematized their solidarity. These were the community elders, as Tho. Paramasivan put it, the leaders of Indians or Tamils, but not people different in kind from their followers.

On the other hand, people such as Ariñar C. N. Annadurai, Kalaiñar Mu. Karunanidhi, Periyar's nephew, E. V. K. Sambath, and others associated with the full-scale politicization of the Dravidian movement—specifically the formation of the DMK as a player in democratic campaigning—recreated public political discursive interaction with the fusion of the rhetorical and devotional models of discursive interaction. The devotional model, deployed within oratorical practice of addressing the public, also established speakers as emblems of Tamil literary antiquity, as indexical icons of an archaic civilization, for devotion embodied both ancient courtly practice (*Pari! Pari!*) and the *bhakti* movements that burned across southern India throughout the previous millennium. What is striking about the taking-up of some of these forms is the way in which long-term elements of Tamil devotional practice, the very stance that worshipers take toward the worshiped—toward both gods and high-status men—were appropriated as elements of antiquity *after* the establishment of the rhetorical model of discourse in Tamil by the previous generation. This history violates a kind of unilinear model of modernity in which people move from the traditional to the modern, from the folk to the cosmopolitan. Indeed, in addition to the emblematization of literary antiquity, the Dravidianists also took up practices of the "folk," particularly those practices associated with the worship of deities and village temple festivals, as indexical icons of their Tamilness.

{3}

WALKING UTOPIA

DEMOCRATIC MEETINGS and processions are some of the most important events of South Indian urban life. They are equaled, and occasionally surpassed, only by the largest temple festivals celebrating the greatest deities. The sounds of the political meeting compete on many evenings with those of temple festivals: recorded *bhakti* or cinema music; live folksingers who make the circuit around the state representing the "folk" to urban and rural audiences; or schoolteachers and college professors debating aspects of contemporary social life with references to the classics of the Tamil literary canon. The Madurai soundscape, fading softer and more distant, growing louder and fading again with the shifting winds, is saturated with aural indices of the celebration of the powerful: deities on the one hand, politicians on the other.

This description the sounds of gods and democratic politicians riding the same night winds is not capricious: the frenetic energy that permeates the nighttime air, the loudspeakers blasting song and voice, the immediate spatial boundedness of the events and their face-to-face celebratory character, and the brightly colored, brightly lighted carnivalesque quality of the political event all combine to suggest a temple festival. This similarity between political and religious events results in a common, obvious, and somewhat problematic observation, namely, that the contemporary public meeting is historically based on the temple festival. Early observers of Dravidian meetings explicitly remarked upon the clever propagandistic move of the first organized Dravidian organization, the Dravidian Association (DK), in using elements of the village temple festival as a means to attract large numbers of rural farmers to their events (e.g., Chidambaram 1987, as cited in Hughes 1991). Most agree that political workers in the early electoral campaigns who first employed what we can call the Dravidianist style of public meetings in towns and villages around the state intentionally conducted their meetings on the model of the village temple festival.[1] Among the questions this chapter addresses, however, are: How precisely does the political event resemble the temple festival and why? And from what other domains of practice does the political event borrow? And what does the form these meetings take tell us about the ways that democracy—and modernity more broadly—is structured in relation to far older, premodern aesthetics of power?

These questions are addressed here via three interrelated sets of problems. The first involves how a charismatic form of patronage was routinized (M. Weber 1946:262ff) in the utopian democratic style of the Dravidian parties. The second concerns how a particular politico-religious paradigm emerged in the longue durée of South Indian political practice, was decapitated in the late medieval and early colonial periods, and emerges again in democratic modernity. The third will show how, ultimately, the practical production of this one urban space-time is a function of that routinized charisma and the coiled potentials of that paradigm unfolding in present-day democratic practice. When we examine democratic events to consider the fusion of the political and the religious we find that it is specifically the spatial and temporal elements that resemble temple festivals. This is the case in the iconic and indexical qualities of the embodiment of worship practices (e.g., public transactions of substance between worshiper and worshiped, citizen and leader) and temple festival forms (e.g., processions). It is also the case in the referential elements of the events and the explicit denotation of temple practice in their decorations and in their oratory.

GODS AND KINGS IN MADURAI

The Dravidianists, recall, built an image of a future squarely upon the imagined past of a pure, independent, and rich Tamil civilization whose primary achievements were embodied within a vast literary canon (or rather set of canons; Venkatachalapathy 2005, 2006), as well as an amazing architectural legacy, including the massive and beautiful Chola and Nayakar temples and the Nayakar rulers' seventeenth-century layout of the city of Madurai itself. In the imaginary of an ancient political practice, the current political expression of this civilization was manifested by the procession of kings and gods: in heroic oratory, in visual media such as posters and murals, in the temporary architectural structures erected as stages for orating leaders, and as arches and cutouts that line processional routes. As James Fernandez wrote in another context, they "collectively state what they do not really believe themselves to be and thus leave open what they can become" (1986:265).

To look at one of these events is to look at a future city, sometimes with forty- or sixty-foot-tall images of leaders and political ancestors looming over their palaces and temples built of bamboo scaffolding, palm fronds (*tatti pandal*), or, sometimes, electric lights. To walk through these processions, to attend these political meetings, is to join a utopian procession of revelers celebrating the coming of a new dispensation, a new world where our gods and our kings would be anointed with the aura of these ancient space-times and the power of the world.

I hope here to engage a broader set of concerns regarding the singular forms modernity takes around the world. Milton Singer (1972) first made the observation that modern signs in India and elsewhere tend to be Janus-faced, looking backward and forward at the same time. Singer evoked Mahatma Gandhi's spinning wheel as a perfect embodiment of the modern sign: it evoked the antiquity and purity of Indian tradition at the very moment of looking to the future of the Indian nation-state. Dravidianist processions also embody this quality of being spatiotemporal and processional enactments of a pure Tamil past within the form of a democratic system of patronage.

But we might also wonder if these signs are something more than merely epiphenomenal to the deeper structure of modernity at large (Appadurai 1996), whether the older aesthetic forms, particularly of the experience of powerful entities such as gods or kings, might have a deeper structuring effect on the forms modernity may take. Sudipta Kaviraj makes this case explicitly in regard to political modernity when he writes that

> politicians might ascend to positions of power by punctiliously/unimpeachably electoral procedures, but those in their field of power might extend to them forms of reverence drawn from a traditional, princely repertoire; and they might draw upon these older repertoires themselves. This is not just a mistake of treating one kind of authority with the deference suited to another; actually, this is the characteristic historical process of the previous practice existing within the newer one as "memory," and substantially altering its operation. (Kaviraj 2005b:518–519)

In the case of Tamilnadu, these memories of earlier regal forms are deeply intertwined with worship practices associated with deities small and large.

The Dravidianist political paradigm takes on the forms of earlier state practices, though the memory of such practices may have been transmitted to moderns rhizomically (Deleuze and Guattari 1987) via worship, that is, in a kind of underground transmission of precolonial political forms within the realm of religious practice that had been divorced from the political under colonial and nationalist modernity. Ironically enough from the position of classic modernization theory (e.g., Rudolph and Rudolph 1967; cf. Appadurai 2006), it is under conditions of postcolonial modernity that an Indic paradigm robustly asserts itself again within the realm of formal politics.

And so we also ask what these forms mean to the specific urban experience of people in Madurai, as they are far from merely the external trappings of a form of European modernity, i.e., democracy; rather, they are the underpinning of how a vernacular modernity may operate. Addressing these questions requires an inquiry into the nature of that city and the production of space-time and meaning in cities, towns, and villages generally. This chapter makes such inquiries by considering the production of urban space and time historically, in the processions of powerful beings, both kings and gods, and in the transaction of gifts and words in worship and in democratic public meetings.

SPATIOTEMPORAL PARADIGMS

The old city of Madurai offers a particularly rich site for such inquiries, as its layout maps a spatiotemporal and cosmological diagram that has been the subject of scholarly and popular discussion for decades, even centuries. Today's Madurai is very clearly centered on the Meenakshi Temple, a massive twenty-plus acre complex housing the two main shrines of the goddess Meenakshi (Parvathi) and her consort, the Lord Sundareswarar (Siva). Around the temple swirl concentric streets named for the months of the year (*Adi, Chitirai, Avani Moola*, and *Masi*) when the principal deities parade through the city during the annual festival cycle.

As has been so often described by scholars (Baker-Reynolds 1987; Beck 1976; Breckenridge 1976, n.d.[a], n.d.[b]; Daniel 1984; Kramrisch 1996 [1946]; Lewandowski 1977; Ramanujan 1971; Redfield and Singer 1954; Singer 1991; Wheatley 1969), the layout of Madurai is said to resemble a lotus flower; it follows the pan-Indic model of sacred space based on the *vastu-pursha mandala*, the "model of the first man" cast down to earth, whose various quarters serve as abodes of the gods. The *mandala* is based on the ultimate template, the human body, which serves in a pan-Indic sociosemeiotic as a primary map for everything from temple and the domestic house to city layout; from an essential, feminine internality to corporeal externality; from ideas of growth and decay in nature (Egnor 1978) to the organization of vowels (*uyirezhuththu*, "life letters") and consonants (*meyezhuththu*, "body letters") in Tamil phonology. It is the archetypal "city as sacred symbol" (Wheatley 1969) that instantiates in its very layout a cosmographic diagram. The city streets are themselves a map of the universe in which the center of Madurai is also the center of a galactic polity (Tambiah 1985) that in theory extends to the very edge of the universe.

Yet the contemporary story of Madurai's cosmographic diagram is incomplete and misleading. The Madurai we come across today in granite and terra cotta—as well as in scholarly articles and tourist brochures—is not necessarily the Madurai that was laid out over time, centered by the Nayakar kings of the sixteenth and seventeenth centuries and recentered by the colonial and postcolonial governments. The Madurai that we see today is only half the city it was. The other half was torn down along with the massive walls and even more massive palace complex in the middle of the nineteenth century (Francis 1906:266); these structures had remained from a time when the city shared two rulers, the goddess Queen Meenakshi and the god-like Nayakar King. Madurai has gone through a long process of centering, decentering, and recentering along with a much wider set of transformations in the spatiotemporal ordering of a divine *cum* political world that spanned one empire and set out a paradigm that was denatured under another (Breckenridge n.d.[a], n.d.[b]; Lewandowski 1977). Curiously enough, and perhaps in violation of some commonly held assumptions about such things, it is during the modern democratic period that the old kings and gods once again walk together in the streets of Madurai. Both the political meeting and the temple festival unfold as similar practices conducted according to interconnected logics that have been redeployed in contemporary democratic practice. Specifically, the Tamil nationalist Dravidian parties appropriated a style that would evoke an ancient, pure Tamil civilization by embodying the ancient kings and gods of a Tamil past as the basis of a new, utopian future. The Dravidianists have found the spatiotemporal model for this imagined past and future in the common experience that most Tamil people have of worship and the temple festival.

Organizers of both festivals and public meetings effect this utopian embodiment by imposing single readings, what we will call simplex spatiotemporal epistemes (Daniel 1996), upon the lived places of the city; they instantiate both simplex time-scapes (such as histories and mythologies) and landscapes (e.g., geographies) onto the streets and alleys of Madurai through the use of signs and practices associated with both the worship of deities and the patronage of kings and other great persons.

This politico-religious paradigm, which we might call a kind of spatio-temporal rhizome (Deleuze and Guattari 1987), evolved within the domain of worship before reemerging in the political sphere as a mode of democratic practice. Deities and kings have long been regarded as similar kinds of beings in pan-Indic social and semeiosic practice and in scholarly discussions of courtly homage and divine worship.[2] Breckenridge's discussion of this similarity, based on her work on the Meenakshi Temple (1976, n.d.[a]; cf. also Appadurai and Breckenridge 1976), offers a striking homology between the worship of deities and the patronage of democratic politicians. Linguistic and, more broadly, semeiotic evidence suggests the identity of powerful humans and deities (Breckenridge 1976:127) as the central sovereigns of political entities. Both deities and kings

> live in a temple-palace designated in Tamil as *koyil* [literally the "place," *il*, of the "lord," *ko*]. Both share a rich pool of ritual paraphernalia (i.e., stylus, drum, sceptre, fly-wisk, umbrella, elephant, etc.) which accompany them during their processional rounds of the kingdom which supports them. . . . Both are referred to as omnipresent sovereign (*iraivan*) or universal lord (*swami*). Both maintain a supporting retinue which forms a royal court (*paricanangal*). And finally, the language of service to the deity is in the idiom of bonded servitude (*adimai*). (Appadurai and Breckenridge 1976:191)

"Worship" (*puja, pucai*) of the principal deities in major temples, Breckenridge writes, "might be described as the giving of homage (*ubagaaram*) to the presiding deity in the temple" (Breckenridge 1976:90). The primary festival, the *thiruvizha,* is constituted as a "royal feast" involving worshipers as donors who offer objects and services for the deity such as silk vestments (*parivattam*) and garlands (*malai*), which are redistributed to honored men after the deity has worn them (105). Great men also offer cash donations for the sponsorship of worship. These exchanges cannot be considered "mere" ritual, as some kind of activity apart from the struggle for political and economic power. The nineteenth-century court cases Breckenridge studied indicated that heads of various social entities, in particular lineages or groups of lineages, vied fiercely for the rights over "first honors" (*mutal mariyatai*): being first to give and first to receive objects of worship.[3]

It is in the minutiae of gift exchanges—gifts such as cloth, garlands, and money—that the broader spatial and temporal unfoldings of political and religious events are strikingly similar. Like their counterparts among the lineage heads vying for preeminence in the eyes of the presiding deity, political subordinates to major political figures vie to be considered first among those who do homage to great leaders: their organizational abilities and financial outlays for campaign materials for meetings and processions (e.g., arches, posters, banners, dancers, etc.) are measured against each other. We will see in both event-types—the festival and the democratic meeting—the pragmatic imposition of a single reading, a single simplex set of meanings, onto the plural or multiplex sensibilities of lived place and time (Daniel 1996).

I will now explore the similarities between the two kinds of events and show how a democratic meeting compares with a temple festival in spatial and temporal terms. How do politico-divine events transform the multiplex dimensions of urban lived places into a simplex meaning of space architecturally constructed and choreographed by event organizers? What are the dynamic qualities of the two event-types that enable this transformation? I will describe and discuss what I call utopian architectural visions, in particular the arches and towers of four prominent events held in Madurai from late July to mid October 1994 by four different political organizations: (1) a DMK political procession that took place on 29 July in association with their Madurai Regional Conference; (2) the brief visit by Vai. Gopalswamy ten days later as part of his 1,100 kilometer Kanyakumari-to-Madras "pilgrimage" (*pathai yathirai*); (3) the visit by then–Chief Minister J. Jayalalitha to attend a ceremony to decorate police officers on 19 September; and (4) a Congress Party conference and procession held on 15 October.

Over a two-and-a-half month period, Madurai was transformed several times from one utopian vision to another. The transformations effected by these events followed a general pattern: these large processions, by virtue of their filmic representations of remote locales and civilizational formations, as well as images of a powerful Dravidian past, a past of kings and heroes, instantiated a far wider set of space-times than the temple festival ordinarily does. And the visions of all of the political parties—DMK, MDMK (Vaiko), AIADMK (Jayalalitha), and Congress-I—were similarly architectured and utopianized; only the characters that peopled and ruled those utopias changed.

SPATIALIZING PRACTICES IN TEMPLE FESTIVALS

It is the political procession's mastery of space and time that is central to ceremonial practice. Both the temple festival and the democratic procession are practices that represent and produce power; they both tend toward aestheticized (or emotionally charged) objectifications of space and time, landscape and history. Temple festivals and citywide democratic processions and events also transform the unmarked everyday experience of a city of lived places—a decentered, nonspecific, multiplex, or diffuse set of meanings—into a highly marked, simplex, and epistemically specific space with a tightly woven set of meanings (Daniel 1996:50).

Valentine Daniel calls quotidian space-times by and through which ordinary people live in their workaday lives "ontic." He opposes the ontic to the epistemic, the latter comprising the practical results of official and institutional practice such as the taking of censuses, the mapping of revenue districts, or the writing of history proper, where multiplicities and fractured and incoherent potentials within any society are fixed, "objectified" (Cohn 1987, 1996), and made "real" (objective) in ways that were only potentialities theretofore. Daniel's terms can be modified, however: the temple festival, though arguably a discursive practice that might be termed "ontic" in the sense of providing a way of being in the world, is also an epistemic discursive practice in the attempt by its organizers and supporters—usually a single *jati* ("caste") or group of *jatis* with a shared socioeconomic status—to place a single meaning onto the space of everyday commerce and life (a normally multiplex set of realities). It also, in practice, provides people a way of seeing and, in seeing, controlling.

Diane Mines, who worked in Tirunelveli district of Tamilnadu, describes the village (*ur*) as a contested site, and the temple festival (*kodai*) and procession as a hegemonic activity that includes certain people and excludes others (1995, 2005). Though the main goddess temple in Yanaimangalam, the town in which she worked in the early 1990s, was said to belong to the "whole *ur*," the *ur* constituted by the "mapping out" operation of the festival and procession was composed of the five streets occupied by the three dominant landowning *jatis* (i.e., the Pillaimar, Muppanar, and Thevarmar). Indeed, the "processional political mapping" that is plotted out by the headmen of the dominant groups contradicts the notions of an *ur*'s simplex unity: "The processions that people walk during the ur goddess festivals in Yanaimangalam spatialize distinctions of local power within the ur. Urs like Yanaimangalam, while talked about locally as unified and total residential units, are in fact spatial products of politically contested actions" (Mines 2005:40).

But the village goddess festival is not the only one, and different festivals impose different "maps" onto the *ur*, each map a new volley in an unending series of exchanges, of attempts at epistemic totalizations of ontic place. Members of groups peripheralized by the goddess procession assert themselves in their own festival processions, which cut across the space of the main town, expand the presence of their gods' ceremonial walks, and force the participation of the dominant groups within their festival by erecting a ceremonial arch over the main road in and out of town. The temple stories that Mines heard revealed a situation of constant competition between various groups and localities within the *ur*. Dominant *jatis* work their festivals to make boundaries around the others; subordinate groups, on the other hand, challenge the dominant *jatis* by "cutting across" those boundaries and instantiating alternative space-times by their actions (2005:191–199). Through their festival activities, the small and excluded make themselves big and inclusive: they expand themselves through spatial, verbal, and other gestures that produce "greatness" (*perumai*) for the temple association and its members, a greatness they would not easily produce without the festival (2005:149–150).

Temple festival organizers attempt to epistemically spatialize the ordinarily multiplex ontic places of the *ur*. This does not, however, result in a transformation of ontic place into epistemic space for all involved; rather, a new onticity is temporarily produced, a simplex ontic place wherein the god of a particular group resides at the center of the *ur*. Do all people recognize this new center, this new mapping of space? No. All such political actions are attempts at temporary transformation made by specific people who are more or less successful at imposing their onticities onto the world in which they live. Their success will only be partly determined in their spatializing practices; indeed, true success (though not foolproof) comes at the moment when a group gains political control of the institutions of legitimate violence (the police), social organization and control (bureaucracy), or knowledge production (schools) and is therefore able to instantiate a more or less durable, more or less hegemonic, set of geographical and historical meanings onto the landscape. Such practices instantiate the structural points of cleavage in the *ur* and reveal a process in which place, itself the lived onticity of any particular location, is a contested outcome of epistemic spatializing practices. In the village, walking itself is the operationalizing practice of these space-times.

EPISTEME AND ONTICITY IN MADURAI

As described above, there appears to be a hegemonic epistemic spatialization of the city of Madurai, a single onticity that has been laid down in granite paving stones, embodied in terra cotta, and mediated to us by temple officials, enthusiastic tour guides, and their scholarly counterparts. Streets radiate out from Meenakshi's temple in concentric rings. The seemingly timeless, cosmographic diagram of the city as sacred center appears to be the single episteme, the only way of knowing the town.

But the man moving from home to work along one of the primary ceremonial processional routes, say, West Masi Street, does not experience Madurai as a sacred *mandala*, as a cosmographic diagram. Rather, he experiences specific places that he knows: the Taj electrical store, for instance, where he buys lightbulbs; the Arya Bhavan, where he drinks rich, milky-sweet coffee or eats steamed rice cakes from time to time; the small shrine of a goddess, whose green face and large eyes move him to offer a gesture of worship as he passes. He thinks of his daughter's upcoming marriage and worries about the loans he has accrued from the loudmouthed money-broker who lives in a house along the way. He remembers that he must buy some tomatoes before going home this afternoon as he crosses Nethaji Road, which has a small market down one of its narrow lanes. He recalls uneasily a lover from his youth as he passes her father's house, and he moves on without turning his head. There is no single "meaning" to West Masi Street: rather this lived place, this street, these temples, stores, and houses are the dead bodies of a million lives, given rebirth as millions more in the imaginings of all who live there or pass by. The street is multiontic, a lived place of being, places of many beings.

These same lived places, West Masi Street and the three other Masi streets that encircle the town, become something else altogether during the annual Chitrai Festival in April. During this festival Meenakshi, the queen of Madurai, conducts a *dik vijya*, a conquering of the Lords of the Eight Directions, in an epic battle that takes place along the Masi streets as she circumambulates the city. Now, West Masi Street and the corners of Southwest and Northwest Masi become sites of conflict, a conflict that is written in the *puranas,* that took place in a time of legends and takes place even now. The simplex onticity of contemporary temple authorities, tour guides, and scholars is reinstantiated; the streets are no longer diffuse in meaning, no longer left to the imaginations of each person. They are now seen as specific places charged with a single set of meanings that all will acknowledge despite their varied lived experiences of the streets in their workaday lives. After she has defeated all the lords save Sundareswarar (Siva), whom the goddess accepts as her lord and husband, the two deities circle the Masi streets again, this time as a Holy Royal Family in a massive temple car.

It is this epistemic spatialization of ontic place that characterizes not only the largest temple festivals but also citywide political events. The temple organization and similarly the political party attempt to put a single "spin," at least temporarily, onto the cityscape, to ritually construct and impose a single meaning or set of meanings onto a space that is normally multivalenced and polysemic. The following section examines the means by which people effect such onticities both at the micro level, at the site of the public meeting itself, and at the macro level, in the instantiation of the utopian space-times of the political procession.

THE FESTIVITIES OF "PUBLIC MEETINGS"

Political events effect the transformation of multiplex to simplex onticity in four ways that share elements with the temple festival. First, public meetings take place in the same spaces and times as temple festivals. Second, they have the same properties of substantive "density" (Mines 2005:157–67), or sensory "saturation"—specifically, the saturation of the visual and aural fields—which is directly proportional to a particular organization's or individual's "greatness" (*perumai*), "name" or "renown" (*peyar*), "influence" (*celvakku* or *vaycu*), "weight" (*kanam*), etc. Third, and related to this "saturation," is the "maximal" (Marriott 1976; Mines 2005:165) quality of the interactions that take place during the events: organizers hope to draw into the spaces of the meetings as many people as they can, thereby transacting with a maximal range of people. The primary speaker, too, engages literally as a maximal transactor, a verbal transactor, a giver of loud, powerful words, a speaker of names, and as a recipient of the various gifts—flowers, shawls, money, and other objects or signs of value—that supporters bestow upon him. The greater the speaker, the greater the crowd, the greater the gifts, and the greater the meeting's extension both visually (with lights, arches, palm fronds [*pandals*], posters, etc.) and aurally (with greater amperage of loudspeaker boxes as well as longer and farther-reaching strings of loudspeaker horns extending down streets and into alleys). Finally, public meetings appear to operate according to the territorial operations Mines recognized as characterizing the activity of village festivals, i.e., "cutting across," "centering," and "expanding" (Mines 2005:191–199; see also 1995:345). To these categories I would also add "reoccupying," whereby a particular group, such as a ward- or district-level youth organization, attempts to reoccupy a particular site upon which a rival group has held a prominent meeting and out-do them in staging and postering, in "greatness" or "name" of main speakers and guests, and in otherwise claiming the space as their own.

Sites and Times of Public Meetings

A series of sites in the main (old) town of Madurai are ideal for gathering large crowds. The corners at North and West Masi and at South and West Masi are particularly popular spots by virtue of the broad spaces that open out at their junctions. These corners are primary gathering points for the population of the city to receive *darshan* (literally, "the sight") of Meenakshi when she performs her *dik vijya,* and of both Meenakshi and Sundareswarar when they proceed through the city after their wedding. These corners are also home to several small, though prominent, temples. The corner of West and North Masi, for instance, has a small Pillaiyar (Ganesh) temple that is famous for its elaborate festival. The festival is well known for featuring a weeklong "music and literature" event that includes a series of literary discourses and debates as well as poetry competitions and musical performances of "light music" (cinema) and *bhakti* songs. It is a popular space, too, with other organizations in surrounding neighborhoods and with citywide groups that need a large space. These corners are normally *purampokku,* the "outside," no-one's land. Like the temple festival, the public meeting creates an *akam,* an "interior," in that "outside" (*puram*) space normally fit only for the dumping of refuse and discourse with strangers (Chakrabarty 1991:21–23).[4]

As I mentioned in the beginning of the book, the "public meeting" is "public" only in the European sense of occurring in "public" spaces. But it is not "public" in either the Indian, and especially Tamil, opposition of interiority/exteriority (*akam/puram*) or its orientation to outsiders and audience alike. *Pothu,* the term that has been translated as "public," is not logically opposable to *conta,* "private," "one's own" (adj), as the term would suggest in English. Rather, *pothu* is logically opposable to *tani,* "singularity," or *suya,* "self," "reflexivity"—i.e., "the general" as opposed to "the singular," "the specific."[5] In addition to "public meeting" the term is also used for "general secretary" (*pothuceyalalar*) or "general good" (*pothunalam*). In a very real way the term *pothukuttam,* which, following colonial practice, translates as "public meeting," is just as easily translatable as "general meeting," i.e., a general meeting of the party members. The *pothukuttam,* then, is unlike the *bazaar* ("market") since the enclosed space is not an "outside" where strangers meet but an "inside," an *akam,* that encloses a familial space where everyone is a brother or sister (at least ideally).[6] The *pothukuttam*, indeed, occurs more as an appropriation of public space than as an instantiation of a concept of a "public" space, "free and open to all." Everything outside this ordered space, this cosmos erected amid chaos, this utopian siblinghood, is *bazaar*, the street, the *mela*, or mixing, of everyday commerce. In this respect, too, the public meeting is more like a temple festival with participants oriented toward a common central focus, the god in the latter case, the main guest and speaker in the former.

Saturation/*Perumai*

Mines describes "density" as that quality of "material excess" so prevalent at a temple festival. Piles and piles of food and agricultural produce, mounds of cloth, garlands, and other gifts heaped upon the god-dancers and vow givers, and the excess that literally overflows (*pongutal*) the pot in that quintessential sign of increase, growth, abundance, and prosperity—the sweet, sticky rice *pongal*—all index what Mines calls density, a quality that iconically represents and is directly proportional to greatness (*perumai*).[7]

It is perhaps in this quality of substantive density or sensory saturation that the political event most clearly resembles a temple festival. Temple organizers attempt to saturate a particular space with signs of their presence, of their occupation of that space. Imitating *toranam*, the strings of mango or *neem* leaves hung about a space marked off for a festival, organizers run strings and strings of flags (also called *toranam*) across and above the meeting space: sometimes the flags are so thick that the area seems to have a *pandal*, a thatched roof, covering it. The space is similarly bound off with various arches and serial-light towers representing architectural structures or with images of the party's leaders.

To attend one of these events is to engage in a unique physical experience that is not merely the result of the large crowds. The mic-sets are often turned up beyond the point of distortion (a typical meeting will have a 750 watt mic-set; large ones may go as high as 3,000 watts—for voice, an immense amount of power). In the spaces dominated by the cinema or political music that usually precedes the meetings, the music does not merely enter the ears but dances over the entire body. Objects in the direct line of the speakers vibrate noticeably, and glass fixtures in homes a hundred yards away shake in their frames. Speech can do the same when a speaker brings his voice to crescendo, especially a very powerful speaker like Vai. Gopalswamy, or DMK leader Mu. Karunanithi in earlier days. Listening to a powerful speaker, one's skin ripples with speech, and ears ring for hours.

Organizers begin blasting music early in the morning on the day of an evening event, though technically, and by law, the music should begin only at the time written on the meeting permit obtained from the police. But amps and loudspeakers—the mic-set—are plugged in before anything else is done, and music serenades the workers setting up the stage, serial arches, and decorations. The music itself declares the space to belong to that organization: any attempt on the part of the police to interfere with the mic-set will be challenged, and ultimately overruled by well-connected event organizers.

A DMK meeting held on 20 May 1995 at Dinamani Talkies (corner of Kamarajar Salai and Munichalai Road) provides a case in point. The horns for that meeting had been extended particularly far into the adjacent neighborhoods and down the main streets and alleys. Police had come by several times to turn off the music, a demand to which junior members of the ward organization responsible had acquiesced. When the senior organizer, V. K. Guruswamy, one of Madurai's young masters in the art of public meetings, arrived he ordered the music turned back on. Police confronting him were warned that if they attempted to interfere in the event he would order his cadres to block Kamarajar Salai and Munichalai Road, major arteries with heavy lorry traffic plying between Ramanathapuram and Rameswaram to the southeast and north to Dindigul, Trichy, and Madras. Aware that the meeting held that night was to be a prominent one with "big" speakers from the DMK headquarters in Madras and several thousands expected in the audience, the police backed off, knowing that Guruswamy could and would make good on his threat.

The meeting space, normally a "public" thoroughfare, is reclaimed and reoccupied by the party staging the event, which saturates the area with signs of their occupation and advertisements about the occasion. The ambiguities inherent in the term *pothukuttam* are exploited here by organizers as one institutional authority—temporarily in control of this space—vis-à-vis another, e.g., the police. Organizers are not engaged in a "public" (*pothu*) event. They are engaging in a "general" (*pothu*) meeting of their party in opposition to the public quality of the space. The ambiguity itself opens up a semantic space, too, for contest.

Maximal Transaction

During the meeting itself a crescendo of aural saturation occurs at the arrival of the main guest. When Mu. Karunanithi (a.k.a. Dr. Kalaiñar) arrives at the meeting venue, for instance, the large crowd will let out great cheers as they throng his car. Whoever is speaking at that moment will be interrupted by whichever organizer is at hand to snatch away the microphone and begin crying out salutations and greetings to their guest.

The caller and crowd break into a frenzy as he ascends the steps onto the stage, flashes his famous "smile of history" and waves. The call and responses may last three minutes or more. It is almost the male equivalent of the women's ululation (*kulavai*) as sweet, sticky rice, *pongal*, "overflows" (*ponguthal*) its pot, the quintessential sign of increase and abundance in Tamil lands.[8] Indeed, the call and response is a *pongal* of sound and crowd, truly a sign of the greatness and renown of the individual.

This saturation of the visual and aural field is also accompanied by the giving of gifts, which tend to pile up on the stage as iconic indices of the regard supporters hold for their leaders. As Mines mentions, primary among the gifts bestowed upon the god-dancers (*samiyadi*) are cloth, which is wrapped around them, flower garlands placed over their necks, and silver and gold armbands and medallions; these, of course, are the "folk" analogues of the silk vestments (*parivattam*), garlands (*malai*), and money exchanged by great men and deities in the big temples such as Meenakshi's (Breckenridge 1976). In public meetings, too, flower garlands and shawls (*tundu* or *ponnadai*) are the primary gifts people bestow upon their leaders. The garlands range from the ordinary Rs. 5 ones used in everyday worship of the deity to the oversized *mandirimalai* ("minister's garland") or *MGR malai* ("MGR garland"), named for their suitability for giving to the very highest status recipient. In 1995 such items might have cost Rs. 2,000 or more, a month's wages for a vast proportion of the population in Tamilnadu at that time.

The three other most common gifts are money, torches, and "shields" (*kedaiyam*). In the case of shawls and garlands, a recipient receives the gift with humility and removes it immediately: one almost never sees a person wearing a *malai* after it is given.[9] When a supporter comes to garland a leader, the latter raises his hands up to receive the gift as it is presented, keeps it about his neck just for a moment, and then removes it and hands it to one of the event organizers or drapes it over the back of the chair.[10] Only with the MGR garland does the leader stand a little longer—time enough for the photographers to get a snap and freeze the image for the newspapers and the presenter's photo collection (to be framed and hung in his home along with pictures of ancestors and deities).

These gifts embody quite different spatiotemporal imaginaries of one's relationship to a leader. Whereas the garland is a very personal gift whose sole value lies in the moment of its giving, shawls are given with the understanding that they will be given away to someone else, often immediately after being received. When asked why people gave garlands or shawls, one man provided a poignant account of the choice. He once gave a garland to MGR when the latter had come to town. Moving his hands to indicate falling rain or flowers, he said he wanted to place the garland about his leader's neck and have the flowers fall down and cover his feet. A shawl, he said, didn't have flowers and would only be given away afterward. He didn't want his gift to go any further than its intended recipient. Others, however, frequently mentioned the continuity of the gift of a shawl, of its "usefulness" after the event was over. After removing the shawl or towel, leaders frequently give them back to audience members, who stretch out their hands to receive them, almost as if receiving *prasadam*, the leftover food of gods received during worship.

At the opposite spatiotemporal extreme from the garland is the *kedaiyam,* a "shield" mounted on a wooden stand. *Kedaiyams* are gifts upon which the giver inscribes his own name. Inscribing one's name on a durable gift is common practice, the logic of which entails the recipient thinking of the giver every time the object is used or viewed. The answer to my question as to why people give such gifts was invariably: *peyar irukku, le?* "My name's on it, isn't it?" It is almost always given by higher-status individuals to the highest-status individuals, thus by people who are vying for reception in the relatively more intimate circles of a major leader.

To give someone a *kedaiyam* takes a certain kind of self-confidence. In accordance with the concept of *perumai* (greatness)—of which spatiotemporal extension of movement and name are the iconic indexes—the gift of a *kedaiyam* embodies an imaginary of greater spatiotemporal extension than the garland or shawl; it is a gift that the giver imagines will be placed in a prominent place in the leader's home or office, occupy his sight and mind in coming years, and extend the name of the giver in space and time. In some respects, the *kedaiyam* is a sign of potential renown, of future "greatness" that will emerge from association with the leader. In spatiotemporal terms, it is the opposite of the flower garland, whose utility extends no further than the moment when flowers fall upon the leader's feet.

Spatiotemporal Operations

People arrange themselves both temporally and spatially in a number of different overlapping and mutually confirming operations that together produce a social coherence in terms of both the hierarchical organization of the collectivity assembled for the event and the identity of that organization. Temporally, a hierarchical order is instantiated in two complementary sequences during the political procession: one unfolds over the course of the event, while the other is cyclically reiterated at the beginning of every speech. The first involves the speaking order, which is organized upon the principle that the first shall be last and the last shall be first. In other words, those who speak at the beginning of a public meeting are lower down the hierarchy (generally) than those who speak at the end. This logic is found all over the world in "public speaking" engagements today, but it is striking in Tamilnadu, where it violates the principle of *mutal mariyatai*, the "first honors" given to the big man at the temple, whose right it is to be first in line to receive *darshan* ("sight") from the deity during a festival. The second temporal sequence reverses and confirms the first. The order of address in the introductory salutations (*munnilai vizhikal*) moves from higher-status persons to the lowest, from particular individuals to groups.

Spatial operations also iconically index hierarchical orders within the group assembled. The stage floor itself comprises an iconic, spatial diagram of the power relations within the local organization conducting the meeting and its particular manifestation during that evening (fig. 5). This diagram can be characterized as operating on two rather obvious dimensions or by two oppositions, i.e., front/back and center/periphery. It finds its most immediate expression in the types, or hierarchies, of chairs, and the seating of participants. The very back of the stage space is usually left empty for standing room, but the last rows of chairs will always consist of humble metal folding chairs. Middle rows, while not folding chairs, might contain metal tube-framed armchairs with plastic webbing. But it is the front row that is usually distinct from the rear rows and most internally differentiated. This row will almost certainly contain armchairs, sometimes wooden framed. The front row also embodies the second axis of distinction on stage, that of center/periphery. It is the centermost chair, reserved for the main speaker of the night, that stands out: the Red Chair. The Red Chair is used at many different kinds of functions, such as weddings (usually for the bridegroom), literary events, and other occasions where all honor must be paid to an important guest or participant. The Red Chair is a high-backed, chrome-tube armchair with shiny red upholstery covering a padded seat and seat back. The top of the chair has a fancy crest that peaks at the top with three finial-capped chrome rods. It is, in other words, a throne for the chief guest, and its distinctive qualities provide a distinct center to the stage, around which all of the action takes place.

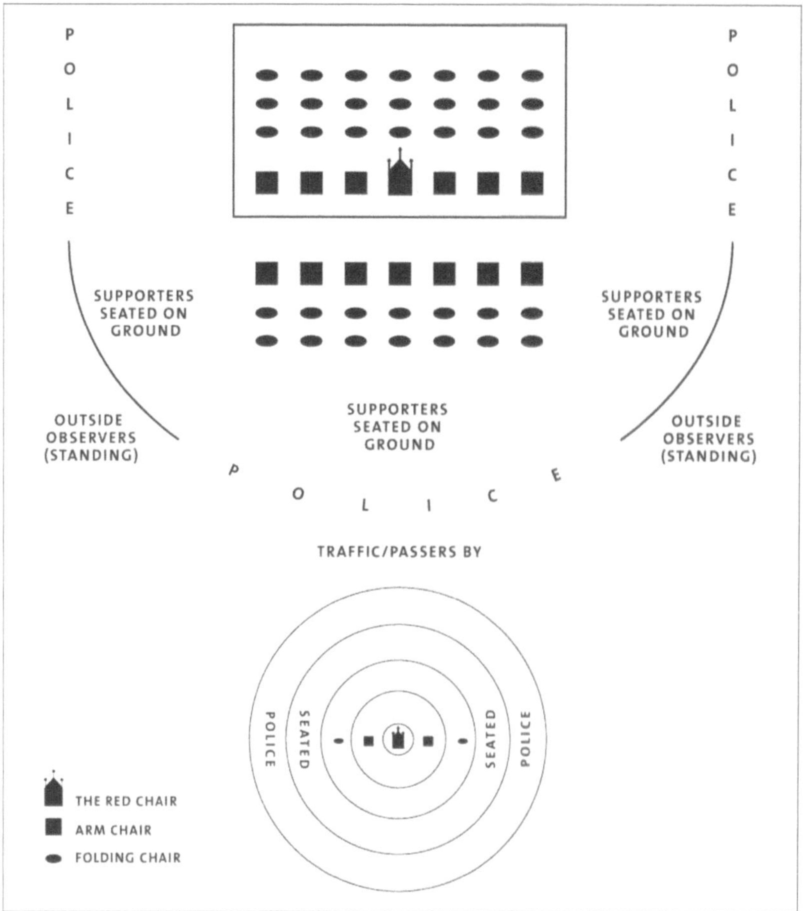

FIGURE 5 Spatial axes of distinction in a public meeting: front–back, center–periphery, *akam–puram*. Line drawing by Mouli Marur.

The front–back and center–periphery distinctions flow off the stage and down onto the street, where they are reversed, and where the external periphery comes into contact with the world outside of the meeting. Of course, another axis of distinction is introduced here: the pan-human opposition top/down. Immediately below the stage are seats placed for other important participants, some of whom speak and some who do not. Here, too, the seating is often hierarchized, armchairs closest to the stage, folding chairs behind them, with most of the audience seated on the dusty pavement just behind the chairs. Snack salesmen with small kerosene torches perched precariously on their trays of peanuts, spiced chick peas, puffed rice, deep-fried *pakkoda,* or the pretzel-like *murukku* carefully seek out spots to place their feet as they make their ways through the crowd.

Finally, the most external periphery of the meetings is defined by the policemen ringing the site. In this external realm, this *puram* to the meeting's *akam*, some of the policemen wear *mufti*—during larger opposition meetings, organizers are convinced that state-level police (Q-branch) or even central government agents (Central Bureau of Investigation or Intelligence Board) lurk in this zone beyond their control. Some of them have tape recorders or have jacked their tape machines into the main amplifier,[11] but most, in uniform, are maintaining a cordon, separating the occupied territory of the public meeting from whatever traffic and passersby may get through the intersection. Beyond the police are outside observers, curious passersby who stand along the sides to listen to a speech and then move on. Others hurry by without any notice whatsoever, or perhaps with irritation at the inconvenience caused by the massive stage and crowd in the middle of a public thoroughfare. The entire diagram can be envisioned as a series of concentric circles that are centered on the occupant of the red chair, as seen in the lower half of figure 5.

WALKING UTOPIA

The public meeting combines many other modes of semeiosocial production of status distinction, greatness, or renown in Tamilnadu, such as weddings, courtrooms, or administrative meetings, university lecture halls, and cinema. And though temple festivals are also quite political—in how organizers exclude or include one group or another, how they center the town in different ways, how a lower-status group cuts across town in order to assert its presence in a higher-status neighborhood, or how groups force the inclusion of other groups by directing traffic through their structures—political meetings are overtly, not covertly, political in the sense of attempting to garner as much support for the party as possible and to raise its profile as high as the organizers can.

Public meetings and their associated processions also tend to incorporate a set of images and signs, often in the form of temporary architectures that are drawn from far wider semeiosocial domains than the temple festival—these are meant to transcend "local" knowledge, "local" history, "local" culture. These space-times may be considered utopian insofar as they weave images of foreign lands and aestheticized Dravidian pasts into images of contemporary and, significantly, future potential polities and histories that will fulfill the promise of the celebratory energies of these political events. Processions move through architectural spaces in which images of the power of the foreign and of the power of the great kings of the Tamil literary canon and history seem to suggest a fantastic potentiality, a qualisign of desire for a coming polity in which the current leaders stand on par with (literal) giants of the past and giants of other lands.

The Towers of the DMK Regional Conference

The procession of the DMK regional conference of 29 July 1994 contained the entire spectrum of images and structures that exemplify these new onticities. It was led off by the state secretary of the DMK youth wing and the unofficial future leader of the party, Mu. Ka. Stalin, Mu. Karunanidhi's son. Stalin, wearing white pants and a white shirt with a black tie, led ranks and ranks of similarly dressed youth wing members carrying the black and red DMK flag, marching in step. The youth wing was followed by a flag brigade of party workers in black pants and red shirts; the women's wing, in red saris; the lawyers' wing, also in white and black; the workers' wing; the literature wing; transportation workers; and finally students. Following these organizations came groups of supporters from all over the state, carrying banners with their ward and district names and salutations to the DMK leader, many accompanied by *karukatham* ("pot-dancers"), *poykalkuthirai* ("false-leg" horses), and "graceful dancers" (*oyilattam*), local drummers called *andipatti* drum groups, and ram's horn (*pantuvathiyam*) players—"folk" performers all. Hundreds of vans and lorries, some blasting party songs from loudspeakers mounted on the vehicles' roofs, brought up the rear in alternating traffic jams and careening dashes.[12]

The crowd moved through approximately one hundred cloth arches, some of them extremely elaborate, with several tiers of fort- or palace-like structures. Each arch carried a message of welcome, the name of the ward in which the arch was erected, and, importantly, the name of the sponsor of that arch. Thirty serial-set towers were also set up. While many of the towers were not specific representations of anything but "tallness," a prominent theme in a number of the arches and serial towers was communal harmony:[13] one tower, called the *mumatha* tower, or the "three religions tower," combined signs of Hinduism, Islam, and Christianity in one structure (fig. 6); and above the entrance to the giant *pandal* set up at the meeting site a giant "rising sun," dawning over two mountains—itself appearing over the walls of a fortress—contained a representation of a temple flanked by a church on the right and a mosque on the left.

Other towers resembled the giant temple cars (*ter*) that carry deities in

FIGURE 6 DMK serial tower, for DMK regional conference of 29 July 1994, North Veli Veethi. The tower features symbols for three religions, Hinduism, Christianity, and Islam, a popular theme for the period. Photo by Elbro Pradeep, Madurai.

the spectacular temple car festivals famous in some towns of Tamilnadu (including Madurai). As the procession approached the main meeting site at the Tamukkam Ground in Tallakkulam, three sixty-foot-tall cutouts of Annadurai, Periyar, and Mu. Karunanidhi—the founding fathers of the main Dravidian parties—loomed ahead. The giants flanked a *pandal* (called a "Thanjavur *pandal*" after the town in which this style was developed) that resembled a palace but was also described by participants as an "entrance to a fortress" (*kottai vasal*). These leaders—legends—past and present peopled a city that one supporter told me was the palace of the DMK rule.

Vaiko's Renaissance

As discussed in chapter 2, Vai. Gopalswamy, a minister of Parliament with leadership aspirations in the DMK, and one of Tamil's most powerful orators, had broken with Kalaiñar at the end of 1993 over the issue of succession to the number-one spot. In founding the MDMK, he brought with him a large number of younger, less well placed leaders, as well as a significant proportion of the DMK's younger supporters from across the state. To steal the thunder and headlines from the DMK's Madurai regional conference of 29 July, on 27 July he held an ostentatious display of youthful political theater by initiating an 1,100 kilometer "Walking Pilgrimage of Awakening" (*ezhuchchi nadaipaayanam,* or *pathaiyathirai*) of fifty-four days from the southern tip of India, Kanyakumari, to Madras. The procession that passed through Madurai on the evening of 9 August—from the city limits at Baikkara in the south to the Mariyamman Teppakkulam on the eastern side of the city—was thus but one 8 kilometer leg of a far longer procession.

Preparations for Vaiko's arrival began just hours after the DMK conference ended. The transformation from the DMK conference to Vaiko's pilgrimage was particularly striking, as the DMK's total saturation of the city space in Madurai—streets, bridges, walls, and the air itself with flags and banners—had been completely obliterated by the morning of 1 August via the saturation of that same space with signs of Vaiko's energy and political support. The day after the DMK leadership and cadres left the city (31 July), giant 24-bit posters, approximately the size of a large hoarding, featuring Kalaiñar Mu. Karunanidhi were covered with even more elaborate posters of Vaiko standing upon fortress walls, raising his fist and his voice to crowds off-picture.[14] The DMK arches welcoming Karunanidhi were replaced with arches for Vaiko. Since Vaiko was still competing in the courts for the use of the red and black DMK flag and other party symbols, the DMK flags were left in place, and a greater number of similarly colored Vaiko flags were woven in among them, giving the viewer an image of even greater saturation of the visual field than the DMK had managed. The semeiotic appropriation of the flags and the thicker saturation of the cityscape with signs of his growing political fortune were iconic of Vaiko's attempt to coopt the party cadres from the DMK.

Dinakaran, a daily newspaper whose editor (K. P. Kandaswamy) was sympathetic to Vaiko, asserted that "the whole city was adorned with the beauty of a temple festival" (*Dinakaran* 10.94:1). "They come from all over Tamilakam by bus—Van—Lorry: Madurai is amazed: 10 Lakhs Gather to Welcome Vaiko.! Women Standing on Rooftops Shower the Processional Route with Flowers!!" declared *Dinakaran*'s front-page headline; if this is true, this gathering would have dwarfed the three hundred thousand–person crowd police officials estimated had gathered for the DMK conference just ten days before.[15]

Vaiko's first major greeting occurred at the Kattabomman Circle, opposite the Madurai Periyar bus stand. A stage had been set up there by the Madurai city youth wing to greet Vaiko with a light music orchestra and several unusual displays. In addition to the "three religions tower" utilized by the DMK, three members of Madurai's religious establishment—a Muslim Imam, a Hindu priest, and a Christian minister—greeted Vaiko from atop a 12-foot dias erected near the circle. Vaiko's final destination, the stage set up near the Teppakkulam, was lit and enclosed with three serial towers, a serial light silhouette of Vaiko, and a grand stage.[16] The meaning of the Vaiko silhouette and the two serial towers depicting Annadurai and Periyar was self-evident, but the other structures of the meeting were less transparent in intent. Most said the tower some 100 meters opposite the stage "resembled a fort" (*kottai mathiri*), and a few suggested to me that it looked like a pyramid. The stage was even more variously interpreted: "Like the Chief Minister's residence," said one processionist; "Like the entrance to a temple," said another. "Like a temple car being driven," "The Eiffel Tower," "A foreign tower," said three other men. Most structures along the route were similarly nonspecific in their representations. It is significant, though, that the interpretations seemed to fall into several broad categories: (1) palaces and forts of a bygone era; (2) temples or temple cars; and (3) foreign structures of one sort or another.

Cutout Culture

The AIADMK—perhaps the most extravagant in their use of that most famous contribution to political culture by Tamil cinema, the cutout—are unparalleled in their ostentatious semeiotic occupation of a city. Charges of "sycophancy" (in English) or "hero-worship" are not uncommonly leveled against the AIADMK by their opponents. Tamil culture, and especially Tamil politics, has become "cutout culture" (*kat-aut kalacharam*), they lament. Utopian spaces celebrated by AIADMK supporters are dystopias to the opponents, spaces that index the decay and cynical manipulation of Tamil culture by self-serving politicians.

Signs of this cutout culture were no less evident on 19 September 1994 during the AIADMK's "beautification" of Madurai for the visit of the "Revolutionary Leader," Jayalalitha, to the city to preside over an awards ceremony for Madurai district police officers. As in Vaiko's procession, the arches and towers were constructed to create a space through which one's leader moves rather than a space through which one's own people move. And, of course, since the leader moves through some of the busiest thoroughfares in town, the entire population is forced to come to terms with a city transformed into "J. Jayalalitha Nagar." Like temple festival arches erected on the main road of Yanaimangalam, everyone must move through her temple and palace gates: ordinary commerce and transportation becomes processional, whether you like it or not. Jayalalitha replaces Meenakshi as queen, and the temple is replaced by her palaces.

Most of the arches constructed for her visit were not the bamboo and cloth variety put up by ward organizations of modest means, but rather the plywood "box" arches that signal institutional (as opposed to individual) financial abilities.[17] Many of the arches, as well as the serial towers, posters, etc., were set up by the two primary rivals for the leader's attentions in Madurai: *Tengaikkadai* ("Coconut Shop") R. Mariyappan, the AIADMK-appointed head of the Madurai District Milk Producer's Cooperative Society (Aavin Milk) and head of the Madurai District Dr. Puratci Talaivi Revolutionary Front, an organization with primary loyalty to Jayalalitha; and Ve. Rajanchellappa, the Madurai district secretary of the AIADMK. These two together, and in competition with each other, spent hundreds of thousands of rupees on arches and other decorations, including large, permanent wall murals painted in prominent (and sometimes controversial) spaces. Other arches were supported by worker associations and the police department. And while many of the arches featured the same kinds of themes that had been promoted in the previous two processions discussed (palaces, forts, temples, foreign towers, religious harmony, etc.), all but three of the eleven cutouts erected[18] were representations of the Revolutionary Leader herself. (The others were of Annadurai, MGR, and Periyar E. V. Ramaswamy.) In one place three forty-foot cutouts stood side by side, featuring Chief Minister Jayalalitha in various poses and costumes.

The same institution-sponsored box arches and cutouts were prominent in the Congress-I's celebration of Rajiv Gandhi's birthday on 15 October. As in the case of the other events, newspapers focused on the decorations of Madurai in preparation for the event: "Narasimha Rao and Sonia Gandhi cutouts proliferate throughout Madurai" (*Dinathandi* 15.10.94:5). Newspapers and casual observers, too, noted how unusual it was for the Congress to use the style of processional arches and cutouts that had become famous in Dravidian party events. "Cutout culture also in Tamilakam's Congress," remarked *Dinamalar*'s front-page caption of a composite photo of cutouts and box arches.[19] One processionist from nearby Thiruvanamalai, who claimed to have been an active participant in Congress political events for thirty-five years, estimated that such arches and cutouts in Congress meetings had been used only in the previous five years or so. Cutouts have become "standard" equipment in political events all over India, another said: "Cutout culture has even gone to Delhi from Tamil cinema." Many others asserted that they had never seen anything like it or on this scale in Madurai before.

A particular tower near the main stage at West and North Masi streets called the "Priya tower" evoked a response slighty different from the usual explanations. One man saw the tower as a *gopuram*, the towers surrounding a temple. Others felt it was the cupola crowning a *gopuram*. Yet a number of others made reference to foreign structures, all of which are the standard explanations given for almost any of the structures. One man in particular, though, after running the gamut of possibilities, suggested a reading that suddenly made me reconsider and clarify some of my thinking about these events. He said, "It's some country or another—is it Russia?" He thought for a moment. "Singapore? It's like something from Singapore, I think." We spoke for a minute or so, and then he burst out: "It's a symbol of China [*cina cimbol*]! It's like something from cinema!" I didn't know at the time that the arch had a name, and that its name was "Priya." I discovered this some days later when I went to interview the owner of the Sri Pazhani Sound and Light Company, which had erected it. When I asked about the name, he explained that it was designed to represent a tower (read "pagoda") that was depicted in "superstar" Rajini Kanth's smash hit film, *Priya*, shot in Singapore.

Listening more carefully during the months that followed, I heard similar answers more and more often. In the end, it was the same man who had made the remark about cinema who took me aside for a tea that night and confided his opinion to me on all of it. He claimed that only with "fanciness" would the people come. Only if one speaks quickly and amazingly would they listen. There is nothing anyone is going to be able to do about it from now on, he said: no one will be able to turn this land around. As he gestured toward the forty-foot towers and sixty-foot cutouts, the architectures and inhabitants of some dystopia, he lamented that politics around the world had decayed, that computers would soon replace human beings, and that eventually we would all starve. Likewise, for the hapless citizens of Madurai, forced to contend with a city shut down by utopian revelers, the fantastic structures erected by any one political organization represent more dystopia than utopia. Yet this is only a function of the level to which the one is able to dominate the lived places of the other.

THE EMBODIMENT OF ANTIQUITY

Ultimately, the fact that urban democratic events in Madurai seem to combine the elements of religious and political practice can be seen in several dimensions, some of which are profoundly ironic.

The Madurai of the Nayakar kings—like a series of other urban centers formed, in Breckenridge's terms, on the cosmopolitan Deccan model—very consciously combined kingly and divine spaces and in many ways focused the city not on the temple but on the palace. Madurai is an ancient city, mentioned as early as first–third-century texts. Yet contemporary Madurai as a politico-religious capital is specifically a product of the Nayakar period of the seventeenth century. The main festivals were established at this time to process through newly reorganized urban space that would provide the Nayakar kings with a cosmological diagram reinforcing their suzerainty. The notion that these cities were "pilgrim centers disembodied from political power," cosmographic diagrams of a strictly "Hindu" "sacred center," was in fact a notion that was produced in and just after the Deccan War period, between ca. 1750 and 1850. It was during this time that the British very intentionally tore down the competing foci of urban space, the walls and the monstrous palace, and left the meaning of the city in the hands of the central temple authorities (Breckenridge n.d.[a]).

Though they left relatively sturdy remnants of the palace standing, the British tore down the vast majority of the compound along with the main city walls in the 1840s. As a part of the "rationalizing" of urban space—the making of a space suitable for the collection of revenue and the establishment of order—the palace complex was diminished, marginalized to the periphery, and framed in the landscape as a relic of the ancient "Wonder that Was India." By the mid to later nineteenth-century, the Tirumala Nayakar Palace appeared like so many other ancient ruins of Indian polities: solitary, broken-down, and empty structures, exhibiting a fecund emptiness that would be filled again in a British royal fantasy of empire (Appadurai 2003).

The contemporary democratic procession in Madurai that appears to occupy "religious" ritual space-times and employs "religious" transactional modalities reappropriates those space-times and practices—which were in fact always already political, whose "merely religious" appearance was a product of the assertion of colonial power. The question may be asked: Why did twentieth-century democratic political practice take these forms? One answer lies in the singular uses of the past in general by agents of the Dravidian or Tamil nationalist vision, the dominant democratic paradigm of twentieth-century Tamilnadu. In this paradigm, indices of an ancient and original South Indian civilization independent of what they considered the relatively more recent Brahminical and Sanskritic North Indian civilization were deployed liberally in the production of their democratic political power. This involved an overall apotheosis of the Tamil language itself (Ramaswamy 1993), which was effected in the oratory and official publications of the major parties. They produced hagiographies of martyrs of the Dravidian cause and the writings of their poet-king leaders, such as "The Learned" (Ariñar) C. N. Annadurai, "The Revolutionary Leader" (Puratchi Tailavar) M. G. Ramachandran, and, especially, "The Artist" (Kalaiñar) Mu. Karunanidhi. When they spoke they embodied ancient kings and gods addressing their people in heroic orations that, as far as we know, never had historical antecedents. In short, an imagined past of a pure and ancient Tamil civilization was embodied on the stage by orating leaders speaking an imagined pure and ancient Tamil language.

The imagination of an orthogenic city (Redfield and Singer 1954), a cosmographic diagram mapped out on the streets of Madurai, is another of the traditional elements that appear to be so commonly evoked in the modernity of democratic Tamilnadu. Along with the notion of a pure and ancient Tamil, it is one more way in which the evocation of "the traditional" and its opposition to "the modern" appears as one of the single most consistent diacritics of modernity in general. And that very articulation of a traditional, "city as symbol" idea, which has been promoted by scholars and tourist officials alike, becomes another sign of the antiquity and cultural authenticity of the Dravidianist paradigm itself.

Madurai has frequently been dubbed *koyil nagar*, "Temple City," by virtue of its thousands—some claim tens or even hundreds of thousands—of shrines: some as large as a city block, others as small as a vestibule on the outside of a shop. But perhaps the sine qua non of the "Temple City" is the Meenakshi Temple itself, the massive 20-plus acre complex that forms the literal and spiritual heart of the city. As mentioned in the first sections above, from this site the streets swirl around in ever-expanding concentric rings, each named for a month of the year, forming a spatiotemporal model of the universe in what scholars have dubbed a cosmographic diagram. The Chitrai Festival articulates this simplex space-time in the movement of Madurai's queen throughout the city. Her *dik vijya*, her triumph over the Lords of the Eight Directions, is at the same time a triumph over space-time, a practice that imposes a single reading onto the lived spaces of the city. The epistemic reading of the city mapped out in the Nayakar layout and instantiated in the Chitrai Festival was so successful that the cosmographic diagram put down in paving stones and traversed by Madurai's deities is virtually the only space-time ever associated with the city, at least from the point of view of the primary institutional productions of knowledge about Madurai by university scholars and tourist officials.

Yet this chapter has demonstrated that there are other space-times possible in Madurai, other possible epistemic aestheticizations of the city that produce onticities that, if not in opposition to the Nayakar model, incorporate and transcend, at least temporarily, that model. Indeed, organizers conducted each of the different events discussed above in an attempt to impose new meanings onto the streets and lanes of Madurai, new potentials, new futures and pasts of ideal polities in an idealized utopian cityscape. The city of Madurai does not always have the same simplex epistemic onticity, and Meenakshi does not always form the center of the city. When the DMK ushers in tens of thousands to walk the streets in military ranks of ordered political action as well as swirling vortices of "folk" energy through a utopian landscape filled with signs of their political future and peopled with sixty-foot-tall images of past and future leaders, a new episteme is inscribed onto the streets. When Vaiko marches through the town a few days later, his pilgrimage reclaims Madurai for him; it recenters Madurai, and even renames it, at least for a moment. But these changes do not occur out of thin air, and certainly not according to some abstract logic inherent within democracy.

I have demonstrated here how politicians engaging in democratic political campaigning conduct their meetings according to a practical logic similar to that which informs a temple festival and procession. Both event types, I propose, are spatializing practices that impose a simplex onticity onto the normally multiplex meanings of the many lived places of the city. They are, in other words, practices in the production of hegemony for the organizers, a hegemony based on a single reading of place that they produce and they control. In agreement with popular perceptions of these events in Tamilnadu—such as those represented in newspaper reportage and by the casual observations of participants—the political meeting does indeed resemble the temple festival in the way organizers saturate space with signs of themselves, promote the maximal transaction of gifts, and conduct spatial operations similar to those conducted in temple festivals.

At the same time, the political meeting draws in a set of signs that transcend those found in the temple festival, signs of foreign lands and ancient times. These wider, global semeiosocial sets are localized, brought into the immediacy of everyday life, and merged with what we might term purely local, distinctly Tamil signs of self in order to construct particular visions of social and political life, utopian visions of a political future in which the leader will occupy the palace of rule. Both the temple festival and the cinematic elements of these meetings transform global spaces and idealized historical time into a space-time that adorns the party's political activity and anoints the organizers and leaders with its aura.

[4]

ON LIFE, MOONLIGHT, AND JASMINE

AND SO we have seen that praise is not merely praise, but an indexical icon, an emblem—of antiquity and of cultural authenticity—and an embodiment of Tamilness deployed in political discourse as an integral element of political legitimacy. As we will see in this and the following chapters, the panegyric can wax somewhat florid: "O, Fullmoon," "O, Jasmine Flower that spreads its essence," "O, Child-like Tamil! O, Budding Moonlight!" Thus do some contemporary politicians of Tamilnadu hail their leaders on wall posters, on ceremonial arches erected to welcome them, and on the political stage itself in fervent, heartfelt oration. Praise by subordinates is (and emblematizes) an ancient cultural logic in the production of power in the Tamil lands, a logic by which the praiser participates in the greatness of the praised at the very moment of naming that greatness. Like *bhakti*, the name for movements of spiritual devotion that burned across different parts of India over the past millennium, praise embodies power and one's relationship to it: one praises one's leader with the desire to participate in the world of that leader and to thereby generate greatness for oneself. The logic of this practice—from its use to its perception as ancient practice—is contained in the very tropic structures found in the vocative phrases, like those above, deployed in mainstream political practice in contemporary Tamilnadu.

This chapter addresses several sets of topics inspired by these practices. One examines such florid vocatives as "O, Child-like Tamil! O, Budding Moonlight" in terms of a trope system found in the medieval Tamil grammar *Nannul* (su. 290). As such, the discussion below contributes to a literature broadly characterized as an anthropology of tropes (cf. Fernandez

1974, 1982, 1986, 1990; Frazer 1940; Friedrich 1979a, 1979b, 1989, 1990, 2006; Jakobson 1956; Sapir and Crocker 1977; Turner 1974) and offers an alternative tropological schema from the ones deployed in that anthropology. Specifically, ethnographers of tropes have sought to understand how people make sense of their worlds by examining metaphor, metonym, and other movements of meaning within the semeiosocial production of human life. In other words, it is not only the case that "all language is always totally tropological" (Friedrich 1990:24). It is also the case that the poetic processes scholars have identified within language, which comprise the very form and movement of language, provide the modalities and motilities of meaning production across the entirety of human action. Here I will outline a uniquely Tamil tropic paradigm called *akupeyar*, "transformed words," a tropology that favors contiguity or indexicality (sometimes—and problematically—called metonymy or synecdoche). These relationships of meaning, I argue, characterize how political supporters understand what they evoke in praising their leaders.

Another set of concerns involves what we can call master tropes, the organizing tropic paradigms of a culture, a people, or an epoch. The poet, linguist, and folklorist A. K. Ramanujan consistently wrote and taught that metonymy appeared to lie at the foundation of a disproportionate amount of Tamil thinking and writing (Ramanujan 1985, 1989). Indeed, he claimed that metonymy appeared to be the master trope of Tamil thought in the way one might say that metaphor is the master trope of Westerners. Now, while we might challenge such essential statements about "Tamil thought" or "Western thought," other scholars, notably Roman Jakobson (1956), made similar claims about how one trope or another appears to predominate among one people or another, or one time period or another. It seems a worthwhile exercise, at least provisionally, to explore such master tropic paradigms as far as we can and to search for what truth they may contain in order to uncover possible meanings that we might otherwise miss.

In this spirit of exploration, then, we will address this essentialism by claiming that a form of contiguity trope called *akupeyar* may well be the master trope of Tamil thought—at least at this moment and in many moments in the past. This is not to claim that twentieth-century Tamil people do not recognize relations of similarity or iconicity in the semeiosocial production of their lives. It is not to claim, in other words, that they see no similes or metaphors. To do so would be to replicate what is sometimes called a strong or naïve Whorfianism, based on a misreading of Benjamin Lee Whorf's theory of linguistic relativity (1956 [1939]; cf. Silverstein

2000)—i.e., the idea that grammatical (or tropic) structures determine the structures of our minds. Whorf's own position was significantly more subtle: the structures of language do have an impact on how we think and act, but they do so via the ideological perception of structure and the instantiation of that perception within specific arenas or modes of practice. So, in conditions fostered under the Dravidianist political dispensation, analogical or iconic relations (i.e., metaphor) are subordinated to those of contiguity or indexicality (i.e., metonymy) as the latter tropic relations appear forefronted in earlier literary and poetic/political practices. And, as with the wider deployment of Tamil literariness and praise as an emblem of antiquity and cultural authenticity, even the logic of the tropic forms themselves have emblematic powers.

MASTER TROPES IN TAMIL

The anthropology of tropes articulated by scholars such as James Fernandez and Paul Friedrich has amply demonstrated the tropological nature of human semeiosocial action to the point that phrases such as "the play of tropes in culture" have entered the anthropological lexicon as workaday concepts. Among a vanguard of anthropologists sensitive to literary analysis and technique, beginning in the 1960s and '70s they each (in very different ways) brought to anthropology a new methodology for and aesthetic of semeiosocial action. Offering an idiosyncratic and partial synthesis here: their work has demonstrated (1) that meaning is never basic, always motile, always "on the move"; (2) that there is no truly formal partition between "poetic" and "ordinary" discourse; (3) that there is a high degree of overlap between the abstractions of "a language" and "a culture"—or "linguaculture"—and that concrete linguistic practice may be the most clearly observable aspect of cultural practice; (4) that the more poetic aspects of language, e.g., figuration of all kinds, intensification of form, and association by analogy, are the very modes by which people produce, reproduce, and transform their worlds; and (5) that anthropologists can analyze performative or organizing tropes operating throughout human action and thereby contribute significantly to their understanding (indeed, such analyses may provide deep insights into the culturally and historically specific meanings that human actors themselves attribute to their worlds and their activities).

This chapter adds to this anthropology of language through its analysis of the aesthetics of poetic action in political communicative practice. I articulate this anthropology, though via a slightly different axiom: every speech community has its own understandings, its own ideologies and aesthetics, of what a language is, what it does, and how it works. The metalinguistic observations of intellectuals born, raised, and trained in their own languages, observations generated through practice, offer a privileged insight into the semeiosocial action with which anthropologists have traditionally concerned themselves. We may thus analyze the poetic action of each society in terms of the tropologies specific to its own phenomenologies of language. Tamil treatises on grammar and poetics, like (and related to) those in Sanskrit, have finely detailed categorizations of tropes. Might the poet-linguists who developed these systems have insights into the production and transformation of meaning not considered by Aristotle, Quintillian, Cicero, Peter Ramus, and all those of the Western semiotic tradition? Below I examine one such set of categorizations, found in one verse of one text, and explore the analytic potential of the system found there in terms of contemporary political practices.

This Tamil system, found in the grammar *Nannul,* consists of sixteen named tropes called *akupeyar,* a term I will use in general for the Tamil system of tropes. As the author of *Nannul* describes it, *akupeyar* depicts one thing in terms of another; but unlike metaphor—(arguably) the Urtrope of Western poetics—the two relata always exist *in praesentia*: both are present in some contiguous relationship with each other. In Western poetics we give the name *metonymy*, sometimes *synecdoche*, to such movements of meaning. The evidence I present here, then, supports A. K. Ramanujan's observation (1985, 1989) that metonym is the master trope of Tamil thought, as evidenced from the earliest literary and grammatical records of the Sangam age some two thousand years ago.

Metonymy is especially evident in the exegetical framework of Sangam grammar and poetics called *thinai*, or "landscape." The land (*idam*)and the seasons and times of day (*kalam, pozhuthu*) are the "first things" of poetry, as "those with the knowledge of the grammar/nature of things say" (*Tolkappiyam, akatinaiyiyal* 4).[1] The Sangam landscape is divided into five regions, each characterized by its own native elements (*karu*) and human occupants (*uri*), which index in turn specific moods and relationships between lovers. To evoke the image of just one of these elements, say the *kurinji* flower, is to evoke the particular landscape in which the *kurinji* blooms (the mountain slopes), the particular people living there (honey-collecting hill tribes), and the mood of two lovers uniting. The *kurinji* flower is in some respects the epitome of an entire genre of poetry that indexes all matters relating to the heart, the "interior," *akam*.

Consider Ramanujan's artful translation of one of the most famous of these poems of the "interior landscape" (1985:244):

What She Said

Bigger than earth, certainly,
higher than the sky,
more unfathomable than the waters
  is the love for this man

of the mountain slopes
where bees make rich honey
from the flowers of the *kurinji*
  that has such black stalks.

TEVAKULATTAR, KURUNTOKAI 3

The mountain slope, "bigger than the earth, certainly," is a simile for the man, as is, of course, the *kurinji* flower itself "that has such black stalks," both signs of love. As Ramanujan puts it, all the elements of the poem—places, times, objects, persons, and moods—are contiguous with each other, each "dwelling inside" (*ullurai*), or indexing, the other. This feature—wherein the terms of the simile, both object and standard of comparison, occupy the same places, the same domains—does not imply the multiverse instantiated in the cross-domain relationships of metaphor; rather, each simile "expresses a universe from within, speaking through any of its parts" (Ramanujan 1985:247).[2]

As we will see below, *akupeyar* is the foundational trope from which all others, including simile, are generated. But to call *akupeyar* a kind of metonym is to miscategorize it, and to place it within an alien system of meaning in which it has no part. Indeed, as the discussion below demonstrates, *akupeyar* is both broader in scope and more foundational in the *Nannul* tropic paradigm than is the concept of *metonym* in English. This difference not only provides us with an alternative mode of semeiosocial analysis of Tamil communicative practice but also reveals to us a logic dwelling inside that practice we might otherwise not have noticed. I will begin with a discussion of the trope system as found in *Nannul*, outline its features, and provide examples both from the commentaries and from American English. Following the outline of the tropes, I will turn to their deployment in some contemporary political practices.

AKUPEYAR IN *NANNUL* 290

Though written approximately eight hundred years ago, *Nannul* stands today as the Ur-text of modern Tamil grammar. While elements of the *Nannul* linguistic paradigm inform school grammar from as early as lower kindergarten, it is formally introduced to present-day students in government schools in the Eighth Standard and continues as the primary source of contemporary Tamil grammar throughout higher education.

Nannul's contemporaneity is due partly to the continuous commentarial tradition, which begins with Mayilainathar's fourteenth-century discussion (Swaminathaiyar 1995 [1918]), written perhaps one hundred years after the purported author, Pavanandhi Munivar, first inscribed his versified linguistic treatise (Dhamotharan 1980:xii).[3] From that time until today approximately thirty commentaries have been written (ibid.). Each of the commentaries appears to build on the previous ones, with similar examples and up-to-date language illuminating not only the original verses but the archaic language of previous commentators as well. A critical reading of the text (e.g., Sadakoparamanujancariyar et al. 1972) resembles an ancient city in an archaeological site, one urban layer laminated upon the previous one, it in turn built on the one before that. For all its ancient laminations, however, the text reads as remarkably modern, transparent to the contemporary student in a way that the Sangam period grammar *Tolkappiyam* (first–third centuries C.E.) is not.[4]

Nannul 290[5] defines *akupeyar* in a way that evokes Aristotle's definition of metaphor (Swaminathaiyar 1995 [1918]:140–142):[6]

> They say that *akupeyar* is one word that, over the course of history, says another word that has its nature (*iyai*).

"Therefore," Mayilainathar continues, "*akupeyar* is a transformed (*akkavakum*) name (*peyar*); all words are either 'natural words' (*iyalpeyar*) or 'transformed words' (*akupeyar*)" (Mayilainathar 289, Swaminathaiyar 1995 [1918]:141). A closer examination of the varieties of *akupeyar* and examples provided for us by various commentators, however, demonstrates that the trope is based on relations of contiguity rather than similarity, closer to metonymy than metaphor. Note that while *Nannul* suggests that the exploration of *akupeyar* is an aspect of etymology, of how words, through history, come to mean what they do at the present, the examples it and the commentators use to illustrate the trope are taken also from more recent, in situ, transformations.

Nannul 290 lists fifteen varieties of *akupeyar,* broken into three unnamed groupings:

> whole, place, time, part, quality, and action; the four measurements; word, thing contained in a space, instrument, effect, and author.

We may break this list up into three sets: (1) the oppositions, (2) tropes of measurement, and (3) complex tropes.

The Oppositions

The first group makes three oppositions between the six terms: *porul* vs. *cinai* (whole vs. part), *idam* vs. *kalam* (place vs. time), *kunam* vs. *tozhil* (quality vs. action). The concepts of the first opposition are very similar to the various kinds of contiguity relationships found in metonymy or synecdoche, but they tend to provide significantly finer-grained distinctions than the latter do. For instance, while our term *metonym* usually covers part-whole or whole-part relationships, the Tamil *idavakupeyar* gives the name of a place (*idam*) to something in or from that place, for instance "china" (for a porcelain plate) or "Tex" (to address someone from Texas). Included among the oppositions is the lovely trope of *kalavakupeyar,* which applies the name of a time or season (*kalam*) to something that occurs in that time or season. For instance, *kar mulaittathu,* "The rainy season (*kaar*) sprouted" (i.e., the crops sprouted), or *chittirai adum,* "(the month of) Chittirai dances" (i.e., festivals occur).

The oppositions also include a term we might call *metaphor,* as it involves a relationship of analogy, although, as with all *akupeyar,* the relationship of contiguity seems to trump that of analogy. Consider *kunavakupeyar,* in which the quality of a thing (*kunam*) becomes the name of the thing with that quality. The examples Mayilainathar provides for this trope appear to always involve the quality manifested in something, such as laundry "bluing" or lime "whitewashing," in which something takes on the name of its color, a contiguity trope.

Finally, the oppositions provide one of the more striking tropes, the *tozhilakupeyar,* in which the action (*tozhil*) of a thing becomes the name of the thing that performs or is created by that action. Two fine English examples include what piano tuners call *the action,* the moving parts of the instrument; or what a clock repairmen might call *the movement* of a grandfather clock, that is, the mechanical gears, springs, and hands of the clock as opposed to the cabinet.

Tropes of Measurement

The second group (7–10) of *akupeyar*, called *alavaiyakupeyar*, "the tropes of measurement," enumerate tropes of "the four kinds of measurements" (*nalvakai alavai*)—*ennal* ("count"), *eduttal* ("weight"), *mukattal* ("capacity"), and *neettal* ("extension"). They do not figure much in the political material to be analyzed below. It should be briefly noted, however, that Mayilainathar's examples are drawn exclusively from the realm of common, everyday things that are purchased in the marketplace or found around the home, e.g., a *quarter* (measure of rice), a *pound* (of sugar), a *bushel* (of wheat), a *span* (of cloth), (walking) a *mile*, etc.

Complex Tropes

The third and final group (11–15) is less internally coherent than the first two, but the tropes in this category are somewhat more complex and are frequently deployed in political discourse. For instance, in *collakupeyar*, the name of a word (*col*) becomes the thing that it means, e.g., a commentary, a sentence of life, or a pronouncement of marriage.[7] In this category are tropes in which cause takes the name of its effect and vice versa, and another (*karuththakupeyar*) in which an object (usually but not necessarily a written or musical composition) takes the name of its author (*karuththan*, literally "he who conceived"): for instance, saying you are reading Shakespeare when in fact you are reading *Romeo and Juliet*.

But perhaps the most important trope for our purposes here is *taniyakupeyar*, in which the name of something in a space/place/object (*tanam*) is transferred to that space/place/object. For instance, in both Tamil and English we call a lamp or a lightbulb a light (*vilakku*), that is, the word for luminescence or photons. In Tamil, one says *nenju nontathu*, "My heart ached," but the term *nenju* actually refers to "feeling," "mind," or "consciousness," and only by transference, "heart." And finally, one might refer to a temple or a direction by the name of the deity that resides there, e.g., Meenakshi for the Meenakshi temple of Madurai, or Nirudhi for the southwest quarter, of which the Lord Nirudhi is its guardian.

As will be seen in the following section, *taniyakupeyar* is one of the primary tropes of political praise. In some respects, the *taniyakupeyar* is the opposite of the *itavakupeyar*, i.e., the trope of place in which something or someone there takes the name of that place (e.g., calling someone by the name of her hometown; referring to a plate as "china," etc.). Contrarily, in *tani* the thing containing or characterizing something takes on the name of the thing contained or characterized, as "feelings" (*nenju*) become the name of the heart, or Nirudhi, the lord of the southwest, is transformed to become the name of the southwest quarter. But in another respect, the transference is effected by a relationship of noncorporeality to corporeality, such as "light" to "lamp," "feeling" to "heart," "deity" to "place."

Before turning to a final aspect of *akupeyar*, it is important to stress that all commentators, from Mayilainathar to the present, note that *akupeyar* may result from several meaning transformations based on combinations of different meaning relationships—very much like, in fact, Fernandez's "syllogisms of association" (1986:103–129). For instance, the term *kar* used above, *kar mulaittathu*, "The crops have sprouted," literally means "black." First, the quality of blackness is transformed into the meaning of "cloud" via *kunavakupeyar* (the trope of quality), which then becomes a sign of the "rainy season" via a reversed *kalavakupeyar* (the trope of time). This transformation is called *irumadiyakupeyar*, "double transference." When *kar* is then applied to "crops," again through *kalavakupeyar*, the transference is said to be "trebled," *mumadiyakupeyar*. Theoretically, a trope may be a combination of many, many meaning transformations; theoretically, meaning may be "turtles all the way down."

A final, sixteenth, trope is mentioned as a variety of *akupeyar* in some recent commentaries and grammars (e.g., Sadakoparamanujancariyar et al. 1972). It encompasses and transforms virtually all other tropes into what Friedrich calls the analogical tropes (1990:37–39). This *aumai*, "simile," or *aumaiyakupeyar*, is a broad categorization of all kinds of analogy, including metaphor (*uruvakam*: literally, *uru*, "form" + *akam*, "interior").

Consider the following rather standard literary example of the following trope:

> *pavai vanthal*
> "A girl came"

The term *pavai* literally means "pupil of the eye." As the pupil reflects a miniature image of the person looking at it, as a homunculus, the term is extended to refer to a puppet or doll, which is in turn extended to the image of a charming girl, a girl as dear as the eye.[8] These transferences are indeed analogical, i.e., metaphor. But grammatical *cum* poetic exegesis of this trope, from *Tolkappiyam* through *Nannul* and to the present day, asserts that this metaphor is actually a form of "reduced simile" (*ullurai aumam*, lit. the simile that "dwells" [*urai*] "inside" [*ul*]), or "elliptical simile" (*auma tokai*; see *Nannul* 366; for discussions of simile in *Tolkappiyam* see Nataraja Sarma 1971:55–57 and Sundaramoorthy 1974:93–113). In such a trope, the standard of comparison (*aumavurupu*) is elided, or "dwells internally," within the trope, which results in a metaphor. To these scholars, the term *pavai vanthal*, "The girl [pupil] came," has the underlying form of *pavai* ponra orutti *vanthal*, "A *girl like* a pupil came" (*Tolkappiyam, aumaiyiyal* 9).[9] Similarly, other tropes that at first glance appear to be metaphors are read as reduced similes, such as an appellation we will discuss below, *muzhumatimukam*, "Full-Moon Face," reduced from something like *muzhumathi* inta *mukam*, "face *equal to* the full moon!"

But it does not end there: the commentators and analysts all suggest that in the case of *pavai vanthal*, for instance, the relationships between pupil, doll, and girl are relationships of *akupeyar*, contiguity: the pupil-to-girl relationship might be said to be based on a relationship of *cinai*, part for whole, whereby the meaning of the pupil, a dear object, expands to the whole, i.e., the girl, who is as dear to us as the eye. Similarly, *muzhumathi*, "Full Moon," applies to the face, which shares the qualities of whiteness and roundness, a *kunavakupeyar*; and the face (a part) expands to represent the entire person, a *cinaiyakupeyar* (Nataraja Sarma 1971:55–57). Hence, according to the Tamil tropic paradigm, what appears at first glance as metaphor is, in fact, simile; and simile is built upon relations of contiguity, *akupeyar*. To the Western-trained scholar, Indian or Euro-American, who considers metaphor to be the master trope from which all others are derived, this categorization of metaphor as a subtype of simile and simile as a subtype of metonymy is rather shocking.

Thus, while simile in Tamil poetics, and Indian poetics generally, is the primary "adornment" (*ani, alankaram*) of poetic composition, *Nannul* recognizes *akupeyar*, of which similes are constructed, as the primary mode of meaning transformation—the master trope—in ordinary language. Indeed, one of the most striking aspects of these tropes is their quotidian quality, indexing the recognition by *Nannul*'s author and commentators of tropic processes on the level of ordinary speaking (as opposed to the European Renaissance categorization of tropes as figures of [a narrowly conceived] poetic language and oratory; see Sonnino 1968:1–14). Notice here, for instance, the examples taken from the home and marketplace given for the *akupeyar* of measurement (*alavaiyakupeyar*): grams and kilos of rice, cooked and raw, "spans" of rope, "cubits" of cloth, walking distances, whitewash and bluing—commonplace, everyday things. Indeed, we might conclude that Pavanadhi Munivar and his commentators recognized some centuries ago what it took contemporary anthropologists and linguists to demonstrate to present generations of scholars—poetic processes of all kinds characterize even the most ordinary discourse in everyday life. "All language is always totally tropological."

ON LIFE, MOONLIGHT, AND JASMINE

In the remainder of this chapter I intend to address the significance of *akupeyar* not in every*day* ordinary discourse but in the extraordinary discourses of every *night*—in other words, political oratory and its associated modes of cultural production. Let us see how they work. The underlying logic of contiguity in *akupeyar* suggests a possible mode of analysis of the speaking practices of local politicians, whose speeches are often interwoven with "literary garlands" (*illakkiya malai*) of praise. The gist of my observation is that the semiotic relationship of contiguity (indexicality) in *akupeyar* is an iconic model of the relationships between powerful leader and hopeful supporter on stage, an icon of indexicality, as it were. An icon of love. I move in this discussion, then, from the semantics of contiguity tropes in Tamil through the pragmatics of semeiotic and on to a phenomenology (an aesthetics and ideology) of language use produced in political praise.

Before getting to these political tropes, however, it is important to review the cast of characters and political positions to which these tropic images refer. This analysis will deal exclusively with two politicians of the Dravidian Progress Association (DMK), a father and a son: a founding member of the party and a great orator, Kalaiñar Mu. Karunanidhi, and his son, the youthful, handsome, and energetic Talapathi ("Leader") Mu. Ka. Stalin.[10] The images and phrases presented below were collected in the early to mid-1990s in Madurai, Tamilnadu, among one set of young political officers and organizers with direct political links to Mu. Ka. Stalin. The DMK emerged in the 1940s as a political party that articulated the Dravidianist political paradigm. This paradigm included promoting Tamil civilization, Tamil literature, and Tamil politics in opposition to what they considered a North Indian, Sanskritic, and Brahmin-dominated Congress party. In their political practice the Dravidianists wove elements of a purported ancient Tamil civilization into their political campaigns and styles of propaganda. So, for instance, Kalaiñar and other founders of the party developed an oratorical style that utilized a "pure" Tamil complete with archaized lexical items and phrasings drawn from the classics of Tamil literature (including, note, the Sangam corpus discussed above; see chapter 1). Such an archaic, pure, language iconically indexed—emblematized—an antiquity of being, of Tamil being, and the politician speaking on stage in some respects embodied Tamil itself and the antiquity of Tamil civilization (chapter 2). Finally, their appearances in towns and cities were highly elaborate affairs involving the erection of temporary monumental architecture such as ceremonial arches, numerous 60-foot-tall cutouts of their leaders and political ancestors (fig. 7), walls plastered with giant posters, murals painted on any available surface, and massive stages and public-address systems (see chapter 3 for a full description of several such meetings). It was in preparation for some of these events that the following materials were collected.

I take for my first examples the vocative phrases printed on arches and posters to welcome party leader Kalaiñar Mu. Karunanidhi to Madurai during the DMK's Madurai Regional Conference of August 1994. Arches and posters commissioned by various groups were inscribed with phrases such as "O, Life of the Siblings" (*udanpirappukkulin uyirey!*), "O, Beat of the Heart that Protects the Party in a Fierce Storm" (*kadum puyalil kazhagham kakka ithayattudippey!*), and, wonderfully, *konju tamizhey, tulir nilavey!*, "O, Child-like Tamil! O, Budding Moonlight." Each one of these similes can be analyzed as built upon the logic of *akupeyar*; they also work within a universe of meaning whereby each vocative phrase indicates not only the leader but the party member or organization praising him. Even though neither is physically present at the arch or in the poster, the use of the vocative postposition –*ey* instantiates a model of discursive interaction in which two parties are present, one hailing, one hailed.

To look at the first phrase:

udanpirappukkulin uyirey!
"O, Life of the Siblings"

To anyone in Tamilnadu today, this vocative shares an obvious intertextuality with Kalaiñar's trademark salutation to his audiences, a phrase he uses at the end of his opening salutations at every public meeting or speaking event:

en uyirinum melana anpu udanpirappukkaley
"O, my siblings whom I love more than life itself"

But here Kalaiñar's phrase is turned back upon himself so that he becomes the very life of the party faithful, who are embodied as a collectivity. Obvi-

FIGURE 7 Cutout of Mu. Ka. Stalin (March 1995)

ously an *akupeyar* of complex transference, the person, Kalaiñar, is called "life" (*uyir*), the animating principle of a person (or that which is contained by a "body," *udal*). This aspect of the phrase is *taniyakupeyar*, a part–whole relationship in which the contained expands to refer to the container, the noncorporeal to the corporeal. But it is not the life of Kalaiñar the phrase is evoking, but the life of the DMK faithful. Kalaiñar, a part (*cinai*) of the party, expands to become the sign of the party as well as its animating principle.

Similar contiguity relations exist within the second example given above:

kadum puyalil kazhagham kakka ithayattudippey
"O, Beat of the Heart that Protects the Party in a Fierce Storm"

The "fierce storm," in this context, refers to the defection of Vai. Gopalswamy (Vaiko) from the DMK in 1993, a staggering blow to the party (Gopalswamy was himself frequently hailed by his own supporters as *puratchipuyaley*, "O, Storm of Revolution"). The phrase is a variant of many, many like it, such as *tayullam kakka ithayattudipey*, "O, Heartbeat that Protects the Mother's Heart/Land." Like in the previous example, Kalaiñar is imagined as the heart (*ithayam*) of an embodied collectivity, indeed, as the very beat, the "pulse" (*tudippu*), that animates the heart of that body. But what the phrase appears to emphasize is the aspect of protection that is the result of the heartbeat. "O, Beat of the Heart that Protects the Party" then involves the double transference of *taniyakupeyar*, as in the previous example, and *karuviyakupeyar*, whereby the effect of something, in this case protection, takes the name of its cause, the heartbeat.

Finally, we have:

konju tamizhey! tulir nilavey!
"O, Child-like Tamil! O, Budding Moonlight"

I admit to some difficulty in translating this isometrical dyad into English, not only because of its maudlin violation of Anglo-American aesthetic conventions but also as the result of its thick resonance with two-thousand-year-old Tamil literary motifs and core Tamil concepts of beauty, value, and life (cf. Egnor 1978). *Konju* is a verb root used adjectivally that means "to fondle or cuddle," as one would a child; "to be full of charm, sweetness, and delight," as a child is; "to blossom, to open, and to be open," as a flower. *konju pecutal*, speaking *konju*-ly, then, is to speak as one would with a child, softly, lispingly, openly, with love and tenderness.[11] To hail Kalaiñar as *konju tamizhey!* is to claim that his very essence is, in some respect, equivalent to the qualities of some beautiful, loving, tender, child-like Tamil—indeed, his Tamil. In regard to *akupeyar*, the term appears to build an image of Kalaiñar based on relations of quality (*panpu*), action (*tozhil*), and the complex trope of instrumentality (*kariyam*), whereby the instrument of effecting something, in this case the speaking person, takes the name of the thing effected, here Tamil. The parallel phrase in the dyad again contains a verb-root adjective, *tulir* (to "bud," "flower," or "put out shoots"), modifying the word for moonlight, *nilavu*. Like the first, this enigmatic phrase is rich with literary resonance and touches on deep notions of Tamil aesthetic value: like the Tamil language that blossoms, lovingly, the moonlight, engendered in Tamil and all over India as feminine, "sprouts, buds, spreads out" softly, tenderly.

Taken together, this elements of this dyad evoke an image of the new, the tender, the essential, the open, and the very energy—a feminine energy—that manifests itself in reproductive fluids, heartbeats, and the physical images of deities (Egnor 1978; Daniel 1984). Though it is the body, a hard, masculine physicality, that encloses and protects a soft, essential, interior, feminine life-force in every living being, this energy itself is what enables the body to act in protection, ergo, "the heartbeat that protects the party," the very life of party supporters.

Similar images are evoked for the praise and welcoming of Kalaiñar's son, Mu. Ka. Stalin, the (then) heir apparent to DMK leadership and head of the party's youth wing. On numerous visits to Madurai the qualities of his youth iconically resonated with the qualities of energetic expansion, increase, (re-)productive fertility, etc. He was called "Murugan," a youthful deity of the mountains, associated with fertility, and considered the god of the Tamils. One poster called him "Youth of Dravidianness" (*diraavidattin ilaiyavaney*!), a phrase applicable to Murugan and thereby depicting Stalin as the very icon of the future potential for the increase of the Tamil universe (*diraavidam*). One of the young masters of the Madurai's political scene, K. Guruswamy, commissioned a poster for Stalin's arrival in April 1993 that hails him as the "Full Moon" (*muzhumatiey*!) and in yet another as the "Dawning Sun" (*ilaiya cuuriyaney*!), a play on the word for "youth" (*ilamai*) and a reference to the party symbol, the rising sun (*uthaya curiyan*). He is called "The Heart of the Young" (*ilainarkalin itayamey*), "Today's Vanguard Leader, Tomorrow's Guardian of the People" (*inraiya talapathiyey*! *nalaiya inamana kavalarey*!), "*Kurinji* Flower" (*kurinji malarey*!),[12] and, finally, my favorite, deployed by "The King," "O, Jasmine Flower which Spreads its Essence/Scent" (*manamparappummallikaiyey*) (fig. 8). These last two eponyms, referring to the *kurinji* flower discussed above, and to jasmine (*mallikai*), a flower fit to adorn young girls, fertile women, bridegrooms, and deities, combine notions of the feminine, the essential, and the fertile as appropriate eponyms of rough, virile, manly politicians.

While these similes are based on iconic resemblances between, say, youth, energetic expansion, and reproduction, the comparisons are them-

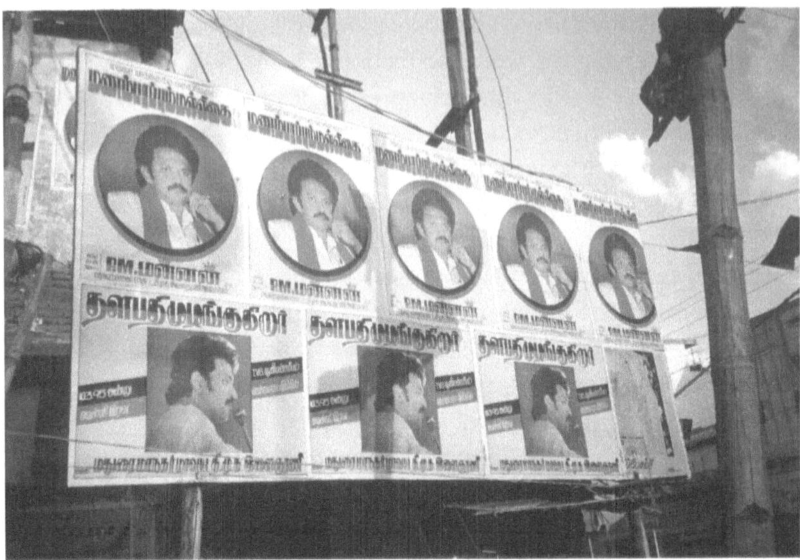

FIGURE 8 Posters of Mu. Ka. Stalin (March 1995). The upper one reads, "O, Jasmine Flower that spreads its Essence" (*manamparappummallikaiyey*); the lower reads, "The Vanguard Leader Roars" (*talapathi muzhangukirar*). Both posters were sponsored by P. M. Mannan, leader of the DMK city and district youth wing in Madurai.

selves constructed on indexical relations of contiguous entities related in vocative phrases such as "The Youth of Dravidianness" or "The Heart of the Young." The use of the vocative itself, the calling and praising of the leader, instantiates a model of discursive interaction in which the participants are present in the same place, each indexing, each "dwelling inside," the other. Such an interaction instantiates, too, a particular ontology, a tableau in which the local politician enjoys an intimate, emotional, and fruitful relationship with his leader. In other words, it evokes a world in which there is an intimate *cum* hierarchical contiguity between praiser and praised.

Consider again the linguist Tolkappiyar, who in claiming that the "first things" of the world were "time" and "place," always meant the specific seasons and times of day, not some abstract temporality; he always meant the specific landscapes with their associated persons, plants, and animals, not abstract "space."[13] In Peircean terms, the linguist remains within a world of secondness, that experience of the world in which all signs are contiguous with all others, in which indexicality draws relations between signs and structures them into unique contexts. This secondness appears as the dominant phenomenology of the Sangam world. Ramanujan claimed that Tolkappiyar never ventures into a description of language or the world that is context-free or "symbolic," that is, characterized by "thirdness"; all such sign relations are always subordinated to indexicality.

Again, to restate the general idea of the argument made above: the relationships of contiguity, of indexicality, and of secondness in the semeiotics of the *Nannul* tropic paradigm bear an iconic relationship to the contiguity, the indexicality—the secondness—produced in the vocatives of political praise as well as in the relationship instantiated between the speaker and the power-that-is; each, like the elements of a Tamil simile, dwells inside the other.

WESTERN POETIC VERSUS CULTURALLY SPECIFIC TROPES

At the end now of our passage into Tamil tropology we might well ask: What difference does it make to the analysis of political language in Tamilnadu whether we employ the four master tropes of Western poetics or the trope system of *akupeyar* found in *Nannul*? Is not a metaphor always a metaphor, a metonym always a metonym regardless of the language used or the metalinguistic systems available in that language? From one point of view, for instance that of a philosopher trained in the arts of Western poetics, a metaphor *is* always a metaphor if it takes an image from one existential domain to describe something from another, say, using the lion, from the domain of animals, to describe a king (to deploy the standard example). Metaphors assume some resemblance between elements in different domains. In the case of the "King who is Lion among Men," we recognize a meta-iconicity between the two entities that is based on fierceness, strength, or hierarchical supremacy. Likewise, metonyms are always metonyms when the standard and object of comparison are recognized as contiguous with one another, say the heart of the person in a phrase such as "He's all heart," the heart as a corporeal part of the person, and the corporeal representing the noncorporeal, i.e., the personal quality of compassion.

But since *akupeyar* shares much with metonymy, we need to be clearer about the anthropological advantages of passing our understanding through a Tamil tropological schema. It is not that Tamil's penchant for contiguity is not familiar. Metonymy is commonly recognized to be one of the "four master tropes" of Western poetics (Burke 1969 [1945]:503), one of the set: metaphor, metonymy, synecdoche, and irony. Metonym posits a relationship based on items *in praesentia*, two terms that are contiguous with each other. We often think of them as part for whole, or whole for part relationships, such as "He's all heart" or "Nice set of wheels."[14] Beyond this formal recognition of the term is the recognition that the trope exists as one within a distinct system of tropes, and often enough in contemporary literature and thought on such things, it exists as something quite distinct from and even in oppositional tension with metaphor. This recognition of metaphor and metonym as being in oppositional tension goes to the very nature of tropology as a body of knowledge and as a method of understanding. And beyond these recognitions there is a corresponding sense of possible dominance of one trope over another as typical of a cultural style, such as in the work of Ramanujan.

As another example of "dominance in tension" we may take Jakobson's well-known discussion of two forms of language disorder (1956:90–95). Jakobson makes the claim that the preponderance or the lack of presence of one or another trope, say metaphor or metonym, in a speech disorder known as aphasia results in two different processes in such speech deterioration. The first one, what he calls contiguity disorder, involves a situation in which the speaker knows the meaning of each and every word but cannot decode how they relate to each other when combined in a sentence. The speaker will be able to correctly identify the color corresponding to "red" and point to the proper object when prompted with the world "house," but the phrase "a red house" will be incomprehensible. In the second one, called similarity disorder, the speaker can make sense of sentences, but will not be able to determine the meaning of any given word outside of context. The word "red," for instance, abstracted from the phrase "a red house," might mean "fish."

> The varieties of aphasia are numerous and diverse, but all of them lie between the two oppositional types just described. Every form of aphasic disturbance consists in some impairment, more or less severe, either of the faculty for selection and substitution or for combination and contexture. The former affliction involves a deterioration of metalinguistic operations, while the latter damages the capacity for maintaining the hierarchy of linguistic units. The relation of similarity is suppressed in the former, the relation of contiguity in the latter type of aphasia. Metaphor is alien to the similarity disorder, and metonymy to the contiguity disorder. (Jakobson 1956:90)

Jakobson's discussion of aphasia suggests a more general inquiry into the nature of language. He explicitly maps metonym and metaphor (contiguity and similarity) onto language's syntagmatic and paradigmatic planes, the planes of combination and selection. Briefly, the paradigm is a set of similar items (e.g., nouns, colors, species, or members of a species) and the syntagmatic chain is the arrangement of elements from potential (paradigmatic) sets onto a real-time instantiation wherein the elements exist *in praesentia*, as in a sentence (Friedrich 1990:35–36). Obviously, paradigms operate in terms of similarity, iconicity, or analogy, whereas syntagmatic chains are systems of contiguous signs. Paradigms operate in terms of metaphor, and syntagms operate in terms of metonym.

Jakobson goes further by suggesting that metaphor and metonym embody a bipolarity that forms the basis of an entire theory of language wherein metaphorical sets existing *in posse* correspond to the abstract "code" of the entire language (*langue*) while the concrete syntagmatic chain of units *in praesentia* within the actual message belongs properly to the realm of speech (*parole*). And not only language: "The dichotomy discussed here appears to be of primal significance and consequence for all verbal behavior and for human behavior in general" (1956:93). Indeed, anticipating an explicitly anthropological theory of tropes by some two decades and providing for it a foundational text, Jakobson takes the opportunity to expand his theory to the work of Freud (1961), in whose analysis of dreams the concept of "condensation" corresponds to metonym and "identification" to metaphor; and to Frazer's famous theory of sympathetic versus contagious magic (1940), in which sympathetic magic (e.g., burning yellow-colored leaves to cure jaundice) operates on the analogical principle of similarity and contagious magic (e.g., entrapping a person with a lock of her hair) operates on the principle of contiguity. This opposition between the metaphoric and the metonymic poles appears universal, and the evidence to suggest that they are at work in all human societies and cultures appears overwhelming.

The global quality of Jakobson's theory, though, allows us at least the recognition that, while analysts might be able to identify metaphoric and metonymic oppositions in all natural languages, "under the influence of a cultural pattern, personality, and verbal style, preference is given to one of the two processes over the other" (Jakobson 1956:90). This is one way to account for the prevalence of *akupeyar* in Tamil political discourse: the desire to enact contiguous, pleasurable, relationships between servant and leader, between devotee and god, is contained within the very tropic figures of the devotee's utterances. As this desire forms the basis of an entire system of patronage within a democratic system (which builds upon the ancient cultural logic of praise), the abundance of the particular trope seems quite natural in contemporary political discourse. But there is also an ancientness here, which is to say, one more element of the Dravidianist political paradigm, which deployed that which was ancient in producing that which was new, that is the democratic modernity of twentieth-century South India. The essential ancientness of the trope, we should note, is one of the key values for the Dravidianists.

But would we have noticed this dimension of the practice had we not looked first at *Nannul* and the tropic system that has such a long genealogy in Tamil culture? Might we have taken "O, Child-like Tamil! O Budding Moonlight!" to be metaphors, as is our Anglo-American disposition? It seems that one of the main challenges to the exegesis of tropes is being able to know and understand how each stands in relation to each and to the others! Even within a relatively coherent system such as our own, as Kenneth Burke points out, any of the four Western master tropes are never pure: "I refer to metaphor, metonymy, synecdoche, and irony. . . . Give a man but one of them, tell him to exploit its possibilities, and if he is thorough, he will come upon the other three" (1969 [1945]:503). "He is all heart" may just as well be analyzed as a metaphor that posits analogical relations between the domain of anatomy, the domain of personal character, and the individual person. And is the term not frequently deployed as an ironic slap in the face of someone who has acted meanly? Furthermore, to speak of "existential domains" in the abstract assumes that all people in all places recognize the same categories of existence—which, of course, anthropologists have spent the better part of the history of the discipline contesting. Jakobson himself noted that the real-time instantiation of textuality involves not only the process of selection from paradigmatic sets but also the combination or contexture of syntactically ordered units at various levels each of which forms the context for units at lower linguistic levels (Jakobson 1959; cf. also Friedrich 1979a:450). In other words, each term deployed within a system is itself a part of a larger context that is built up by the concatenation of linguistic elements. And the contexture built of "O, Full Moon! O, Budding Moonlight!" is hardly the Western tropological system. In fact, from the Dravidianist point of view, the trope makes full sense within the larger system of *akupeyar*, not only a system of praise but also an emblem of Tamil linguistic and civilizational antiquity.

The use of the vocative ending *-ey* in the examples cited itself instantiates a model of discourse in which both parties, praiser and praised, are co-present, and in which the vocative forms the highest level of contexture for all the other units (at least upon the formally linguistic plane). In the light of this, the very use of any particular trope both presupposes and entails the categorical domains evoked in the trope itself; it is not enough to presuppose existential domains apart from their instantiation in particular practices, verbal or otherwise (Duranti and Goodwin 1992). It seems, therefore, that knowledge of this Indian system enlarges our understand of tropology generally, something that would have been missed had we too easily sought to universalize the tropology of Western poetics. Indeed, a too-easy supposition of the universality of Western poetics may blind us to the ways other people understand the modalities and motilities of meaning in verbal interaction and ultimately the kinds of categories they might presuppose and entail in the production and reproduction of meaningful ontologies.

By contrast, the exploration of tropic figuration in terms of indigenous categories and systems, such as the *Nannul* paradigm, provides the analyst with potential models of thought and categorization that may have remained unnoticed through reliance on the Aristotelian/Ramusian system alone. The overwhelming preponderance of contiguity in the transformation of meaning in *akupeyar* supports Ramanujan's observations regarding the "master trope" of Tamil (though within a different paradigm). It also suggests a deeper analysis of contemporary political behavior, one in which the desire to develop intimate and pleasurable relationships between servants and leaders, devotees and gods—an ancient cultural logic—appears to be operative as a primary modality in the production of and relationship to power in democratic Tamilnadu.

[5]

BHAKTI AND THE LIMITS OF APOTHEOSIS

Every movement of your tongue
Results in beneficial development schemes!
Even wastelands flourish
If your foot steps there!

THOUGH POLITICIANS will ridicule their opponents for engaging in what they describe as "hyperbole," they will do so in the very same breath that praises their own leaders with equally, and even more, florid images. Posters plastering the walls and advertising hoardings of Madurai for Vai. Gopalswamy's pilgrimage from Kannyakumari to Madras hailed him as "The Storm of Revolution," "The Third Chapter" (of modern Dravidian politics),[1] and even "The Alexander of the South Lands."

Remarkable as these epithets are, political praise generated by the AIADMK represents the most extreme manifestation of this logic. The poem below was placed in a small box on the front page of a newspaper by the Kamarajar district secretary of the AIADMK, Sathur K. Sundarapandian, on the occasion of Jayalalitha's visit to Kamaraj district. It was entitled, "I Worshipped Your Golden Feet" (*porpatham paninden*):

O, Auspicious Leader
Who has ushered in
  a Golden Era of Government!
O, Revolutionary Leader
Whom we worship daily
  turning evil-doing wastrels
  into question-marks!

Every movement of your tongue
Results in beneficial development schemes!
Even wastelands flourish
If your foot steps there!
I bow my head
   at the coming of your golden feet.
I put my hands together
   and it cools my intellect
   to welcome you
   bowing down to worship your feet.

(MALAI MURASU 22.08.94:2)

This poem exemplifies the kind of poetry that dominates the pages of Tamil newspapers, as well as posters, arches, and other signs of welcome, when any major politician comes to town. Most of these poems slap together stock phrases of adulation to weave a new poem that says nothing different from a hundred others in the newspaper that day. But the poems I will examine in the rest of this chapter, and visual images associated with them, all attribute to Jayalalitha a certain divinity, worthy of worship, even of the most physical forms of worship such as prostrating at one's leader's feet or self-mutilation; they all attribute to her the sole agency of the state ("every movement of your tongue [*navacaippellam*] results in beneficial development schemes [*nalatittam*]"); they all assert that her mere presence in a particular place will bring forth abundance and fertility, growth and greenness ("even wastelands flourish if your foot steps there"); they all claim she is the very embodiment of such qualities as love, compassion, intelligence, the Tamil language, and history itself; and finally, they all address her in very familiar terms, such as "family deity" or "deity of my heart," and most significantly, as "Mother"—as an intimate, fertile, and powerful being.

This chapter examines some of these poems in order to describe an aspect of the imaginings of power in the political practice of Tamilnadu. In the case of the chief minister, the notion that her bodily presence in a wasteland will produce abundance or that her tongue is the source of all development projects suggests that the image of Jayalalitha in these poems is a condensation—specifically an aestheticization (Daniel 1996)—of an abstraction, i.e., the state (Abrams 1988). I use the term "aestheticization" to describe what Cohn (1987) calls "objectification," with the difference that the discursively constructed object is imbued with emotional charge—plus or minus, attraction or repulsion. The significant effect of these practices is to bring about a feeling, a mood, an affective relationship to the object of the poem. The realm of the aesthetic, then, might be characterized as occupying one end of a continuum of possible phenomenological "takes" on the world, from an embodied, emotional, "gut," reaction to a more "rational"—perhaps (better) "rationalized"—"ideology" of human action, products of action, and institutions. The "state" (or other aestheticizations of power), no matter in what form it may be imagined, probably partakes more of the realm of imagination on a workaday basis, more within the aesthetic end of the phenomenological continuum, than in the rationalized realm of ideology. The state is never a neutral imagining but always an image to which we either tie ourselves in devotion or patriotic love or defy with parricidal hatred.

But these imaginings do not merely follow some logic peculiar to the nation-state or to modernity at large (Anderson 1991 [1983]; cf. Appadurai 1996; Chatterjee 1993; Kaviraj 1993, 2005a, 2005b); rather, these practices are informed by common potentialities within Tamil society that are produced and reproduced according to aesthetics and ideologies more specific to phenomenologies peculiar to the Tamil people. Praise and *bhakti*, or devotional love, appear to be master aesthetics of the practices discussed in this chapter—and, indeed, in many of the speaking practices covered in this book. Praise, as I have argued, is an ancient Indian cultural logic (Appadurai 1990; Ali 1996, 2004; Davis 1985; Cutler 1987) that informs the discursive practices whereby one aestheticizes power as an intimate being, such as a family deity or mother, who will grant us the benefits of her presence and respond to our appeals. Appadurai describes the praise of superiors in Hindu India, especially kings, as anchored in the logic of worship. Praise is, above all, a ritual activity, which produces a "hierarchical intimacy" (Babb 1986, quoted in Appadurai 1990)[2] between the worshiper and the worshiped, who is, often enough, a deity. The ritual practice, though intimate, is performed for others to see; it is meant to be observed and evaluated by onlookers. As such, it is an aesthetic practice in the sense both that it is a practice that can be evaluated positively or negatively and that it has emotional content—which in the case of praise poetry is the content of devotional love, or *bhakti*.

Usually translated as "devotional love," *bhakti* has characterized many moments of South Asian devotional practice over the centuries and among certain sects (Ali 1996; Cutler 1987; Davis 1991; Peterson 1989; Ramanujan 1992 [1981]; Singer 1972). But the logic of *bhakti*—not strictly a religious logic per se—informs not only the devotional practices associated with deities, but also relationships to powerful entities in general. Richard Davis' tripartite definition of *bhakti*—i.e., "recognition of the god's superiority, devoted attentiveness, and desire to participate in his exalted domain" (Davis 1991:7, as quoted in Ali 1996:144)—serves equally well to describe the practices of local politicians vis-à-vis their sponsors and political leaders. As the poems and images that saturate city spaces on walls, over streets, and on the pages of newspapers described below demonstrate, these three characteristics—praise of superiority, devotedness, and participation—are integral aspects of Tamil political practice.

What better image to illustrate these characteristics of praise, devotedness, and desire in the patronage of esteemed leaders than the poster designed and commissioned by Durai for the DMK regional conference in 1994. The 8-bit poster (approximately 4 feet by 8 feet), plastered all over Madurai—including, significantly, opposite the main entrance to the conference venue—featured a large image of Kalaiñar Karunanidhi standing alongside a large, red, block-lettered vocative phrase: "O, Sacred Image of Sacrifice" (*thiyagathin thiru uruvey*). The image was reproduced extensively in newspapers throughout the state. What made the poster particularly remarkable was that a lithograph of Durai's face was placed in the heart of his leader as if to declare both his allegiance to Kalaiñar and his fervent desire to be always in Kalaiñar's heart/mind (*manam*). Durai declared to me that intent exactly.

Another large banner (fig. 9), commissioned by P. V. Poppaiyan, a trustee of the Koodal Alagar Temple in Madurai and a prominent supporter of Jayalalitha, depicted a smiling Jayalalitha opposite a young man—presumably an idealized image of Poppaiyan himself—spreading open his chest to reveal another face of the chief minister. This image, like Durai's, appeared in numerous newspapers and magazines, whose editors were seemingly as astonished by it as I was. And like Durai's poster, the banner clearly resonated with both the Christian image of the sacred heart of Jesus Christ—a very common image in Tamilnadu—and the famous depiction of Hanuman, Lord Rama's monkey general and *bhaktar extraordinaire*, opening his chest to reveal Rama constantly dwelling in his heart.

Both Durai's and Poppaiyan's images, though in complementary opposition, provide the same ultimate message: the devotee resides in the heart of the leader, and the leader, in turn, resides in the heart of the devotee. That both images received statewide media coverage fulfilled another desire as well: the posters were seen by the leaders; and just as one is seen by the god when undertaking *darshan* and receives benefit by that sight (Eck

FIGURE 9 Banner showing "Poppaiyan's Heart" (March 1995). Hoarding erected by P. V. Poppaiyan near the Kaththabomman Circle (near the city bus stand) on the occasion of Chief Minister Jayalalitha's forty-seventh birthday. The poster reads, "Tomorrow's Prime Minister who has achieved her 47th Birthday, the God of Our Heart, May You Live Many Years."

1981), Durai and Poppaiyan's acts of devotion and praise no doubt resulted in various unspecified, but no less potent, benefits. Perhaps most important, the posters were seen by us, by all who walked by and marveled at them or saw them in the newspapers, and by the readers of this book, who now know the names Durai and Poppaiyan. We, too, participate in the production of this greatness.

I will begin with a description of the praise poetry, found in newspapers, that appears whenever a "big" politician comes to town. Following an analysis of the poems and their layout on the page, I will turn back to a discussion of the streets and how similar images are produced there, and I provide a more detailed discussion of the iconography of political praise. In the final section I look at various reactions to two incidents of the praise of Jayalalitha by opposition leaders and by Christians (who felt that certain practices had crossed a line). Indeed, while the aesthetics of *bhakti* are evident in the ways people produce and relate to power, the Tamil people appear to place a distinct limit to the apotheosis of politicians in contemporary democratic practice.

CONTEMPORARY PRAISE POETRY AND ITS ANTECEDENTS

The advertisements I examine here were taken out by local politicians on days of their leader's arrival in their towns or districts. The hundreds of ads that dominate the pages on those days spill out of the regular sections into special sections (*ciruppumalar*) issued by the newspapers in order to hold them all. The sudden appearance of the excess of Jayalalitha images and the sudden storm of praise—"O, Amazon Warrior"; "O, Protector Deity"; "O, Doctor Revolutionary Leader"—never efface the fact that these ads are taken out by specific people who direct their messages not only to their leaders but also to their constituents, their colleagues and competitors within the party, and their political enemies. The larger and more extravagant the ads, the greater one's presence in that town's political organization, and certainly the greater one's image in the sight—literally, in the early morning gaze—of the "big person" thumbing through the local newspaper. Almost invariably, a politician's welcome contains a large image of the "big person," her name or appellation in the boldest print, and a poem addressed to her. The inclusion of the local politician's photograph—placed prominently at the bottom of the page, those names always in the second-boldest print—ensures that this "enchanted forest of adulation" (Mbembe 1992) never entirely bewitches the reader as some "authorless" text expressing timeless truth.

The overall structure and main motifs of these poems have a number of antecedents that reveal the overall logic of praise. Of the many possible, I discuss three: the welcome address of stage speaking; medieval *bhakti* poetry; and the praise of kings found in *prashasti* and *meykeerthi* poems of kingly praise.

The "welcome address" (*varaverpurai*), a performance genre of oratory, ends with the phrase *varuka! varuka! enru varaverkirom*, "saying 'Welcome! Welcome!' we welcome you." The most common vocatives printed boldly in the advertisements also iconically resonate with the moment of welcoming a leader to a speaking event. The event organizer at the microphone shouts out "O, Doctor Revolutionary Leader"—and the crowd responds "Long Live!"; he shouts: "O, Amazon Warrior who Protects Social Justice"—they respond: "Long Live!"; "O, Family Deity"—"Long Live! Long Live! Long Live!" The event becomes marked by the rhythm of the chant-and-response (which may last for five minutes or more), the passion of the party cadres as they throng the stage, and the frenzy that frequently erupts as the faithful struggle with organizers and bodyguards to garland their leader or give her a gift with no regard to the proper time and place for such things. The welcoming of the "big person" with its vocative chanting is always a moment of intense energy and enthusiasm, one of the aspects of political meetings that marked them, in my mind, as sites of intense desire and longing.

Listening to the chants or looking at these vocatives in newspapers, we get a sense of the range of appellations Jayalalitha's supporters generate for her as well as the variety of images that are deployed in the aestheticization of her power. She is hailed, first, as a leader of specific groups, such as "the poor," the "common people," or "the Tamil lands" (*tamilakam*); she is a "Golden Leader," a "Leader equal to a Lion," a "Leader whom all the world praises." Second, she is characterized as a reincarnation of famous historical figures: kings (e.g., Pari, a Sangam Age king known for his philanthropy), queens (e.g., Jansi Rani, a Rajasthani queen who is said to have strapped her newborn crown prince on her back and died fighting off Muslim invaders of her kingdom), and literary figures (e.g., Andal, the famous author of Vaishnavite *bhakti* poetry; see fig. 10). Third, she is hailed as a deity: "O, God of our Heart," "O, Goddess of Dharma," "O, Protector Deity of Social Justice," "Family Deity." I've broken the remainder of the vocative appellations down into the categories of history/literature/language ("O, Tamil"; "O, Golden book of History"), light/lamps ("O, Sacred Lamp of the Southlands"), the heart ("O, Vital Heartbeat of the Poor"), land or architecture ("O, Land that sprouted Heroism"), intimate beings ("O, Mother"), and a series of abstractions such as bravery, love, statecraft, sacredness, and motherhood. It is all these qualities and identities that are woven together in this aestheticized image of Jayalalitha as the sole agency of the state—indeed, as the state itself. Her appearances at opening ceremonies for multibillion-rupee state-development projects or all-women police stations—which are the impetus for the praise poetry—become celebrations of her personal largesse; her movement across the landscape of Tamilnadu is praised as the movement of state power itself (cf. Tennekoon 1988).

The second most obvious antecedent for the praise poem, as suggested at the outset of this chapter, is *bhakti* poetry, or the poetry of devotion to a personal deity. Such poems seem to particularly resonate with the poetry of the medieval devotional text of Tamil Saivism, *Thevaram*; these are poems with which vast swaths of the Tamil population are at least acquainted if not intimately familiar.[3] Reading the same basic structure in the newspaper poems over and over again resembles a reading of the *Thevaram*, which is organized in thematic cycles in the praise of Lord Siva.

FIGURE 10 Newspaper advertisement showing Jayalalitha as Andal, placed by P. B. Selvasubramaniyaraja of the Revolutionary Leader Front, Rajapalaiyam, Kamaraj district. The ad reads, "O, Reincarnation of Mother Andal! / O, Excellence whom All the World Praises! / Welcome! / Shower Riches upon Us!" Quarter-page ad, *Malai Murasu* 28.8.94:1.

One example, taken from the *Appar Thevaram*, composed perhaps in the seventh century, might here suffices to indicate the obvious connection between the two poetic traditions:

. . .
bright flame, celestial being
who stands as the pure path,

bull among the immortals,
honey who dwells in Tiruvaiyaru!
I wander as your servant,
worshipping and singing your feet.

(APPAR THEVARAM 4.39; TRANS. PETERSON 1989:286)

Compare the above with the poem below placed in the *Malai Murasu* (22.08.94:3) by a minister of the Tamilnadu Legislative Assembly from Kamarajar district, and District Secretary of the Revolutionary Leader Front, Mr. J. Balagangatharan:

O, sacred lamp of the Southlands!
O, light of the Dravidian family!
O, burning torch of poor people!
O, Athiparasakti
  vital ruler of this earthly world!
O, esteemed Doctor Revolutionary Leader
  who transforms these Tamil lands into a Golden Realm!
I welcome you
I touch your golden feet and worship you!

Obviously, a number of motifs have been borrowed directly from medieval *bhakti* poetry, not least of which is the evocation of lamps, lights, and fire, elements of worship and icons of power. In addition to the massive parallelisms of the lines ("lamp of the Southlands/light of the Dravidian family/Burning torch of poor people"), the poem (as are most of these poems) is shot through with the ancient trope *taaniyaakupeyar*, the trope of space (*taanam*) in which the thing contained (light) expands to represent the container (lamp). Recall, too that *taaniyaakupeyar* also moves from corporeal to incorporeal, and vice versa, from instance to generality and back again, as in the following poem, placed by two of the chief minister's lieutenants in Madurai, in which Jayalalitha is praised as the very embodiment (*uruvam*) of a series of positive abstract values and strengths (*Malai Malar* [special section] 19.09.94:11):

O, Mother
Who has given us life
Our God of personal grace
The very embodiment of

> Intelligence, Ability, Refinement, Discrimination, Love, Compassion, Achievement, History, Epoch, Honesty, Ability, Strong Will, Political Talents
>
> Welcome! Welcome!
>
> We touch your feet and worship you.
>
> —C. Singam, Asst. Secretary, Madurai District AIADMK, Madurai
> Sellur K. Raji, Secretary, 16th Ward, AIADMK, Madurai

So in every respect, from the subject matter of light that so characterizes literary appellations applied to deities to the logic of the trope itself, the poems embody that Dravidian antiquity indexically instantiated in a second-order emblematization of a literariness, of an ancient (and culturally authentic) mode of political patronage, of a past.

Third, as the mode of worship is hyperbolic (at least from some points of view), intensely emotional, and aesthetically crafted, the contemporary praise poem appears to partake of the same logic of the pan-Indic Sanskrit *prashasti* inscriptions dating in Tamilnadu from the same period as the first *bhakti* movements (Appadurai 1990:110ff, n. 1). *Prashasti* were inscriptional "praise prefaces" that identified the king as a divine descendant of a deity and bestowed titles (*virutu*), "emblems" or "honors" upon the king from a subordinate. The Tamil counterpart of the *prashasti* prefaces, which develop during the Chola period (ninth–twelfth centuries C.E.), are *meykeerthi*. *Meykeerthi* differ from *prashasti* in their far more standardized formats and their attention to the achievements of the king and not to his genealogy (Davis 1985:5). The Chola king was praised for his conquests on the hot battlefield and the protection of his home landscape, cool and green under his all-encompassing royal parasol. In other words, the king's actions and accomplishments are more important than any authorial claims of legitimate pedigree. *Meykeerthis* praise the king's works, by which the land is transformed, made lush and fertile ("even wastelands flourish if your foot steps there").

In each case, the welcome address, the *bhakti* poem, and the *prashasti/meykeerthi* inscription, the leader is praised publicly, emotionally, and, from at least some viewpoints, hyperbolically.

Consider the following example, placed in a newspaper by a member of Parliament upon the occasion of the chief minister's visit to his home town of Palani (*Malai Malar* 23.09.94:5):

O, Sacredness! O Sacred Lamp!
O, Great Light of Dravida!
O, Encyclopedia of History
  who achieved [a policy of] 69 percent caste reservation!
O, Fantasy who brought the Kaveri River
  to fatten this golden fertile country for all of history!
O, Lamp of the Lighthouse!
O, Golden Light of the Lion Throne
  which is the cradle of the Child who came to show the world the
  Grammar of Motherhood!

O, Our Goddess of Love
  who has placed her foot
  in Anna District!
O, Leader equal to the Lion!
Mother, May you come! O, Welcome!

Forever Your Faithful Servant,

P. Kumaraswamy, B.Sc., B.L., M.P.
Palani Parliamentary District

The MP's poem contains aspects of all three of the antecedents mentioned above. It is first organized as a complex vocative phrase directed toward Jayalalitha. Second, its characterization of the leader through the use of motifs such as lamps, lights, and majestic creatures such as lions, as well as its overall mood of praise, resonates clearly with medieval *bhakti* poetic practice. Third, Kumaraswamy publicly praises the chief minister's works, such as her political struggle to ensure that 69 percent of state government appointments will be filled by members of Scheduled Castes and Tribes and the Backward and Most Backward Classes. And despite the fact that Tamilnadu's ongoing dispute with neighboring Karnataka over the water rights to the Kaveri River had not been resolved at that time, the poem attributes to Jayalalitha not only the successful settlement of the problem but the very flow of the river itself and the unending fertility of the Tamil lands! And the invocation of such images of lamps and lights—common among all the Dravidian parties—suggests that her presence casts a light in the darkness (of opposition rule), and brings cool greenness to lands that were parched; the imagery appears to parallel the old *meykeerthi* opposition of arid battlefields and the cool, fertile lands of the parasol landscape.

LAYOUT AND ICONOGRAPHY

In print, the poetic descriptions of Jayalalitha as a deity, king, or queen are framed by borders and boxes that confirm her royal *cum* divine identity; and the layout and iconography too suggest the imagining of both hierarchical and intimate relationships to the leader. In addition to rather standard borders of red, white, and black, the colors of the AIADMK, we see Jayalalitha standing framed by temple pillars or in a temple or royal *mandapam*; she is shown shaded by the royal parasol; she is seated in the Lion Throne reviewing her all women police brigades—which she has just instituted—as they march by. The lion, so frequently mentioned, has numerous resonances in contemporary Tamil culture. The lion, as in Europe, is the sign of royalty par excellence; it is also said to be Jayalalitha's zodiac sign. One woman examining the lions arrayed around her in an ad placed for a ceremony to decorate police officers suggested to me that the lions were policemen standing guard around the chief minister. Finally, just as each deity has a vehicle, so too does Jayalalitha have the lion—the same vehicle, by the way, of the pan-Indian goddess Durga and the local Tamil deity Mariyamman.

Such hierarchical intimacy is also achieved by other elements of the layout on the page: hierarchy in top-to-bottom oppositions, and intimacy in the choice of portraits as well as their orientation vis-à-vis each other. One P. Balasubramanian, head of the Tamilnadu Produce Sales Board, placed a full-page, full-color ad in the *Malai Murasu* (fig. 11). Other than a small picture of himself with some text at the bottom of the page, the ad features a large central photograph of the chief minister dressed in a white sari, smiling pleasantly and gazing down and off page. The central photograph is surrounded by sixty smaller "thumbnails" of exactly the same image, the larger one and most of the smaller ones appearing to gaze warmly at Bala himself! Orienting the CM's picture so that it smiles intimately at the ad's sponsor is a frequent technique in these ads.

Hierarchical relationships are equally transparent. Numerous ads place Jayalalitha just below figures such as Dravidian leader Periyar and the DMK and AIADMK founders Annadurai and MGR, respectively. In such a position she channels praise to and benefits from those late, great political figures and the local politician pictured at the bottom of the page. This same configuration is repeated by lower-level political workers, who insert their district-level leaders in between themselves and Jayalalitha; or, to forefront their local patronage to an even greater

FIGURE 11 Newspaper advertisement taken out by P. Balasubramanian. Note that many of the images of Jayalalitha appear to be smiling on the ad's sponsor. *Malai Murasu* 1994.

degree, the local leader's picture is placed in the same line as the leader's name (a strategy that has, on some occasions, been the subject of controversy).

Balasubramanian's image is striking in its use of repetition, the repetition of the image, the same image over and over again, almost as if we are gazing upon Jayalalitha with the complex eyes of bees. The image is suggestive of another very common Tamil formal (or structural) trope (Friedrich 1990), *madakku*. *Madakku* is one of those terms one occasionally encounters in a good lexicon or etymological dictionary that fills up a page or more with its myriad uses. When Tho. Paramasivan first pointed it out to me, he translated it as "a fold" or "folding," and he folded a piece of paper like an accordion to demonstrate the concept. The verbal form has, in addition to "folding," the senses of "to deflect," "to repeat," "to subdue in war," "to overpower," "to stop with argument," "to shut someone's mouth," "to destroy," "to kill," "to tame," "to humble," "to counteract," "to parcel out and enclose a piece of land," and "to repeat, as words or phrases." The substantive includes nominalizations of the above verbal forms in addition to the senses "inflection," "refraction" (as light through a prism), and the named "verbal adornment" (*ani*) in poetics, as specifically mentioned in the medieval treatise on verbal adornment, *Dandiyalankaram* (*su.* 92): "repetition of a word, foot, or line of poetry in a stanza, each time in a different sense."[4]

What is often popularly referred to as "the Tamil Bible," *Thirukkural*, contains perhaps hundreds of couplets organized according to this adornment of repetition. Reading the following example aloud gives one the sense of a repeating sound:

tupparkku tuppaya tuppakii tuppararkku
tuppaya thum mazhai

In addition to making good food for people to eat
the rain, itself, is also food.

(THIRUKKURAL 12)

The verse, about the goodness of rain (*mazhai*), "refracts" three primary senses of the root *tuppu*: the verb "eat" and two substantives, "food" and "excellence" (or "good"). In this case the metrical foot (*adi*) is refracted to form a pleasingly staccato alliteration between *tupparkku* "for those who eat," *tuppu* "good," *tuppakii* "make food," and *tuppaya thum* "is also food."

The sense of "repetition" combines and illuminates the connections between the many senses listed above; *madakku* has the rhetorical power to dominate in argument, to subdue one's opposition with the saturation of the semantic field with a single, yet fluidly morphable sound. It particularly illuminates the senses of "folding" and "refraction," whereby a particular term, phrase, or even metrical pattern will repeat in such a way that the meanings are "bent," each term appearing as if refracted from its own specific, unique facet of a single prism.

Tho. Paramasivan argued that *madakku* was visually instantiated in such advertisements as the one Balasubramanian produced in figure 11, claiming that it has the saturating effect discussed in the previous chapter. It is strikingly embodied in the massive saturation of the newspaper advertisements when the "big person" comes to town and, as we shall see in the next section, in the manner in which such images saturate the visual field within the cityscape.

A RETURN TO THE STREETS

These ads constitute but one of a series of activities local politicos undertake to welcome their leader and, importantly, to tie their names with her. The placement of the praise poem is thus one practice in the context of a series of related practices, most notably in street-level activities that are structurally similar to the newspaper poems. The ceremonial arches described in the previous chapter were inscribed with the same vocative salutations, especially "Revolutionary Leader," "Mother Tamil," "Family Deity," etc., and, during the caste reservation agitations, "Amazon Warrior who Protects Social Justice." And the use of *madakku* has the effect of utterly saturating the space of the city: by plastering the same poster dozens of times, many right next to each other (as again in an example earlier in the book, fig. 8), or by the use of cutouts lining streets, providing a sense of the omnipresence of the leader throughout the city.

The very same phrases that are printed in newspaper ads appear throughout the city in posters, on banners, and on wall paintings. One example is the mural sponsored by one of Madurai's most prominent supporters and (therefore) benefactors of Jayalalitha, "Coconutshop" R. Mariyappan; it was put up in a place he dubbed "*JJ Tidal*," or "The Space of J. Jayalalitha" (fig. 12), and it read:

> O, Lioness
> who appears as a burning lamp to light the Tamil lands
> which have been cast in darkness!
> O, Goddess of Revolution!
> O, Mother!
> O, Tamil!

This painting, along with several others in Madurai commissioned by "Coconutshop" Mariyappan's supporters, has the same structural properties as many of the ads as well as other visual representations of praise. Mariyappan's supporters commissioned a number of painted images on

FIGURE 12 Mural at "*JJ Tidal*" (1994), showing the crisscrossing gazes from Mariyappan to Jayalalitha, from Jayalalitha to M. G. Ramachandran and Ariñar C. N. Annadurai, and back again up to Periyar E. V. Ramaswamy. The two leaves are the official voting sign of the AIADMK. The mural reads, "O, Lioness who appears as a burning lamp to all the Tamil lands, which have been cast into darkness! O, Goddess of Revolution! O, Mother! O, Tamil!" The writing at the bottom notes that the mural was sponsored by "The Madurai City Self-Protection Force."

structures throughout Madurai in 1994 and 1995. There appears in this and other paintings a crisscrossing of gazes and postures: from Mariyappan, in the lower right-hand corner, worshiping, Jayalalitha; to Jayalalitha, on the left, worshiping MGR and Annadurai (who appear to float like ghosts); and back again to Periyar, framed not unlike a revered ancestor's portrait hanging on the wall in the hall of someone's home.

This spatial logic is equally evident in a painting from along Workshop Road (fig. 13). Also commissioned by political workers of Mariyappan's camp, this brightly painted mural depicts Mariyappan reverently saluting Jayalalitha, who lights a lamp over a sun-drenched Madurai, its landscape dominated by the towers (*gopurams*) of the Meenakshi Temple. The portraits of their political forebears (MGR and Annadurai) appear above here, too, to balance the names of the mural sponsors below. Again, as in *bhakti* poetry such as *Thevaram*, praising the servant (Mariyappan) of the servant (Jayalalitha) of the lord (Meenaksh) is a long and

FIGURE 13 Mural along Workshop Road (1994), picturing Jayalalitha and Mariyappan in an almost familial tableau. The work was commissioned by subordinates of Mariyappan, Pon. Arumugam, R. T. Paramasivam, and M. G. Pandikumar. The heading reads, "34th Ward Revolutionary Leader Front."

fruitful strategy in Tamil practices for the production of political power. But this mural goes even further: Mariyappan and the chief minister appear framed in a familial tableau, a domestic scene of husband and auspicious wife of child-bearing years (*sumangali*) reverently worshiping their god. Taking in this image with one glance, our minds shift back and forth from the image of hierarchical salutation to that of a fantastic Holy Family wherein our local leader—himself a source of great benefit—dwells married to our Mother/Goddess. What fruits, what benefits, such a union produces!

A final mural commissioned by Mariyappan's nephew, M. G. Pandi Kumar, and his nephew's colleague, Pon Arumugam, both replicates the logic of the two murals discussed above (and *mutatis mutandis*, the visual structure of the newspaper advertisements and posters) and pushes the extremes of the identification of god and politician (fig. 14). The mural was painted in celebration of Jayalalitha's accomplishment of inaugurating the 8th World Tamil Conference in Thanjavur in January 1995. The phrase printed in the painting is rather standard for these kinds of images and hails the chief minister: "O, Historical Achievement of establishing the 8th World Tamil Conference! O, Mother Tamil!" The painting itself is remarkable, though, for several reasons. First, Jayalalitha is seated in the royal "Lion Throne" (*seemasanam*) guarded by a lion lying to the right of her chair. Opposite her, and slightly below, is painted a framed portrait of Coconutshop Mariyappan, who is depicted in a reverent posture facing Jayalalitha. Despite the fact that his portrait appears slightly below the image of Jayalalitha, the image of his face is larger than hers (and I can't help but find his gold watch and ring, prominently visible on his left hand, significant in indexing his status as a professional man). Images of MGR and Annadurai, like the portrait of Periyar in the JJ Tidal mural, are framed as ancestors on the walls of someone's (Mariyappan's?) home.

But the most remarkable aspect of this painting is its location: the mural was created directly on the back side of the Vinayakar (i.e., Ganesh) Temple, which sits on the traffic island, built for it, that divides North Veli Street (ironically named the *Vazhi Vidum Vinayagar Koyil*, or "The Ganesh Temple that Gives Way") in the area of Cimmakkal. The placement of the painting on this temple was not initially a problem. But, as we will see below, the painting became the focus of some controversy within the context of other events that were to transpire over the next few months.

FIGURE 14 Mural with Jayalalitha and Mariyappan painted on the back wall of the Vinayakar (Ganesh) Temple (1995).

THE LIMITS OF APOTHEOSIS

I have argued thus far that the logic of these political practices partakes of the same logic that informs religious practices or practices associated with the worship of god (*viz*: that of praise, *bhakti*). To say this, however, implies that there is a clear division between what Tamil people call "religion" (*anmigam, matham, bhakti*) and "politics" (*araciyal*), which is a matter of some considerable debate. It is clear that gods and politicians (along with movie stars) reside in an ethical realm quite different from that of ordinary human beings. (Arguably, Jayalalitha is—or has been at one time or another—all three!) But gods, politicians, and movie stars resemble each other more they resemble than those who worship/honor/revere them. They appear to get away with sexual impropriety, marital infidelity, and polygamy, with trickery, lying, and cheating—even murder. And yet they hold the love and affection of people. Curious.

Despite the obvious similarities, however, there appears nevertheless to be a limit to the extremes of the identification between these two sets of practice. In fact, the two interrelated events I discuss below both further illustrate the identity of the logic that informs both religious and political practices and demonstrate the limits this identity may take. Like the sixteenth-century Nayaka rhetoric of kingship described by Narayana Rao, Shulman, and Subrahmanyam, which "stretched" the identification of god and king "to the snapping point" (1992:182), in these incidents the identities drawn between Jayalalitha and deities surpassed that point and snapped. There are limits to apotheosis.

Jayalalitha and the Virgin Mary

On the morning of 23 February 1995 posters commissioned by C. R. Gopi, a district-level leader of the AIADMK in Madras, appeared in several places in Madras in commemoration of Jayalalitha's forty-seventh birthday. One of the posters featured images of the Virgin Mary with Child and the other depicted Athiparasakti, the focus of a popular middle-class goddess cult. Both goddesses were shown with the face of Jayalalitha. On 24 February newspapers around the state took note of the images, carrying photos of them as well as the other extraordinary hoardings, cutouts, and arches erected in honor of the chief minister (including Poppaiyan's open-heart image, discussed above). On 25 February, however, papers reported that leaders of different Christian communities and denominations had met to criticize the identification of Mary with Jayalalitha. A statement issued by a group of Catholic priests who had met at the Catholic bishop's bungalow in Madras strongly rebuked Jayalalitha and her supporters for the blasphemous treatment of the sacred image of the Virgin:

> The poster depicting Tamilnadu's Chief Minister violates the basis of the Catholic faith. It is not appropriate for any woman, other than the Virgin Mary herself, including the Chief Minister of Tamilnadu, to depict themselves as the Virgin Mary, Mother of Jesus Christ.
>
> Therefore, we vehemently oppose this disgraceful act of comparing the Virgin Mary with the Chief Minister of Tamilnadu. This insults our deeply felt Catholic and Christian beliefs, and represents a grave disturbance to [good] relations among religions. We, the members of the Catholic Christian Community, unanimously demand that posters of this kind be immediately removed and that those involved in this deed apologize. We are also announcing that if [these things] are not done, appropriate actions will be taken against North Chennai Assistant Secretary C. R. Gopi. (*Malai Murasu* 25.02.93:3)

On 26 February Jayalalitha issued an announcement stating that some people had celebrated her birthday in a manner she did not appreciate, and she asked "lovingly" that people stop putting up posters and cutouts depicting her as a deity. The posters in question, plus several similar cutouts, were removed by that evening.

But the damage had been done. Christian leaders met again on 6 March and demanded that all Christian AIADMK ministers and MLAs resign their offices and that Jayalalitha herself apologize. Their joint resolution threatened mass protests by all Tamil Christians. Of course neither demand was met, and protest meetings erupted all over the state. An enormous meeting of some forty thousand people, conducted by various Christian groups, spun out of control in the port town of Tutucorin: traffic was blocked, a stage set up by AIADMK workers for a public meeting was destroyed along with associated hoardings, arches, and mic-set, and buses were set on fire. Jayalalitha was burned in effigy (an illegal act in India). In Madurai approximately one thousand women blocked buses and shut down businesses around the collector's office; students of various colleges went on strike and blocked traffic; illegal (i.e., homemade and unregistered) posters appeared throughout the city.

Protests continued throughout the month: churches all over Tamilnadu flew black flags starting on 12 March, and a week of mourning and protest was called. By 14 March protest meetings had so crippled the state that the collector of Madurai issued orders to the police to arrest those who blocked traffic or upset commerce. Thousands were arrested on 17 March during cross-bearing processions by women—including four hundred nuns—and mid-road hunger strikes by men—including ministers and priests—in Madurai. On 26 March papers reported that some 4,500,000 Christians had prayed in their churches during special sermons.

Politicians of opposing parties immediately began to criticize the chief minister for encouraging sycophancy among her party faithful. Vaiko echoed the Catholics by denouncing the imagery as both blasphemy (*mapathagam*) and a violation of core Dravidian Party beliefs (i.e., atheism). Tamilnadu Congress Committee General Secretary Kumari Anandan also issued a statement condemning the deification of the chief minister by her party.

But perhaps the most vociferous, and creative, opposition was undertaken by Jayalalitha's chief rival, Kalaiñar Mu. Karunanidhi. Kalaiñar penned a "small-screen [i.e., TV] cinema" story that was published in the *Dinathandi* on 1 March 1995. He wrote the story not to appear on television, but to "play on the screen of the minds" of the people of Tamilnadu. I reproduce it in its entirety here not only because of its discussion of the Virgin Mary and Athiparasakti posters but for its wider critique of the kinds of newspaper images discussed above as well. The Kalaiñar screenplay, more than any other single statement, both points out the limits of the identity between religious and political practices, and gives a negative description of the practical logic underlying both.

> *First scene, camera: Thiruvetharu Temple tower* (gopuram). *The temple bell swings fiercely, as if swaying in a strong storm, but it does not raise a sound. The camera leaves the bell. It pans the inner sanctum.* ADHIKESAVA PERUMAL *[Lord Vishnu] awakens panic-stricken from his eternal sleep and sits up.* "Alas," screams PERUMAL, "last year we received 20 million rupees, this year only 15? It's thievery, thievery!"
>
> *The snake that serves as his bed is named* ADHISESHAN. *He stands opposite eternally the sleeping* PERUMAL, *worships him, and politely says,* "O, Lord. This is the result of your eternal sleep." "O, Adhiseshan! You lie here as my bed and spread your hood in a protective parasol. How can you tolerate it when those good-for-nothings come in here? You have one thousand tongues! Couldn't you loudly protest 'Thief! Thief!' with just one of those tongues?" *asks* ADHIKESAVA PERUMAL *angrily.*
>
> ADHISESHAN *gives a measured reply*: "O, Lord! I fear what you might

do if you hear my voice. What has happened has happened. Let us see what happens next."

ADHIKESAVAR: What must we do next?

ADHISESHAN: We can complain to the police, and post haste!

ADHIKESAVAR: What happened to the complaint we issued to the police when those 20 million rupees were stolen back in 1992? It's been three years, and a charge-sheet hasn't even been prepared! Even if we give a complaint now it will be the same story. I think we should go to Siva Peruman and petition him. Where is Garuda, my vehicle?

Before ADHIKESAVAR *can close his mouth* GARUDA [an eagle, Vishnu's sacred vehicle] *comes flying in to background music, "gnoy!," and stops in front of* ADHIKESAVA PERUMAL. *Although trembling a little,* ADHISESHAN, *with the courage of knowing that he stands next to* PERUMAL, *arrogantly asks,* "Hey Garuda, how're you doing?" GARUDA *laughs and says,* "We are well indeed, standing where we are." "Garudalvar!" *says* ADHIKESAVA PERUMAL *in a commanding voice.* "I, your servant, await your command," GARUDA *replies.*

PERUMAL *climbs atop* GARUDA *and sits down.*

The scene changes from one showing GARUDA *beginning to flap his wings to one showing a helicopter flying in the open sky. As the helicopter alights in Kailasa* [Lord Siva's heavenly abode], *it changes back into* GARUDA. ADHIKESAVA PERUMAL *descends from it briskly. As he enters the main gate of Kailasa,* LORD NANDI [a bull, Siva's vehicle] *welcomes him with a worshipful* "Namaste."

ADHIKESAVAR: Lord Nandi! I need to see Lord Paramasivan [Siva] immediately! I have an urgent matter to discuss. A robbery of many millions of rupees has occurred in my temple! Where is Lord Siva?

LORD NANDI: O, Lord! Lord Siva hasn't been in Kailasa for a few days.

ADHIKESAVAR: Is that so? Where has he gone?

LORD NANDI: He said he didn't even need me, his vehicle, and he has gone on a pilgrimage, by foot, in search of the goddess Parvathi.

ADHIKESAVAR: What's all this? Is Parvathi Devi missing? Is Devi angry at Lord Siva or something?

LORD NANDI: Yes, Lord, she is unimaginably angry!

ADHIKESAVAR: Why, what happened?

LORD NANDI: Paramasivan and Parvathi went down to Earth and saw that people were saying that Parvathi had taken on an avatar in the form of a woman Chief Minister; they say that there are posters and cutouts of her all over Tamilnadu.

As they are talking they see in their minds' eyes the scene of the Chief

Minister's cutouts and posters in the form of Parvathi. Near the Parvathi image erected at the seashore cars stop, and ten or fifteen ministers get out. They stand directly in front of the image, fall down on the ground, and begin to worship it. From that place the camera moves to many different sites: some ministers eat earth-rice; some perform angapirathachanam[5] *in temples; some ministers walk on fire. Again,* LORD NANDI *speaks in Kailasa:*

LORD NANDI: Just because it is some woman's birthday, they're saying that Parvathi has taken on her avatar. She [Jayalalitha] is cheating the poor people! Parvathi became angry with Siva when he did nothing about it; they had a fight and she left him.

ADHIKESAVAR: What can Siva do about it? Real *bhakti pandits* should have criticized it, no?

LORD NANDI: The police couldn't stop the thievery at your temple, so you come to petition Lord Siva; Parvathi complained to Siva in the same way, got angry, and left.

ADHIKESAVAR: It's that woman Chief Minister! We should issue a statement asking that she henceforth never place a picture or depict herself as a deity, shouldn't we?

LORD NANDI: They've plastered up a picture of the woman Chief Minister as the Virgin Mary! The Christians have risen up in a fury! There is protest in all the four directions! Given no alternative, *that woman* has issued a statement. During the past three years, they have depicted the Chief Minister as Mookambika [the three main Goddesses-in-One; i.e., Parvathi, Lakshmi, and Saraswathi], as Murugan's wife, Valli, as Mariyamman [the smallpox goddess], as Kali, and as Parvathi. They have even issued full-page advertisements in newspapers! Her party's ministers and prominent members have commissioned advertisements in the newspapers with Veda-like hymns to her feet! Nowadays, without even opening her mouth, that Chief Minister arrogantly considers all Hindus her creatures. Now she seems to be wondering if "this cat will drink this milk, too,"[6] and the Christians have risen up in anger. She pretends that she doesn't know anything about it.

ADHIKESAVAR: O, Lord Nandi! I came here to speak about the many million of rupees worth of jewels that have disappeared from my temple, and now you tell me that Parvathi is missing!

While the two are talking, the conches of Kailasa are sounding as if all the worlds are shaking. LORD NANDI *leaps up, runs to get the Mathalam Drum, and begins to beat it. The camera showing the conch and the Mathalam Drum pans over to show two rough and callused feet ascending the cloud stairway of Kailasa. Ashes from the cremation grounds appear as a vast cloud of smoke.*

The camera focuses on the feet coming. It rises up to show SIVA *coming with a sad face. As soon as he sees* ADHIKESAVA PERUMAL, *his sorrow overflows:* "O, Brother-in-Law!" *they both cry out in one voice as their sorrow gushes forth and they embrace each other.* "Where is Parvathi? What has become of her? Lord Nandi told me you went looking for her." *Our* LORD SIVA *swallows hard, unable to answer* ADHIKESAVA PERUMAL'S *question; his eyes become waterfalls.*

ADHIKESAVAR: If my sister Parvathi were here now, she who protected you by stopping the Alagala Poison when you swallowed it, she would be in agony to see you sob so. O, Brother-in-Law! What has become of her?

As ADHIKESAVAR *and* SIVA *are embracing each other their flood of tears forms into a great ocean. First there is a scene of gods and demons churning the ocean of the world; then a scene depicting the trick of the creation of ambrosia and poison; and then the scene of Parvathi squeezing* SIVA'S *throat and keeping the poison from entering him. . . . After all this,* ADHIKESAVAR *speaks*: "O, Brother-in-Law! After seeing all these things—the Chief Minister as the avatar of Parvathi, as the rebirth of Mookambika, a woman who equates her feet with the Vedas—after seeing these advertisements for the past three years, the *bhakti pandits* do not stir at all. You don't get upset! But on the very day that the Chief Minister puts up posters of herself as the Virgin Mary, Christians rise up like waves on the roaring sea, voice their opposition, and humble that Chief Minister!"

LORD SIVA: What is my salvation from this? Parvathi chastised me; she became hot [with anger]. She left me because she could get no satisfaction from me. I have searched for her, I have been wandering in search of her. It's been no use. I don't know what has become of my Parvathi! Who would dare compare herself to her? She grumbled that even if these so-called *bhaktars* have no shame, do I have no shame as well? Has she fallen into a tank? Has she leaped to her death in a well? Has she hanged herself? I don't know! I ripped down just one of the hundreds of posters that were plastered on the doorway of the Chief Minister's house.

SIVA *then produces a poster that he had hidden under his tiger-skin shawl, and sobs as he weeps.*

The scene ends in a freeze-frame shot of SIVA *and* ADHIKESAVAR. *The film ends with the words* "Parvathi is Missing" *above the picture, as its title.*

O, Siblings! This letter has been written that this TV movie may play on the screens of the people's minds!

Jayalalitha and the Ganesh Temple

Kalaiñar's attack on the practices of Jayalalitha's faithful was perceived by members of the Hindu establishment as an attack on them as well. Indeed, less than a week later (5 March), in a speech given at a wedding celebration in Salem, Kalaiñar explicitly questioned the Hindu lack of response to AIADMK excesses:

> When a poster was printed depicting Jayalalitha as the Virgin Mary Christian organizations vehemently protested. But what do Hindu religious organizations such as the RSS, the Hindu Front, the [Hindu Bhaktar] Jana Sangam, and Bharatiya Janatha [Party] do when Jayalalitha is depicted as Madurai Meenakshi and Parvathi? Full-page ads for Jayalalitha appear in newspapers saying "We worship your feet which are equal to the Vedas." (*Dinamalar* 6.03.95:10)

Ramagopalan, the leader of the Hindu right-wing group "Hindu Front" (*Indumunani*), immediately responded by issuing a statement on 6 March to the effect that tolerance was a characteristic of the Hindu faith (and not, seemingly, of Christianity):

> Hindus have never been bothered when who knows how many posters have been placed or cutouts erected hailing Tamilnadu Chief Minister Miss Jayalalitha as Ambikai or Adhiparasakti. . . . [In the same way] they sell firecrackers with the name "Lakshmi Crackers." No Hindu's heart has ever been wounded by the thought that when this cracker explodes into pieces, Lakshmi Devi also explodes into pieces. . . . The reason for this is the unshakable quality of the Hindu faith in God. (*Dinathandi* 8.3.95:8)

Ramagopalan rebukes not Jayalalitha but Kalaiñar for fanning the flames of communal discord by writing and speaking against the Hindu community's lack of opposition to AIADMK practices. But P. N. Vallaracu, All-India Forward Block Party Secretary of Tamilnadu, took up Kalaiñar's challenge, and Ramagopalan's declaration of tolerance, and condemned the painting of Jayalalitha on the back side of the Vinayakar (Ganesh) Temple in Madurai (fig. 14, described above). From the wording of his statement, issued on 12 March, it is clear that the Christian response to the Virgin Mary incident was the model of a new kind of protest by some Hindus against AIADMK excesses of praise:

> Because AIADMK partymen have depicted Chief Minister Jayalalitha as the Virgin Mary, Christians have felt wounded and a great protest has arisen from them. Now, AIADMK partymen, who have depicted the Chief Minister as Adhiparasakti and Madurai Meenakshi, have begun to paint Jayalalitha on temple walls. The famous Vinayakar Temple is in Madurai's Cimmakkal. They have painted a picture of Chief Minister Jayalalitha on an entire wall of that temple. Milk production leader Mariyappan, whose picture is also prominent on the temple wall, has desecrated the sacredness of the Vinayakar Temple.
>
> Hindu Front leaders will not come forward to erase the picture. The reason that Ramagopalan is not prepared to criticize either the painting of Chief Minister Jayalalitha or the theft of millions of rupees from Hindu temples is the AIADMK's financial and authoritarian might.
>
> Therefore, I hereby announce that if the paintings of Jayalalitha and milk production leader Mariyappan are not taken down in one week's time Hindus under my leadership will gather together and destroy the paintings. I also call upon Hindu Front leader Ramagopalan to take part in this. (*Dinakaran* 13.3.95:9)

While Ramagopalan, allied with the AIADMK, did not answer Vallaracu's call, Vallaracu was joined by several other individuals and organizations, including leaders of other organizations associated with the Hindu right, such as Hindu Bhaktar Jana Sabai leader Thiyagarajan, who also called for the painting's removal. But the outcry appeared to die out as the one-week deadline passed without incident and several months went by. Their call to protest seemingly did not have the popular appeal that characterized the Christian agitations.

It was not until the early morning of 5 July 1995 that the Ganesh Temple painting again gained public attention, when some substance, variously described as black paint or tar, was found splashed on the faces of the painted images of Jayalalitha and Mariyappan and (significantly!) on the names of the painting's sponsors. *Malai Murasu* (5.07.95:1) reported that news of the painting's desecration "spread like wild-fire," and by 10 A.M. a large crowd of AIADMK supporters had blocked traffic around the Cimmakkal temple: "Buses on both sides (of the temple) stood still like standing water." One Velmurugan, a student at Madurai Law College (notorious for its flamboyant protests), poured kerosene on himself and threatened to set himself on fire; he was prevented from doing so by his comrades.[7] AIADMK party supporters began smashing scooters and bicycles, setting them afire in the street, and throwing stones at any cars that were unlucky enough to get caught in the melee. Shops all around Cimmakkal closed their shutters. *Dinakaran* (6.07.95:1) described the scene as a "riot" (*kalavaram*).

Police rushed to the scene and conferred with senior partymen and supporters who had gathered there, including Coconutshop Mariyappan, Minister of Parliament Rajanchellappa, Poppaiyan, and others. Assuring the leaders that parties responsible for the painting's destruction would be arrested quickly, the police commissioner managed to convince Mariyappan and Rajanchellappa to call an end to the roadblock and disperse the crowd. Apparently, the commissioner also agreed to something else: constables were present at the temple twenty-four hours a day from the next day on as work began to restore the painting (*Nakeeran* 12–18 July 1995). Hindu Bhaktar Jana Sabai leader Thiyagarajan claimed that his life was in danger. He was arrested on 17 July.[8]

WORSHIPER AND WORSHIPED

The opposition to the excesses of praise by AIADMK partymen appears to confirm the observation that people relate to powerful leaders in ways similar to the ways they relate to their deities. And we found, too, that there appear to be limits to the practical identification of logics that inform "religious" and "political" forms of association with powerful beings, both gods and men. It is not insignificant that the opposition to these excesses was voiced first and most vociferously by members of the Christian community, whose see themselves as a community under siege and make a far clearer distinction between God and human being than most Hindus. Neither is it insignificant that the call-to-arms by leaders of politically motivated Hindu organizations was never heeded by the vast majority of Hindus in Tamilnadu. Hindu Front leader Ramagopalan's observation—that Hindus are not bothered by such things as the depiction of Jayalalitha as a goddess—is correct, though perhaps not for the reasons he mentioned: the Hindu Front, the RSS, and similar Hindu nationalist organizations are not known for their "tolerance."

As many observers of Hindu statecraft and kingship have observed (Appadurai and Breckenridge 1976; Dirks 1987; Narayana Rao, Shulman, and Subrahmanyam 1992; Price 1996a; Waghorne 1994), the relevant distinction in religious and political practices is not so much between gods and men (as Western and Abrahamic ideology maintains) but between the worshiper and the worshiped (Moffatt 1979:234n, as quoted in Pandian 1992a:134). Dirks, for instance, writes in his discussion of early British period kingly practice and its relation to social order (including caste), that

> not only is there no fundamental ontological separation of a "religious" from a "political" domain, but religious institutions and activities are fundamental features of what we describe here as the political system. Kings derive much of their power from worship, and bestow their emblems and privileges in a cultural atmosphere that is permeated by the language and attitudes of worship. . . . Religion does not encompass kingship any more than kingship encompasses religion. (Dirks 1989:60–61)

It is important here to note also that the ontological separation of the terms "political" and "religion" is highly suspect, very recent, and probably based more on Western enlightenment notions than on anything developed in India (Asad 1993, 2003; Balagangadhara 1994; Daniel 2002; King 1999). The carving out of a political space by Christians in the Virgin Mary debacle and the subsequent Ganesh Temple controversy is a delightfully explicit model of how the various practices of "Hinduism" gelled, over the past two centuries, into something that all agree today is a "religion" (Mishra 2004; Van der Veer 2001; Lorenzen 2006; Pennington 2005).

But Dirks' remarks regarding the mid-nineteenth century coincide with similar observations made for Chola period court practices (Ali 1996, 2004), the Nayakar courts of Thanjavur and Madurai (Narayana Rao, Shulman, and Subrahmanyam 1992, 2003), and kingly practice in seventeenth- through nineteenth-century Ramnad (Price 1996a) and Puthukkottai (Dirks 1987; Waghorne 1994). Indeed, the idea appears to be as old as the earliest texts in India. As McKim Marriott has observed on many occasions, Hindu macrosociology (like microbiology)

> presents explicit cosmogonic theories (for instance Manu 9:3–5, 14–18, 32–35) in which the gods, the Brahman *varna*, and the king, divinity, morality (*dharma*), and royal power (*ksatra*), the power to give punishment (*danda*) subtly with speech or grossly with weapons—all are seen as transformations of each other and of the original undifferentiated cosmic energy or protoplasm (*brahman*). . . . Recent ethnography tells of the same sorts of cognitions among Hindus in rural areas, where the categories of gods and men are thought to be mutually continuous, uninterrupted by distinctions such as "sacred" and "profane," "spirit" and "matter." . . . All beings are gradable by "power" (*shakti*, etc.), and power is understood to be synonymous with both religious virtue and effective worldly dominance. (1976:112–113)

Again, as with the larger argument of this book, this is not to make a claim regarding some direct and unmediated continuity between precolonial courtly practices and the practices of contemporary political patronage (as explicitly argued, for instance, by Dickey [1993a] and Price [1996a]). Indeed, as I argued in the preceding chapters, the kind of practices surrounding the political patronage of Jayalalitha appear to be the culmination of a far more recent development associated with democratic campaigning by the Dravidian parties (Price 1996b); there was nothing like this during the late British and early postindependence Congress period in Tamilnadu among politicians and their supporters (with the one glaring exception—precedent?—of the subcontinent-wide treatment of Mahatma Gandhi, see Amin 1988:288–348). And according to most interlocutors in Madurai there was nothing approaching the deification of politicians among the Dravidians until the rise of MGR and his successor, Jayalalitha.

Furthermore, there is one aspect of the classical practice of praising the god/king that is markedly absent in contemporary political practice: the erotics of the king. In both Chola (Ali 1996) and Nayakar (Narayana Rao, Shulman, and Subrahmanyam 1992) court poetry the king's erotic exploits were explicitly praised as an index of his godlike virility and suitability to rule; indeed, the "major diagnostic feature" of Nayakar praise poetry was the king's "hypertrophied eroticism" (Narayana Rao et al. 1992:62; for examples of a similar aesthetic of eroticism in Chola *ula* poetry see Ali 1996:175–215, 2004; Wentworth 2009). Today this aspect of the leader's persona is not generally discussed in either public meetings or newspaper reportage. The facts that Kalaiñar has several wives or that Jayalalitha's life partner is a woman are widely known, occasionally ridiculed by vulgar speakers on stage (see chapter 7), but never made topics of praise by their supporters.[9]

Clearly, even though today the distinction between religion and politics is a strong one, something of the old "traditional" logic informing relationships between the powerful, be they gods or humans, and those who patronize them has managed to remain even after the old kingdoms were "hollowed out" by British colonial hegemony and the rational modernism of the Congress period—or else that tradition was reinvented precisely in the modernity that is democratic practice. Of course, the deployment of what appears to be a traditional, Indic mode of patronage—in this case likening one's leader to a deity—appears to be another element in the larger meta-traditional deployment of such forms within the larger Dravidianist paradigm.

[6]

KAVITHA'S LOVE

THE DEVOTIONAL practices described in this book—this *bhakti,* this love written large on the streets and walls of Madurai, in newspapers and in epic dramas—is of course not subjectless, authorless, *bhaktar*-less. It is also not mere sycophancy, as one level of analysis and much popular discussion of these things in Tamilnadu might suggest. Rather, people with genuine emotional stakes in their leaders produce this material, call their leaders "Mother" and "Family Deity"; most important, they believe it. The leader enters the *bhaktar*'s dreams at night, protects her in times of trouble, offers hope to her on a personal level, becomes the object of her desires. What follows here is the story of one of these *bhaktars* and her desperate desire, her "frenzied love" (*veri pacam*), which, she believes, will be attained through the use and mastery of the Tamil language. This *bhaktar*'s speech and speech about speech suggest the link between the *bhakti* of old and its current incarnation vis-à-vis the red-tongued gods whose temple is the Legislative Assembly and the *Kottai,* the "Fort," in Madras.

N. G. M. Kavitha was perhaps unusual insofar as she was a woman, a relatively rarer, relatively more marked occupant of the political stage. As a woman she was held to a stricter exemplification of the values inherent in the act of public speaking, and she was more vulnerable to the dangers and fantasies to which those occupying the lower levels of the political hierarchy are subject. She was at the base of several hierarchies; and as I came to understand such things during my stay in Tamilnadu, those on the lower end of the semeiosocial scale often have a unique (perhaps clearer?) view of the structures of domination in which they dwell—if only because they frequently experience the effects of such domination on their very bodies.[1] Ultimately, as will become clear in the unfolding of her tale, Kavitha's story demonstrates for us, in her words on and off the stage, the purest ideal of the poet-politician and the aesthetic impulses that drive political cultural production of semeiosocial form in Tamilnadu.

This chapter is based on two texts[2] produced on two occasions: one a speech delivered upon a stage at a political meeting, and the other produced in an interview situation. Both texts, though quite different in interactional emergence and structural organization, were produced with the key participants well aware of the interactional presuppositions and entailments of the two performance/interactional genres. In the first case, Kavitha and I attended and participated in a public meeting, a genre of interaction with very clear discursive and interactional parameters in which both of us could reasonably anticipate the unfolding of the event. Kavitha came to participate fully in the great game of political speaking and advancement both for her party and for herself; I came to the meeting to listen to and record these speeches, also for my own advancement as a scholar working on a doctoral dissertation. In the second case, Kavitha came to me to tell me a story that she hoped would be told elsewhere; she hoped, too, that this story, like her speeches, would be extended in time and space to some unknown but possibly fruitful place from which a higher power would benefit her. She was quite explicit about this:

> *solla vendiya suzhnilai achchu. sari, ningal terinjukonga; velinattukkarar tana? Tamilnattile oru pennukku ippadiyellam irukku nu ninga poy solla num, ile?*
>
> What I needed to say happened. Right, you should know it; you're just a foreigner, right? (*laughs*) You should go and tell people that it is like this for a woman in Tamilnadu.

HOW I MET HER

It was at a meeting put on by Durai that I first heard Kavitha speak on stage. The meeting took place just in front of Durai's home at Arappalaiyam Crossroads in the neighborhood of Madurai called Ponnagaram on 24 April 1995. It was a *kandana pothukkuuddam*, literally, "a public meeting to criticize," entitled *Kutravalikundil irukkum Jayalalithah: nee rajinama cey!* "O, Jayalalitha who is in the docks: Resign!" DMK leader Kalaiñar had recently submitted a list of corruption charges to the governor of Tamilnadu detailing the CM's crimes and those of her ministers. At the same time, the DMK was continuing its attack against Vai. Ko. Gopalswamy (Vaiko), who, as discussed already, had defected to form a breakaway party, the Renaissance Dravidian Progress Association (MDMK). Because he was a longtime leader of the DMK, a minister of Parliament, and one of Tamilnadu's most talented stage speakers, the defection of Vaiko was met with great anger and dismay by the DMK, and tirades against what Kavitha called the "Traitor from Kalingapatti" and the "Party Traitor" also dominated the speeches of that night.

When I first heard Kavitha speak I noticed immediately a difference between her and the other speakers. I could not understand her, for she was too fast for my alien ears. But there was a distinct rhythmicality to her speaking, a dancing staccato energy in her voice that fascinated me and drew the attention of the audience gathered there. A run-of-the-mill speaker in Madurai frequently enjoys a less than attentive audience: organizers will be in a constant buzz sending out their underlings for tea or barking other orders to them, greeting important guests, whispering cheerfully head-to-head with someone or other seated on stage, or otherwise engaged in all the minutiae of running a public meeting, including the details that hadn't yet been accomplished before all got underway. Others will chat among themselves, go off in twos and threes to the tea stall around the corner, fiddle with their clothing as they arrange themselves on the pavement for the evening, whatever—anything but giving rapt attention, especially during the several hours of speeches by the less renowned that invariably take place prior to the featured guest. As Kavitha began her speech, though, the normally distracted fixed upon her, and their attention did not waver throughout her eighteen-and-a-half-minute speech.

I thought at the time she was a very young woman, perhaps in her early or mid twenties. I felt, therefore, somewhat awkward approaching her for fear of frightening her or invoking the wrong kind of attention to myself. But I was keen to talk with women politicians at the time, to get a sense of their roles in and perspectives on the world of political speaking. Women usually came on stage early in the meetings to deliver what always appeared to me to be very well crafted speeches; sometimes a little girl with precocious speaking skills (the daughter of some party member) would deliver an intricate memorized speech right after the singers, poets, and other entertainers organizers enlisted to get the meetings going. And a small group of women are almost always there on the side, dressed in red saris with black boarders, sitting in the chairs arrayed on the side of the stage; a small group of them were there that night.

Through an introduction by the King, I met one of them, Mrs. Parvathi Annamalai, a woman in her mid sixties or so. We chatted for some time; I indicated my interest in speaking with her, and received an invitation to her home the next day. Kavitha left shortly thereafter, along with the other women, just as the "vulgar" Theepori Arumugam was taking the stage, and before I got a chance to meet or talk with her. I felt helpless as she crammed into an auto rickshaw with the others and rode away.

The next day I went to Mrs. Parvathi's home and spoke with her and an associate about their experiences in politics. At the end of the meeting, I indicated to Mrs. Parvathi my interest in speaking with Kavitha. When I told her of hesitating to approach her at the meeting she laughed at me. "Kavitha is a married woman with two children," she said.

About three weeks later, on 10 May, I was home working, frantically trying to tie up my research, which was to end along with the month. My little room had taken on the appearance of a full-scale field-shop: newspapers in various degrees of vivisection, clippings strewn around the room. Several friends were organizing them into clip books; another was busily transcribing tapes trying to put down the hundreds of hours of speeches that I'd accumulated. As I listen to the recording of the interview, I also hear the usual suspects, neighborhood children such as the ever-present Murugapandi, running in and out of the room.

Into this scene entered Kavitha, escorted by three of the neighborhood kids who had helped her to navigate the streets and alleys to my place. She wasn't sure I'd recognize her, and made haste to mention several times that she had spoken at Durai's meeting and that she had seen me there, and that Parvathi Annamalai had indicated to her that I wanted to meet her. It took several minutes to convince her that I knew very well who she was and that I was very happy that she had come to see me. After settling down with tea, we arranged ourselves at my desk with a tape recorder and began a three-hour conversation about her life and her work.

THE INTERVIEW

As it turns out, she had been born only a few houses away from the meeting venue of 24 April at Arappalaiyam Crossroads, right behind Durai's house. It was there, sitting on the doorstep of her home after she had become a "big woman" (*periya pen*) and couldn't go out alone anymore, that she had first listened to the political speech that was piped her way by horn speakers strung throughout her neighborhood for political meetings. "You couldn't help hearing what they were shouting in the microphones," she said, "we didn't have to go to the meetings because we could hear what they said while doing our housework." She particularly appreciated the speaking energies of Theepori Arumugam, the so-called vulgar speaker.

> His words and all, he won't speak with propriety, he'll speak vulgarly. Not a single old women would be able to sit at such a meeting, that's how vulgar he speaks! Even so, we'd be very interested, we had to hear his forceful, shouting speed [*ongi kathura speedu*]. We'd enjoy listening to his speeches on the sly.

In fact, it was the voices of the speakers that she identified as the sources of her own speaking abilities. I tried repeatedly to discuss her training as a speaker, seeking to understand how she came to be so proficient. Did she attend speaking competitions like other future stage speakers? Did any teacher take particular interest in her and help her to become a great public speaker? Did she read poetry and grammar? No, she said, there were no teachers of note in her early education, she never read poetry, and she never competed in oratorical competitions. Like so many children I met with extraordinary abilities but meager family recourses, she excelled in math and Tamil but lagged behind in English and science (in which English proficiency is necessary). She talked of one speech competition held for the older children that, in true character, she attended despite being told repeatedly to leave by the teachers. She stood in the back and listened, fascinated, the grownups ignoring her, having finally given up the effort.

It was the power of the great speakers, she claimed, that transformed her into a stage speaker.

> I've never heard Periyar's voice or Anna's voice—I've seen pictures of Periyar but never heard Periyar's voice. When we hear the voices of the great leaders we develop enthusiasm for politics. I have heard Kalaiñar's voice. I have seen him in person.

The contrast between seeing and hearing is important to note insofar as it violates certain long-standing stereotypes of Hindu phenomenology in which seeing is considered the primary sense, the primary mode and point of worship (Eck 1981:7–9); here Kavitha evokes the sense of hearing—specifically hearing the voices of great leaders—as the transformative sensation, a sensory experience equivalent to (or greater than) the experience of seeing one's god. Kalaiñar's voice, especially, is central:

My education is little
I've no political experience.
I pay close attention to the tongue [*nakku*] which Kalaiñar speaks with
When he speaks I pay attention to the way he brings his arm around.
I pay close attention no matter which leader speaks.
That's [the trick].
That's [the trick] for the speaker:

the tongue [*nakku*]
how to improve it, to speak
when we speak in "stacked utterances" [*adukkumozhi*] the tongue
she will develop, right?

But there is also a dual relationship in this hearing: if Kalaiñar hears her voice, too, the benefits for her may be vast. "If Kalaiñar hears me speak I'll get an MLA (Minister of the Legislative Assembly) seat," she thought. Again, the parallel of the reciprocal exchange of voices between subordinate and superior political figure with the reciprocal exchange of gazes between devotee and god is striking. The experience of hearing the voices of the great founding leaders, or the lack of such experience, and having them hear you, becomes important not only personally but politically, too, as we see in the speech to follow.

Persistence in the face of adversity characterized Kavitha's story in general. She was married when she was twenty-one years old to her own mother's brother's (*taaymaaman*) son, a romantic ideal for many in Tamilnadu (Trawick 1990:148–151). He was a tea-stall owner in Madurai. In the beginning the marriage worked out well enough: two children, both girls, were born within the first few years. Her husband's family sought her younger brother for their daughter—"give a girl, take a girl," they say (*pen koduttu, pen edukka*). It is thought to be a reasonable financial solution for some poorer families insofar as the amounts of dowry and other marriage gifts can be exchanged reciprocally (in the ideal case). But that practice is also considered fraught with danger: if one marriage goes bad the other family might begin to mistreat the bride in their home. Her brother said, "We've given our sister, let that be enough." And that's when Kavitha's troubles began in earnest. Her husband's family began to mistreat her, to be cruel to her.

K: After all that some cruelties began.
B: By cruelties, you mean . . . ?
K: By cruelties I mean that there was no happiness in my life. At a stage of

> life in which one should really live we have the desire that on our street, when a husband and wife walk down a street. . . . And this way would my husband be? I cried to someone next to me once, "Why, sister, after so many days since getting married, my husband has never taken me to a temple, never taken me even to the cinema, sister."

It got worse. Her husband eventually took another wife and moved down to a town in Ramanathapuram district. She found a job in a medical clinic as a receptionist, but her meager salary was not enough to support her two daughters (now her sole responsibility): she sent one to her sister and another to her mother. Finding the salary too little even to be able to feed herself, she began to turn her attentions to politics as another possible source of income.

In 1988, during the general elections, she was asked by members of a women's political organization to go canvassing, putting up flags bearing the Rising Sun sign of the DMK. It was at this time that she came under the influence of a man named A. S. Kani, who had been involved in politics for more than fifty years. She told him her story and begged him to introduce her to stage speaking. He advised her on what to do on the stage: read the "notice" (the list of organizers, speakers, and sponsors for an event), and then speak for two minutes or so. He also encouraged her to sing songs that she composed herself. Her songs focused on prices, how the cost of living under the rule of Jayalalitha had risen (a prominent theme in her speeches of 1995 as well). Two songs became three, three became five. "All the people sitting at a public meeting look forward to hearing what the ladies will say on stages."

KAVITHA'S LOVE

Kavitha spoke of many kinds of love, or lack thereof, often in the most poetic terms. The two forms of love that were most prominently evoked in her conversation with me were love for her deity and, most important, love for her leader, Kalaiñar. Love in Tamilnadu, of many, many kinds, is intimately associated with—some would say necessarily entails—suffering; it is a dangerous emotion that if outwardly displayed can lead to injury or death for the object of one's affection as well as for oneself. In some ways it is akin to any strong positive emotion directed at another, such as admiration or appreciation, that can have deleterious effects upon the object of desire. In general, love must be very carefully—usually surreptitiously, ambiguously—demonstrated (Trawick 1990:93–97).

But not in politics, nor in worship. She makes no ambiguities regarding her feelings for her leader, perhaps because the statement itself has the possibility of reaching Kalaiñar's ears and providing some benefit to her. Regardless, Kavitha attributes much of her suffering to her love for her leader:

I don't have proper food to eat,
I'll tell you openly.
I don't have proper clothes to wear—
That's how poor I am.
I'm in dire straits in this movement.
What is the reason?
The love [*pacam*] I have for Kalaiñar.
When I say Kalaiñar I mean—it's somehow . . .
Our grandfa—it's like seeing our father's father to me.
Do you understand or not?

What is important to see in the above fragment as well as in the one to follow, though, is the specific creative construction of this love that both follows and transcends already extant models for love among Tamilians. But the parallel structure of identification in her utterances clearly, unequivocally, equates her suffering with her love, her *pacam*, for Kalaiñar. The notion of the grandfather is further fleshed out in an account of a particular moment in her childhood. At this moment in the conversation she waxes ebullient: "I have a frenzied love [*veri pacam*] for Kalaiñar," she says, almost as if she were talking of a lover or a god:

I have a frenzied love [*veri pacam*] for Kalaiñar!
They say it, don't they?
If my father asked if I were the most beloved child (in the house):
If he asked, "Grandfather, which child do you like?"—
"I like this second one best," he'd say, my Grandfather.
It's like that for me.
Grandfather, like knowing my father's father
when I see him.
In the place where I didn't see Thandai Periyar,
I have seen Kalaiñar.
Instead of seeing Perariñar Anna,
I have seen Kalaiñar.
When I say that

> I may have a grandfather and I may have a father, too
> to us it's a—just like he says,
> like saying, "My sister with whom I was born"
> as our Elder Brother with whom we were born
> we have accepted him.

Many kinds of possible loves are interwoven in this fragment, loves that exploit inherent possibilities in Tamil political culture as well as a broader aesthetics of interaction in general. She continues the idea of Kalaiñar as her grandfather, specifically her father's father. On some occasion still poignant in her memory the grandfather expressed his special love for Kavitha. The scene is very familiar, something that truly happened to her. The language she uses to describe this incident and its significance to her—the model of love which she and her "grandfather" Kalaiñar inhabit—is noncontinuous, "ungrammatical," we might say; it more resembles a kind of free verse built on a series of parallel phrases that build up a complex set of identifications between Kalaiñar, her grandfathers, and the two great leaders, Periyar and Anna, whom she never saw. Though there is also the mention of Kalaiñar as the "elder brother, and she as "the sister with whom [he] was born," it is not a contradiction; neither is it a contradiction later in our conversation when she mentioned that she would never use Kalaiñar's name, Karunanidhi (in the same way, note, that a wife would never speak the name of her husband). Rather, all of these identifications are layered one upon the other to develop a complex of different modes of loving that might be applied to the ideal relationship she imagines between herself and her leader: a "frenzied love" that also leads to her suffering.

THE SPEECH

The speech that Kavitha had given that night I heard her was, she says, a fragment of a longer speech (speech$_1$) that kept on getting longer and longer; it was only for lack of time—time being a function of her relative status—that speech$_1$ had not yet been instantiated in some real-time performance. Her citations of speech$_2$, during our interview, then, are citations of a citation, instantiations twice removed from the original speech$_1$ that was to be delivered eventually upon a stage on which she would be the *sirappuppechalar*, the "special Speaker," the primary guest, the last to speak and the first to be greeted. There is in Kavitha's account an understanding of the political economy of speaking, a dialectical relationship between the speech$_1$ that she has prepared and not yet delivered and the speech$_2$ that she performs at the public meetings of that time; speech$_2$, being heard by greater and greater persons—ultimately by Kalaiñar—will eventually lead her to deliver speech$_1$. And her citations to me (speech$_3$) are also delivered in the hope that this, too, will extend her name, her "weight."

Her speech (see the appendix, "Kavitha's Speech," p. 199ff) begins the way all such speeches must, with "introductory salutations" ordered according to the principles outlined in chapter 2—i.e., the highest ranked are mentioned first, the lowest last. It is important to note here the use of kinship terms for—almost[3]—every one of the party members addressed: Elder Brother Mu. Ka. Alagiri (Kalaiñar's son), Elder Brother Nannilam Natarajan, Elder Brother Theepori Arumugam, Beloved Mother Parvathi Annamalai, etc. Also of particular interest is the fact that she addresses not only her childhood neighbors among the "middle classes who live in this area," but also the people of other parties who are listening "on the sly" (*ozhinthiruunthu*) to her oration (lines 26, 27), just as she had listened "on the sly" to speeches while doing her housework as a girl.

Following the introduction, Kavitha's speech appears to be composed of five more sections, each thematically distinct, some with clear indications of topical shift, e.g., line 131, "But let us not fret over that" (secs. II/III); line 182, "I don't have time to speak any more about you" (secs. III/IV); line 201, "I do not have time to speak a long time" (secs. IV/V); and line 234, "I have neither the time nor the opportunity to speak for an extended time" (secs. V/VI). Based on these and other obvious topical breaks, the speech as a whole can be diagrammed as in table 6.1. But more clearly, each section, or pair of sections, cycles through distinct contrasts between the greatness of her leader Kalaiñar and the depravity and the moral and historical unfitness of DMK opponents, specifically Chief Minister Jayalalitha and former party member Vaiko.

Section II begins with a literal, worshipful stance: "Our Tamil people's leader, who stands in protection of our party after chopping to pieces the plots of that cabal of traitors / I face the place where that leader resides, worship/salute [*vanangu*] him / and I will put to you just a few thoughts and then take my leave" (lines 33–34). This section is the most "rhetorical" of all (as defined in chapter 2); she locates Kalaiñar both in opposition to Vaiko and Jayalalitha and within the lineage of the great leaders Periyar E. V. Ramaswamy and Ariñar Annadurai. She takes special care at this point both to historicize the fear that Jayalalitha feels at the rising prospects of

TABLE 6.1 Outline of Kavitha's Speech

Section Number	Title	Line Numbers
I	Introductory Salutations	1–31
II	Jayalalitha's Fears vs. Kalaiñar's Deeds	32–131
III	The Party Traitor	132–182
IV	Rape and Corruption	183–201
V	Kalaiñar's Praise	202–233
VI	Conclusion	234–247

NOTE: See appendix.

the DMK, and to demonstrate Kalaiñar's historical fitness to rule. Specifically, in lines 66–106 she documents his historical record of generosity and wise rule—e.g., free electricity, loan write-offs, and material subsides for farmers; free bus passes and augmentation of the "Nutritious Noon Meal" scheme for students; material aide to women for marriage and widow support, etc.—and she also emphasizes his record *in regard to history* (which great and not-so-great leaders were unable to do), of erecting statues: along the Marina Beach in Madras to such personages as the great Chief Ministers Kamaraj and M. G. Ramachandran; for the Poligar Virapandi Kattaboman, an eighteenth-century king who defied the British and was hanged for it; and for Kannaki, the heroine of the Tamil epic *Silappathikaram,* who embodies the powers of a chaste and righteous Tamil woman. That this particular section was delivered more spontaneously than the ones that follow is indicated by the flow of the speech, the topical "drift" indicated by the shift at line 107 between the discussion of a statue erected to Rajiv Gandhi and the one dealing with the dissolution of the DMK government in 1976 by Indira Gandhi.

The other sections, however, are each organized by radically contrasting shifts between "rhetorical" abuse of enemies and "devotional" praise of Kalaiñar. Section III exemplifies her poetic gifts in both respects. She begins with a relatively straightforward account of how the "Party Traitor," Vaiko, emerged as a player in Tamilnadu politics not for the sake of the Tamil people but for that of one of his "community" (*inam*) fellows and for his own prestige and economic advancement (as Panchayat Head and later as the head of several banks). She also ridicules his ouster from Parliament as an MP after taking a clandestine boat trip to Sri Lanka to meet with LTTE leaders in 1989; she takes care to point out that he was ousted by a woman (line 154).

But in the next lines she seems genuinely outraged that this "Party Traitor" (*kazhagattin durohi*), who "wears a black shawl and delivers heroic orations on stages," has claimed that her leader, Kalaiñar, has begun to "stammer" (*tadumaruthal*) when speaking Tamil! In examining this section note how the phrase "[he] stammers [in] Tamil" (*tamil tadumarukirathu*) appears over and over again and appears to anchor specific breath groups; note also that each breath group repeats an interrogative structure, /-*a*/, syntactically marked as ironic:

indrakku medaiyile karuppu tundu pottukondu veeravacanam pecukirar
These days he gets up on stages wearing a black shawl and gives heroic orations.

Thandai Periyar neril parttiruppara
Did he ever see Thandai Periyar in person?

Anna kuralai kettiruppara neril parttiruppara
Did he ever hear Anna's voice, or see him in person?

ivarkalellam talaivar Kalaiñar avarkalai parttu tamil tadumarukirathu *endru collavillai*
All of those who saw our leader Kalaiñar never said that he stammered in Tamil.

Kalingappatti kazhagattin durogi collikirar tamil talaivarkku tamil tadumarukiratham
The Party Traitor from Kalingappatti says so. The Tamil Leader stammers in Tamil, he says!

yarkku tamil tadumarukirathu
Who stammers in Tamil?

sanga tamil vilakkattirka tamil tadumarukirathu
Does [one] stammer when discoursing on Sangam Tamil?

eetradi kuralukku oviyam teettitta durogi turikai yetrivarukka tamizh tadumarukirathu
Will one raising a brush to paint a painting stammer in Tamil in poetic two-line stanzas?

Parada! Ceran Senkottuvan Pandiyanai Colanai Palluvanai
"Hey, Da, look at Ceran, at Senkuttuvan, at the Pandyan King, at the Colan King, at the Pallavan King."

endru adaiiyalam kattiya anta paintamilukka tamil tadumarukirathu

Will one stammer in pure, ancient Tamil when pointing [these kings] out?

sivi cinkarittu rattakkavi pidittu val koduttu 168a
Having groomed and decorated [her son], having placed a blood *thilagam* on [his forehead] and given him a sword,

sendru va makaney pormuai nokki enru 168b
and turning to the battlefield said, "Go and Come, O, my son!"

anuppiya tamilachchiyar 168c
this mother who sent [him] to the battlefield

namakkellam adaiyalam kattiya anda tamilarivukka tamil tadumarukirathu 169
Will the Tamil knowledge stammer that identifies to us all [this woman?]

In our discussion after the speech, Kavitha pointed to this particular section to illustrate what she called *adukkumozhikal*, or "stacked utterances," a recent coinage of meta-oratorical discourse that appears to be based on the principle of *madakku* ("refraction," "folding") described in the previous chapter. Kavitha demonstrates throughout the speech her mastery of the trope; she was quite explicit in our discussion about her continued attempts to extend her repertoire of *adukkumozhikal* by devising new phrases that were "appropriate" (*poruththamana*) to the previous ones. When I asked what she meant by "appropriate" she pointed to how she used *tamil tadumarukirathu* over and over again as a primary organizing or anchoring phrase. Though she had not heard of the trope of *madakku*, *adukkumozhikal* are essentially refractions of a similar thematic and metrical structure, each one built—"stacked"—one upon the other.[4]

Following Kavitha's lead, notice how the repetition of the phrase *tamil tadumarukirathu* "[he] stammers [in] Tamil," contrasted with *tamil tadumaravillai* "[he] doesn't stammer [in] Tamil" (lines 161–169) structures the entire section of the speech fragment (just as the *pola*, *pothu*, and *odu* endings and *tailavar* of Vaiko's speech structured the sections cited in chapter 2). Syntactically, lines 164–167 are refractions of one another—"stacked" transformations, in Kavitha's terms—structured by ironically marked interrogatives. The interrogative marker /*-a*/ is suffixed onto a dative verbal noun followed by the subject and finite verb; an unmarked equivalent to line 164, for instance, maintains a standard SOV syntactic structure, suffixing the interrogative marker onto the end of the finite verb:

sanga tamil *vilakkattirku* *tamil tadumarukiratha.*
Sangam Tamil illuminate$^{\text{-VN-dat}}$ stammer$^{\text{-IIIsgnr INT}}$
Does Tamil stammer for illuminating [discoursing on] Sangam Tamil?

There is a further use of *adukkumozhikal*, which Kavitha pointed out in our discussion, in the sequence of questions that immediately follow the segment reproduced above. In this segment note how a series of terms end in the interrogative marker /*-a*/, tying together these terms into a description of her leader:

*Kalaiñar tuppum echchil kuda kanni tamil irukkirathu endru kazhagattin durohikku teriyath**a*** 170
Doesn't the Party Traitor know that even Kalaiñar's spittle has Virgin Tamil in it?

*Kalaiñar avarkal yeratha malai uchiy**a** ulavatha pulkal mudikal**a*** 171a
Is there a mountaintop Kalaiñar has not climbed, a crown of fame not acknowledged?

*adaiyatha malar malaiy**a** nadai poda raja veethiy**a*** 171b
a flower garland he has not worn, a sacred street on which he has not walked triumphantly?

*Kalaignar avarkal amaratha ceemasanam**a** aniyatha kritam**a*** 172a
Is there a throne upon which Kalaiñar has not sat, a crown he has not worn,

*talaivar Kalaiñar avarkal pesatha medaiy**a** icaikkatha todikal**a*** 172b
a stage on which our leader Kalaiñar has not spoken, music not composed,

*eluthatha ilakkiyam**a** ennatha cindanaikal**a** vadikkatha tamil**a*** 173a
literature not written, ideas not considered, Tamil not formed,

*varkkatha kavaithaikal**a** kathaiy**a*** 173b
poetry not composed,

*katturaiy**a** cirukathaiy**a** naval**a** natakam**a** cinemav**a** kalaiyarang**a** karuththarangal* 174
stories, essays, short stories, novels, plays, films, art competitions, debates,

latchakanakkana madalkal kavithaikal eluthakkudiya 175a
hundreds of thousands of letters, poems?—

tanga tamilanukku tamil tadumaravillai 175b
does the Golden Tamilian who is able to write [all these things] stammer in his Tamil?

ada paiththiyakkara kalingappatti durohi 176
O, You crazed man, Kalingappatti Traitor!

tamil tadumarum *endral unakkum enakkum tan* tamil tadumarum 177
If you speak of stammering in Tamil, it is only you and I who stammer in Tamil.

enna karanam? 178
Why?

[in Telugu] telungula mattaducchi tamil mattudu tamil tadumarum. 179
A Telugu speaker who speaks Tamil stammers in Tamil.

namathu tay mozhi telungu 180
Our mother tongue is Telugu

talaivar Kalaiñar avarkal tay mozhi tamil mozhi anda tanka tamilanukku tamil tadumaravillai 181
Our Leader Kalaiñar's mother tongue is the Tamil language. That Golden Tamilian never stammers!

enakku itharku mele unnai patri pecuvatharku enakku neram illai 182
I don't have time to speak any more about you.

Though she casts the topic of the Party Traitor aside in disgust with "I don't have time to speak any more about you," Kavitha's description of Kalaiñar is built upon the dynamic tension resulting in the contrast between the two. The Traitor never saw Periyar or heard Annadurai speak, was never anointed by their munificent gazes, never transformed by their poetic voices, but Kalaiñar saw and heard them and has the historical depth the other lacks; though Vaiko claims that Kalaiñar's ability to speak, and by iconic extension, his ability to rule, is stammering as he ages, it is really the Traitor whose knowledge of Tamil language—and, by indexical and iconic extension, culture (*panbadu*)—is faulty. The ironic questions of lines 165–167 apply both to Kalaiñar, insofar as he doesn't stammer when discoursing on Sangam Tamil, for instance, and to Vaiko, whose vulgarity is manifested in his "two-line stanzas" (*eetradikkural*) even as he pretends to be a cultured painter.

Line 166 perfectly illustrates the dual implication of a single phrase:

> Will a pure, ancient Tamil [*paintamil*] stammer when identifying to us [these great persons] by saying, "Hey, Da [*parada!*], look at Ceran, at Senkuttuvan, at the Pandyan King, at the Colan King, at the Pallavan King"?

The implication here is that while Kalaiñar's speech is characterized by a "pure, ancient Tamil" (and Vaiko's is not), the Traitor would be so vulgar as to introduce the kings of the Sangam Age with singular endings /*-an*/ suffixed to their names (i.e., Cer*an* vs. Cerar, Pandy*an* vs. Pandyar, etc.) along with a marker of casual spoken Tamil *parada!*, "Hey, Da, look!" (The /*-ada*/ of *parada* is a rude second-person singular ending equivalent to "look, you.") Again, the transparent iconicity of their speech with their characters, Kalaiñar's *paintamil*, and Vaiko's *kochchaittamil*, beautifully suggests that whereas Kalaiñar would understand appropriate linguistic behavior in the courts of Sangam kings, Vaiko's language is fit for nothing better than the streets. Language is explicitly iconic of an inner being.

It is also iconic of a larger ethnic being. Kavitha provides the final trump against Vaiko by pointing out that the Traitor, like herself, grew up in a Telugu-speaking household. Standing on a modest stage on a Madurai street corner, she addresses the fallen prince directly in lines 177–180: "It is only you and I who stammer in Tamil," she says. But, of course, considering the footing of generations of poets, grammarians, and saints vis-à-vis their kings, elder forebears, and Gods, the move is, in the end, well in accordance with historically established tactics in the production of personal and political power.

When I asked her about *adukkumozhikal*, Kavitha claimed that she was working on developing more and more of these stacked utterances, because as she wrote more, collected more from newspapers, her lot in life would surely improve. Her desire for *adukkumozhikal* seemed to me a passionate collecting of "valuable meaning/objects" with which she might purchase a way out of her current straits. For Kavitha, *madakku* not only organized her speeches, it represented for her a kind of wealth, "a precious jewel of prosody" (*yappalungaram*), with which she would be able to increase her fame (*perumai*), properly care for her daughters (a formidable task even for stable middle-class families), and rise into history.

Let me highlight two striking elements of Kavitha's theory of communication: first, her speech is explicitly not merely denotational text (reference and predication) but is a fortiori interactional text (Silverstein 1993), a stacking of utterances, a compiling of recursive, isometric parallel phrases that, in her own estimation, is produced to instantiate a relationship between herself and the subject of her speech, her leader Kalaiñar. In so doing she subordinates that somewhat-crucial nexus of representation—one greatly overestimated in Western folk and formal linguistics, i.e., the nexus of reference and reality (Hill 1992:264)—to the far more crucial and fruitful relationship extant between the speech of a suppliant and her deity. The representational function of speech that draws a connection between reference and reality is the lesser function in this particular rhetoric. The delivery of this speech, then, is an explicit production of her political and economic position within the DMK.

Second, her speaking is not monologic, but dialogic. We tend to think of political oratory as monologic, a single active speaker who addresses a relatively inactive audience. This fits with Western models of speaking and rhetoric whereby the speaker packages information in the form of a "speech" that is then "delivered" to an audience, or in some semeiosocial imaginaries, a "public." But Kavitha's theory of the linguistic practice of stage speaking reveals that she is involved in a dialogue with Kalaiñar that is not unlike the one between the saints and deity in *Thevaram*, or the poets and kings in a thousand-year-old tradition of panegyric. Hers is a dialogic monologue, a speech delivered to offer a referential text to an immediate audience and an interactional text to both the immediate audience and to a wider audience of transcendent beings. We see here, then, a double audience, and a double rhetoric$_1$, one that combines the traditional Western rhetorical$_2$ function of offering a stylistically pleasing oration to "persuade" an immediate audience to one's point of view, and the more peculiarly Tamil devotional model of discourse, whose "function" is to instantiate a fruitful interactivity between suppliant and powerful being.

Though both were a part of Kavitha's own understanding of what she was doing, the devotional element of the speech was clearly that element that brought her to the stage night after night. It was the point.

[7]

SPEECH IN THE *KALI YUGAM*

I'VE ARGUED in this book that with the advent of mass democratic politics in Tamilnadu, a new mode of oratory emerged in political communication. Spoken primarily by elite, literate leaders to an illiterate electorate, this new mode of political oratory is marked by a form of Tamil modeled on the written word called "beautiful Tamil" (*centamil*), in contrast to the language of "everyday life" (*nadaimuraitamil*), "bent," or "vulgar" Tamil (*koduntamil, kochaitamil*). What most people speak at home and on the streets, with family and friends, is called "vulgar" (*kochai*), as opposed to what only the very privileged few have mastered and can wield on the public stage: the "cultivated" (*panbadutta*) and "fine" (*cemmaiyana*) Tamil. I've also argued, building on the observation of Tho. Paramasivan, that the distinction between *cemmai*—"fineness," "refinedness," "beauty"—and *kochai*—"coarseness," "crudity," "vulgarity"—corresponds to a "proper" distinction (Certeau 1984:xix) of statuses between speakers and their audiences. Finally, the system of iconic relations between sociological positions and speech genres was taken up as a mode of formal political practice within the Dravidianist paradigm of democratic campaigning as an emblem (an indexical icon) of Tamil civilizational antiquity and purity. The *centamil* revolution thus instantiated a proper distinction between speakers and listeners, a political distinction between the Tamil and the Indian nationalists, and a civilizational distinction between the Dravidian and the Aryan.

While most speakers have adhered to the prescriptive norms for Tamil oratory, a few speakers have intentionally violated these norms in their public speeches. Theepori ("the Roman Candle") Arumugam was the best known of these speakers during the period of my fieldwork, in 1992–1995.

His speech is frequently characterized as "vulgar" (*kochai*) or "dirty" (*asingam*) by the standards of elite public discourse, and yet he maintained the ability to attract some of the largest crowds of any contemporary public speaker and the praise of members of the lower—and, interestingly, the highest—classes.

In this chapter I will consider what makes Theeporiyar so popular, what makes his speech vulgar, and by what standards his speech is evaluated as "vulgar." I will discuss his intentional violation and inversion of normative rules of Tamil public discourse (as these were demonstrated in Kavitha's exemplary speech in the previous chapter). I begin with a brief biography of Theeporiyar. I then look at a speech he made in Madurai in March 1995, a speech that, as we shall see, demonstrates a mastery of his art, especially the manipulation of the social and gendered registers, or speech genres, available in Tamil. The hypermasculinity of Theeporiyar's vulgarity also suggests the need for a reexamination of the gendering of Tamil public discourse in general, which highlights another counterintuitive element of the Dravidianist adoption of signs of cultural antiquity and authenticity. In the end, vulgarity itself will come briefly under our consideration, as will the varying standards by which any evaluative statement of Tamil speech can be made.

THE MAN WHO SPEAKS FIRE

"My life is the public meeting. I have no other income," says Theepori Arumugam, smiling, snapping his fingers, punching his fist into his hand with a popping sound. He speaks virtually every night, often from 11 or 12 for a solid two hours; the only times he gets a break, he claims, is when it rains. And during those two hours, Theeporiyar expends vast energy, dancing from foot to foot, stabbing the air, and snapping his fingers in rhythm with his oration. Some say he has asthma, which gives his voice a certain breathless quality. When his speech reaches its stride and his energy level is at its peak, Theeporiyar seems to gasp for breath, inhaling for each breath-group with his trademark rasp, which sounds like wind rushing through a tunnel. He truly evokes the idea of a "sparkler" (*theeppori*), a roman candle of speech. To listen to Theeporiyar is to sit mesmerized, not by the beauty of his speech, but by its brute physical energy.

He was born the youngest child and only son of seven siblings to a Saiva Vellala[1] accountant in Madurai. He studied up to the second form (officially the equivalent of the seventh standard, but probably comparable to a secondary school learning certificate [ninth standard] or above in today's curriculum). "There are educated speakers and uneducated speakers," he told me. He claimed the latter status—like Periyar E. V. Ramaswamy, he hastens to add, the founder of the Dravida Kazhagam (DK). It was as a boy listening to the speeches of Periyar and DMK founder Ariñar C. N. Annadurai, he says, that he yearned to become a speaker like them. He took first prize in a speech competition during his last year as a student, and he probably began his speaking career shortly thereafter. People said he had been a Congress speaker earlier, but when asked, Theeporiyar denied it: he claims that he joined politics as a DMK man. And it was Annadurai himself who gave him the title "Theepori" after a meeting at Villupuram in 1966. Annadurai claimed that Arumugam had "sparked" the crowd, had set them on fire, after the other party workers had been striking the match without effect.[2] The next day posters appeared announcing the speaker called Theepori Arumugam.

When I met him at his home on 26 February 1995 he was a thin, wiry man of fifty-six years, about 5'2", with bright eyes and a great shock of white hair that seems to stand on end. His face is deeply scarred in several places, marking the attack on him by the hired thugs of another party—he was quite certain it was the ruling AIADMK—on 29 May 1992. A gang waylaid him near the Madurai bus stand late one night when he was traveling home in an auto rickshaw after a meeting. It was probably 2:30 or 3:00 A.M. They tried to cut his tongue out, but he managed to draw it back in time, he claimed, as he mimed how he slurped his tongue back into his mouth like a snake retreating into its burrow. He claimed that they also attempted to cut a nerve in his throat, the nerve that controls speech, and the very nerve that had been severed in MGR's throat, leaving his speech slurred, after he was shot by M. R. Ratha back in 1967 (Pandian 1992a:17). The attack on Theeporiyar came ten days after another outspoken critic of the ruling AIADMK, Indian Administrative Service (IAS) officer and former collector V. S. Chandralekha, had acid thrown into her face. It was the beginning of a general climate of intolerance against outspoken opposition to the current chief minister and AIADMK leader, Dr. J. Jayalalitha.

Up until that point Theeporiyar had been arrested only once, during the Emergency and the dismissal of the DMK. At the time of my interview with him in February, he told me that he had had eighteen cases filed against him in three years, only one of which had been thrown out. This represents an extraordinary number of arrests within a very short period, and during a time in which he had been behaving no differently from how he had been before. He was arrested again—shortly before I left Tamilnadu the following May—after a disturbance at a meeting in which he was scheduled to speak. These disturbances had come more and more to mark his speaking engagements. It was a rare meeting at which something unusual did not occur, such as a power outage or, like the meeting of 21 March 1995 that I discuss below, an incensed ruling party worker poking a cow with a stick on a sensitive part of its body, thereby provoking it to run wildly into the crowd that had shown up that night. Whether trying to cut out his tongue, sever a nerve thought to control speech, or disrupt his meetings via angry cows or darkness, members of the ruling AIADMK wanted this man silent.

Why? Theeporiyar can draw a crowd and keep it sitting in front of him laughing for two hours or more. His particular ability to draw a crowd, though, is a phenomenon new to Tamil politics—not that large crowds at public meetings are new, but the style of his speech is. To draw these crowds, he does not follow the formula used by Ariñar Annadurai or Kalaiñar Karunanidhi; rather, he breaks with the historical pattern that brought the Dravidian parties to power by consciously violating the linguistic and normative rules that had served them so well in the past.

As we discussed in chapters 1 and 2 above, during the early period of the full-blown democratic politics of the 1940s, refined stage speech was marked not only by phonological, lexical, and syntactic "refinedness" (*cemmai*) but by a refinedness of character as well. As Thiru Vi. Kalyanasundaram (Thiru. Vi. Ka.) writes in the "introduction" to Devasigamani Achariya's *Medaitamil*, the quality of "eloquence," *navanmai*, literally "tongue-power" or "tongue-strength," is something that marks not only speech but the entire person (Achariya 1987 [1949]:7):

> It is said that one needs *navanmai* to speak on stage. What do those who are called *navalar*, those who have the quality of *navanmai*, say is *navanmai*? Is *navanmai* hastily vomiting up [the contents] of a rumbling [stomach] into mere piles of words? No. Then what is *navanmai*? *navanmai* is maintaining one's tongue without evil. *navanmai* is the attempt to espouse only goodness. *navanmai* is speaking having carefully measured out words pregnant with meaning. *navanmai* is the result of learning, knowledge, and right conduct.

As a part of this habitus of power, one did not use common terms of abuse, nor did one speak disrespectfully and in vulgar or obscene (*kochaiyana, abasamana, asingamana)* terms of one's political opponent. The rules of stage speech also dictated that one never made explicit mention to sexuality due to the potential of mixed audiences (rare though they may be). It was (and continues to be) incumbent upon the speaker to maintain a relatively rigid posture, to keep his language and his body in general under the utmost control. Like dance, like poetry, there is a hyperregularity to both the movement and the speech of the performer that embodies an idealization of both person and language, resulting in a kind of consubstantiality of speaker and speech.

But let us examine this consubstantiality further. For Thiru. Vi. Ka., refined Tamil was could be envisioned as goddesses residing in different parts of the body. He cites the "implicit similes" (*ullurai aumam*) of the goddess Lakshmi dwelling in Vishnu's heart, Kalaimakal (Saraswathi) residing on Brahma's tongue, and the half-man, half-woman image of Siva as Siva and Parvathi together (Ardhanareeswara). These similes, he claims, reveal the truth that "our heart (*manam*), language (*mozhi*), and body (*mey*)—that is, our thought (*ennam*), speech (*pechu*), and actions (*ceyal*)—must have goodness (*nanmai*) and power/energy (*sakti*)" (Achariya 1987 [1949]:7). "If Kalaimakal dwells there, your tongue will have *navanmai*." The essense of Thiru. Vi. Ka.'s simile, then, is that eloquence is an aspect of a certain feminine quality—as represented by the image of the goddess Saraswathi—and that this quality is necessary for stage speaking.

I want to take Thiru. Vi. Ka. at his word: the public language of the stage itself is feminine. Perhaps this is why Kavitha represented to me the purest ideal of the poet-politician.

MOTHERHOOD, VIRGINITY, AND THE PURITY OF TAMIL SPEECH

Let us return briefly to some of the tropes we examined in chapter 5 regarding Jayalalitha. The trope of "motherhood" is one of several primary tropes in discourses about Tamil. Others include "history" (*cariththiram*), whereby the refined oratory of the stage instantiates what is thought to be an "original" form of the language unchanged since the Sangam period almost two thousand years ago; "grammar" (*illakkanam*), which characterizes formal Tamil as opposed to *kochaitamil* and is thought to be the normative essence of any particular quality or substance; "culture" (*panbadu*), or the "cultivated" and "fertile" quality of language and people as opposed to an uncultivated and barren form of Tamil spoken by "uneducated" and therefore unproductive people. The following analysis represents only one of several aspects or tropes.

This identification of speaker and language is paralleled on a larger scale in the identification of the Tamil language and the people of Tamilnadu.

As C. S. Lakshmi (1990), Sumathi Ramaswamy (1992, 1993, 1997), and others have noted, Tamil itself was constructed in the Dravidian movement as a person, specifically a woman, whose purity and honor (*karpu*) was to be upheld in the face of invasion, or even miscegenation, by foreign languages such as English and Hindi. The figure of *Tamiltay*, or "Mother Tamil," along with "virgin tamil" (*kannitamil*) emerges early on in the Dravidian nationalist movement and becomes a focal sign for rallying the Tamil people against imperialism from abroad and from North India. This personification of Tamil as Mother is characterized by "sweetness" (*inimai*) and "virginity" (*kannimai*; Ramaswamy 1993:712). The purity of Tamil women and the Tamil language became both presupposed for a linguistic and cultural nationalism and entailed in statements about right conduct and the political duty of all Tamilians, especially women, to be pure and refined and to speak purely.[3] Indeed, in almost all discussions I had with different people regarding the concept of Tamil *panbadu*, or "Tamil culture," the dual ideas of the purity of women and the purity of Tamil emerged within the first few breaths as central, definitive concepts of Tamil identity.

We can now understand more of Kavitha's speech in the previous chapter. Women personify in their stage behavior the canonical image of pure Tamil. While men may frequently slip out of *centamil* to enact various registers for humorous or theatrical effect, the female political stage speaker almost never does; she will maintain an absolutely rigid bodily posture, keeping her head and torso motionless, perhaps only moving her arms in gestures. And her language will be characterized, more than her male counterparts', by strings of *adukkumozhikal*, "stacked phrases," language contained, controlled, and beautified in metrical couplets. It is not therefore merely the purity of women and language that characterized what folks call *tamilpanbadu* but the rigid control and containment of those categories lest they be lost, diluted, or defiled by foreign categories (non-Tamil men and languages; see Ramaswamy 1999). This is an old story in Tamilnadu that is paralleled in many arenas.[4]

Reconsider, again, the praise that dominates political practices in Tamilnadu, the kinds of praise applied to the leaders. Jayalalitha and her supporters exploited the particular metaphor of the pure Tamil mother/speech to a maximum extent. "The Leader of Pure Tamil" (*centamil talaivi*), "The Mother of Good Tamil" (*natramil tay*), "The Reincarnation of Mother Antal" (*annai Andalin maruppirappu*), "The New Avatar of Mother Tamil" (*pirappedutta tamilannai*), "The Very Grammar of Motherhood" (*taymaiyin ilakkanam*), or simply "Mother" (*tay*). She is also hailed not only as the Tamil Mother, but as Tamil itself: her supporters address her in their advertisements as "O, Sangam Tamil" (*Sangattamiley!*) or more prosaically, "O, Poem Surging from (the ocean of) Sangam Tamil" *(Sangattamil pongum kavithaiyey*!), "O, Golden Book of History" (*Sarittirattin pon yedey!*), "O, Elegant Tamil" (*Theentamiley!*), and finally, and most commonly, "O, Tamil" (*Tamiley!*). In the near daily-heard vocative, *Tayey! Tamiley!*, the chief minister mastered the potential inherent in contemporary Tamil culture to identify herself as the very incarnation of motherhood and of Tamil.

While we might expect feminine signs to be applied to Jayalalitha, they are not exclusively applied to women. Once we are alerted to the phenomenon, the political world appears pervaded with feminized signs of power applied to the persons—and sometimes bodies—of men. As we saw in chapter 4 and its *akupeyars* of jasmine and *kurinji* flowers, heartbeats and pulses, supporters within Dravidianist modes of political communicative practice apply notions of femininity and feminine quality and, indeed, power (*sakti*), all drawn from such diverse fields as Tamil literature (*kurinji*), ayurvedic medicine (pulses, heartbeats), and the practices of everyday life (jasmine).

Kurinji is the sign par excellence of ancient Sangam poetry's "interior landscape," the poems of the "interior" (*akam*), of the heart and of love versus the poems of the "exterior" (*puram*), the poems of kings, battles, and war. Given that the gendered moieties of interior and exterior are associated with female and male voices, respectively, the *kurinji* flower is a feminine sign. Most critics would not be satisfied with such an interpretation on its own, and indeed, in all fairness, some have objected to it. But the association of *kurinji* with other feminine signs—in particular, heartbeats and pulses—gives critics pause. Consider the phrase applied to Kalaiñar on a poster by Durai and the King, ca. 1994: "O, Heartbeat that protects the Motherland" (*tayakam kaka ithaya tudippey!*). Ayurvedic and more broadly Tamil Saivite and folk conceptions of the body (Daniel 1984; Egnor 1978:11–31, 140–174; cf. Ramanujan 1967) will separate out the internal essences and powers of an essentially feminine interior from the more external substances and corporeal elements of the body as male. The pulse (*tudippu*) is a sign of a feminine force (*sakti*) coursing through the body, animating it, giving it life. The wonderful image of Ardhanareeswara evoked above by Thiru. Vi. Ka., the half-Siva/half-Parvathi figure of Siva, embodies the larger principle of the universe composed of male and female attributes, a masculine corporeality and a feminine essence. Finally, jasmine is arguably a feminine sign as it is a flower used to adorn young girls and married women on a quotidian basis. Jasmine is also used to adorn the bodies of men on ritual occasions: as bridegrooms (as a sign of their feminine powers and, therefore, virility) and as corpses (as a feminine sign that replaces the feminine pulse that has been lost in the brute masculine corporeality of the dead body). And in the phrase *manam parappum malikaiyey!*, "O, Jasmine Flower that Spreads its Essence/Scent," applied to the warrior-prince Mu. Ka. Stalin, jasmine does not imply that Stalin is effeminate but rather that he is an essence-like being, young, virile, and active—a lifeforce, the very opposite of a corpse.

The purity of *centamil*, its virginity, is but one more element—among many—of the feminization of Dravidianist political practice: the political speaker embodies the very person of Tamil when speaking on the stage. In some ways, and for most speakers, the use of *centamil* in this context is a kind of semeiosic drag, a "passing" of men in a feminized language, taking from that pure Tamil notions of purity, antiquity, cultural authenticity, and power. Again, ironically enough, this embodiment is enacted in distinction to the audiences who gather to witness these avatars of Tamil, audiences that are almost exclusively male (except in the carefully marked off spaces for women, the very marking that indexes the masculine gendering of the ordinarily unmarked space of the public meeting). In keeping with this distinction between the speaker and his audience, indexed by the use of *centamil*, whatever occurs in casual conversation among ordinary people off the stage should never enter the mouth of the speaker on the stage.

Theeporiyar's "vulgarity" is marked exactly by the violation of these rules. His style of speaking, including sexual innuendo, is not unusual in common parlance, especially among members of the lower classes and especially among men. But on a stage, over a mic-set hooked up to speakers and loudspeaker horns positioned to blast into every house for blocks around, his behavior is a violation of "proper" norms of "public" speech that, as it turns out, is equivalent to a masculinization of speech that is canonically feminine in the Dravidianist paradigm.

21 MARCH 1995

The organizers of the event discussed below had been having trouble with the police in trying to hold the public meeting that night (a common occurrence for opposition parties, especially the DMK during this period). About a month earlier a ruling party event was held at the main junction of the neighborhood in connection with the month-long celebration of

Chief Minister Jayalalitha's forty-seventh birthday. It was a gala affair attended by some of the AIADMK's leaders and *talaimai pechalarkal*, "chief speakers," including the speaker of the Legislative Assembly. The meeting featured lavish decorations, cutouts of the chief minister, massive and expensive color posters featuring the lithos and names of the chief minister and speaker (as well as the primary organizer of the event), two musical and dance groups, and an ostentatious display of regal magnanimity in the doling out of five hundred 5-kg bags of rice, five hundred saris, five hundred dhotis (*veshti*), and various cooking pots. The mic-set for that meeting had been set up the previous evening, and on the day of the event MGR and AIADMK songs were blasted from the early morning onward. Despite its being a primary intersection within the city connecting the north and south banks of the Vaigai River, the road was blocked off at 7:00 P.M. and was not reopened until 1 A.M. That very night the DMK leaders of that ward printed out and began distributing flyers for a meeting to be held one month later at the same spot.

It was not to be. Most DMK organizers during that month were harassed by the police; public meeting permits were issued late; electricity was cut to an area during a scheduled meeting; in the case of this meeting, the desired and high-profile site was unavailable for traffic reasons, and a less desirable site off the main road was chosen. The tone of the speeches preceding Theeporiyar on 21 March was angry and defiant regarding police interference. Theeporiyar started his oration that night by violating the rules governing one of the most important moments in any speech, the "introduction and salutations" (*munnilai vizhikkal*), which, as we have seen, should be used for praise rather than rebuke. During the first part of any speech, a speaker will address by name the various members of the organization that has invited him, important members of the audience, and the general public—and always in the most "chaste" *centamil*. As discussed in chapter 2 in regard to Vaiko's allegiance to Kalaiñar, from the local point of view, who the speaker addresses, or omits, is observed with great interest, and the *munnilai vizhikkal* might be the only moment of a two-hour speech that is remembered and discussed. Often, to earn some points with the local police, the speaker will salute "our friends of the police department" (*kaval thurai nanbarkaley!*). Considering the troubles the organizers of the event had had that evening and the anger of earlier speeches, Theeporiyar ended his introductions with an unusual twist, with greetings to "naive police department officers" (*kaval thurai appavikaley!*), to the nervous chuckling of the audience. But throughout the introduction he spoke in pure, fluent *centamil*.

Within two minutes, however, he had switched to varying genres of common Tamil, elongating vowels for emphasis, raspberrying his *p*'s with a somewhat obscene effect (in vintage Theepori style). The theme of this night's speech was speech itself, speakers' rights, and the history of Tamil oratory.

Periyar "tolarkaley" appadi nu arambipparu
Periyar would address his audiences "*tholarkaley*" [O, Comrades]

ana Anna tan "periyorkaleye, taymarkaley," appadi nu arambipparu
But Annadurai would begin "*periyorkaley, taymarkaley*" [O, Gentlemen and Ladies]

ana kangrashkaranga "maha janangaley, kankrash maha shabaiyiley"
But the Congressmen, "*maha janangaley, Congresh maha shabaiyiley*" [O, Great People in this Congress Party])

Here Theepori points out the linguistic markers of different political positions in their introductions and salutations: Periyar's creaky-voiced *tholar*—the same term used by Marxists, "Comrade"—indexes his proletarian and progressive associations in an elderly, grandfatherly, voice. Annadurai's invention of the terms "*periyorkaley, taymarkaley*," for "Ladies and Gentlemen," deployed the Tamil root */per-/* or */peru-/*, meaning "big" or "great," and included women in the audience via that quintessential Tamil word for "mother," *tay*. Annadurai's development was in direct opposition to Theepori's third set of terms, used by Congressmen and pre-DMK politicians generally, the Sanskritic *maha* (great) and *janangal* (people), an Indo-European term related to the root */gen/* as in "gens," "generation," "genus," etc. Theepori doesn't fail to hyperpalatalize the */s/* in "Congress" to */sh/* and pronounces it with a triple consonant cluster */-nkr-/*, marking the speech—and the politics—as Brahminical, northern, very not-Tamil.[5] In Theeporiyar's brilliant linguistic excursion, phonology, morphology, lexicon, and suprasegmental features all index an entire sociopolitical universe in a manner that delights as few linguistic analyses (of the formal variety) can ever do. But he begins here to move away from the strict rules of the stage, to characterizations of caste dialect and a descent into a new set of linguistic conventions far removed from "proper" modes of Tamil oratory (in de Certeau's sense of the term).

The most obvious violation of the principles of stage speech is his use of sexual innuendo, called "double meanings."[6] Continuing his discussion of the current political conditions of public speech, Theepori decries recent attempts to silence him. At one point he makes the analogy of a full meal to illustrate the necessity of different speech styles:

innikki
Today

ippadi pecalama appadi pecalama
"May we speak this way, may we speak that way?

medaiyile ippadiyella pecalama appadi pecalama enna
May we speak on the stage this way?" If we (have to) ask like this

pechchukkalai enkratenna?
what has become of the thing called "the Speaking Arts"?

pechchukkalai enkarathenna atu mothile Jayalalithavukku teriyappaduttukiren
The first thing I'm going to do is inform Jayalalitha about what the thing called "the Speaking Arts" is!

ippadiyellam pecalama pothukkuttattile ippadiyellam pecalama oru sappadu enna karam irukkum, svittu irukkum
"May we speak all like this, may we speak all like this in a public meeting?" A meal has pungent tastes and sweet tastes

sambar irukkum rasam irukkum moru irukkum ideyile payasam [unclear] *undu*
it has *sambar, racam*, buttermilk, maybe *payasam* in between;

kadaiciyile payacattile mutale moru vittu kadaaici payasattile nakkirathundu
And in the end—first pour a little buttermilk into the *payasam*, and in the end you'll have some licking too!

payasam utrama sathareshaam podurathundu
If you don't add *payasam* there'll be *sathareshaam*

Sappattile inippu irukku, karam irukku, tovappu irukku ella athu tan sappadu
In food there's sweet, hot, pungent—it's all like that:

verum inippave sappitta niroli ondivarum
If you only eat sweet you'll get some blood deficiency.

ella narmala irukkanum

Everything should be balanced.

antha adippaiyile pechchu kalagnar ellam
In the same vein, all speaking artists,

ellarum talaivar mathiriye pecina
if they all spoke like our Leader,

ellarum pallattile kal tukkarathukku yaru?
who all would get down in the pit and throw out the stones?

athu nalu peru tukkirathukku venduma illaiya
You need a bunch of guys to lift, right?

antha mathiri pechukkalai
It's the same way with the speaking arts.

Theeporiyar accomplishes much in this piece. He casts himself as a laborer who has to get down into the political pit and do the hard work that needs to be done. His use of the term "licking," in association with mixing the creamy, white buttermilk (*mor*) in with the sweet, sticky *payasam*, draws hearty laughter from the audience, which picks up on the obvious "double meaning." He makes this remark, with accompanying gestures, exactly in the moment of criticizing political power for attempting legally to regulate his speech. It is clear that as a political laborer it is his business to do the dirty work that no one would expect his leader to do. And it is also clear that Theeporiyar is exactly like his audience: a laborer whose work is sometimes unpleasant.

But he isn't exactly like them; he is a powerful man who speaks on stage, something relatively few people can do, or feel they can do. And this difference is marked from time to time in his speech: the introduction is one obvious place—despite his less than canonical welcome to the police—for it was delivered in a "chaste" *centamil*. But perhaps more revealingly, he shifts back to *centamil* again when events—the aforementioned cow—threaten to disrupt his meeting. About thirty minutes into his speech Theeporiyar refers to the chief minister as a prostitute (*vibachari*) several times; shortly thereafter the cow makes her entrance:

tayavu ceythu appadi irungu 1
Please, just sit down.

madu, madu, onnumille madu
It's a cow, a cow, it's nothing, just a cow.

onnumille ninga okkarungu, ceranai cernthavarnga okkarunga
It's nothing, please sit down. Will those joined in this meeting please sit down.

ellam okkarungaya, onnumille ninga okkarunga
Hey, y'all, sit down. It's nothing, please sit down.

His speech is this fragment remains colloquial, common; "*ellam okkarungaya*" ("Hey, y'all, sit down") would not be out of place at a family gathering, or with friends talking among themselves. Thinking this would be enough to settle things down, Theeporiyar then continues the speech from where he left off. After about fifteen seconds, though, he finds that the cow has not yet finished her work, the meeting threatens to get out of control, and he shifts back into *centamil* to get the crowd to settle down.

tayavu ceytu nammudaiya tolarkal
Please, my Comrades

amaitiyaka, appadiyey
peacefully, just like that

udkarungal pannivumpadi kettukkolkiren
sit down please, I request most humbly.

kuttam todarntu nadaiperum . . .
The meeting will resume shortly . . .

"I most humbly request our comrades please to quietly, calmly sit down. The meeting will resume shortly." The shift is significant, for it indexes Theepori's new, if momentary, differentiation between himself as stage speaker and his audience. His Tamil is suddenly hegemonic, privileged, a lapse into a "proper" mode of speech just long enough to reestablish authority over the meeting. As the meeting settles back to normal, he quickly shifts back into his standard, common mode of speech. With the exception of one moment some time later in which he "humbly requests" (in *centamil*) that those sitting on the stage be quiet, he maintains various common registers until the end of the speech. But these moments provide us with an insight into the practical, privileged use of beauty in a political economy in which the cultivation of such beauty is valued.

Theeporiyar fully admits that his speech is vulgar. I asked him what he said to those who called his speech vulgar: "*Athu tan colren*," he said, "I would say exactly that." He also pointed out that his speaking style varies according to such factors as time of day, venue, audience, and town.[7] He is proud of the fact that he was invited by one of Tamilnadu's most prominent literary speakers, Solomon Poppaiya, to deliver a speech on the speaking arts at American College in Madurai; his speech there was devoid of the "vulgar" elements that usually characterize it. And when he speaks in the area hill station, Kodaikkanal, where public meetings are often held during the day on account of the cold, his speech is similarly sanitized of his more colorful phrases. Clearly, Theeporiyar is well aware of his audiences and modifies his speech accordingly.

SPEECH IN THE *KALI YUGAM*

When Theepori Arumugam first came to my attention, I was immediately struck by a seeming contradiction: most middle-class people I asked would wrinkle their noses and vehemently denounce Theeporiyar as an abomination, as vulgar and indicative of the general degeneration of the times (oratory in the *kali yugam*, one might say, the speaking arts in this Iron Age). Many of the professional speakers I was working with, however, characterized Theeporiyar as a creative genius. These teachers and college professors felt he was probably among the very best speakers alive today. At the same time, they found the normal run-of-the-mill political stage speaker obnoxious and distasteful. These latter were the true representatives of the general degenerative state of Tamil today. Indeed, that sentiment was frequently echoed in a number of my interviews with people living in my neighborhood in 1995. One of my neighbors said that the sheer sound of *centamil* coming over the wind on any evening was distasteful, "hateful" (*veruppa irukku*), representative of the fundamental hypocrisy of the current political environment and the Dravidianist paradigm itself. And so it was not only speech, he added, but the staging of political events in general, with their *pandals*, posters, flags, cutouts, banners, loudspeakers—the whole blooming, buzzing spectacle of a Dravidianist political meeting. It was a lie told by the powerful to the "uneducated."

My neighbor was hardly alone. In the 1990s numerous social critics complained bitterly over the brute vulgarity of political public culture, including the grand public displays (e.g., Aravanan 1994:35–39). But there is special attention drawn to the speech as a mark of this vulgarity. The use—they would say "abuse"—of Tamil literature is frequently cited as a marker of this vulgarity. Recall in the previous chapter when Kavitha evoked the image of a Tamil woman who happily sends her son out to a battlefield. The reference specifically resonates with the following Sangam poem:

The old woman's shoulders
were dry, unfleshed,
with outstanding veins;
her low belly
was like a lotus pad.

When people said her son had taken fright,
had turned his back on battle
and died,
she raged
and shouted,

"If he really broke down
in the thick of battle,
I'll slash these breasts
that gave him suck,"

and went there,
sword in hand.

Turning over body after fallen body,
she rummaged through the blood-red field
till she found her son, quartered, in pieces,

and she rejoiced
more than on the day
she gave him birth.

(Nacellai Who Sang of the Crow, PURANANURU 278;
TRANS. A. K. RAMANUJAN [1985:182])

Poems such as this—and this one in particular—are so associated with Dravidian boilerplate that anti-Dravidian party poets have taken particular aim at the hyperbole of such sentiments when it is applied to contemporary political competition. The following poem, "Kalavazhuvamaithi," by the Madras poet Gnanakoothan (1994:31), parodies the maudlin sentimentality and vulgarized citation of the above *Purananuru* poem at a typical public meeting.[8] Most of the speech depicted comprises the formal, structural necessities of a public oration, such as the introductions and salutations and the concluding remarks. Note, in passing, the casual mispronunciation of the standard greeting, *vanakkam*, as well as the title of the text cited, *Purananuru*, iconically forefronting the hypocrisy of the political hack exploiting Tamil literature, and the language itself, for political gain; in typical fashion, a member of the organizing committee, presumably from an urban neighborhood, Vannarpettai (perhaps in Madras Tirunelveli), demonstrates the typically exquisite lack of timing by interrupting the speaker to garland him:

"To the leaders
and great Tamil people . . . *Vanakkom*!

I am very happy to have been given the opportunity to speak
in the 90th ward. Today,
we see a meeting of people
gathered here in the sorrow of hunger,
in tears . . ."

"A garland on behalf of Vannarpettai"

"Shall we allow the great Tamil people to languish?
Shall we forget the mother in *Poranantru*
who told us to go to the battlefield?
We see today piles of corpses laid out by those who plotted and schemed
who lead Tamilians to a life of sorrow.

Come all,
we will destroy our enemies,
those cats, those foxes,
who have deceived us with their false ways.

O, leaders!
O, people!
Since I have two more meetings to speak at
I take my leave, *Vanakkom*."

*"There are two more here to speak
Quiet now . . . quiet . . . "*

Writing his "Introduction" in 1949, Thiru. Vi. Ka. notes that the speaking arts developed by Congressmen were slowly becoming something else. A man of complex political allegiances, Thiru. Vi. Ka. was among the first to take *centamil* from the literary to the political stage, thereby instantiating what we call today *medaitamil*. But, I wonder, was he expressing misfortune regarding that move when he wrote the following? Was he speaking of "uneducated" speakers such as Periyar and Theeporiyar? Or was he referring to "fine" speakers like Annadurai and Kalaiñar? One's politics and view of the times will provide the answer.

> As the numbers of the Congress party become rarer, others increase. What has been the result? Look at our country. Alas! There are class/faction quarrels! Religious wars! Rivers of blood! Mountains of corpses! Horrible sights, unseemly, horrible sights! The stages are the same, but what is the difference? The tongue—the change has come from the tongue. . . . (1987 [1949]: 8)

AN ASSAULT ON THE "PROPER"

In closing, I wish mention an encounter I had with a young man while I was conducting interviews in my neighborhood in April 1995. The man and his wife made *appalam* (*pappadam*) in their rented home of 10 by 6 feet overlooking the southern bank of the Vaigai. He was young, but like many of his class, looked considerably older, his hair already graying although he was not yet even thirty. In these interviews I asked people to tell me who they thought were the best speakers of Tamil in the land. In answer to this question, the *appalam* maker, generally quite quiet, gave the only animated answer of the entire session: "Theepori Arumukam." "Why?," I asked. He grinned broadly when he answered, "He chastises everything" (*ellatheyum thittuvaru*).

Theepori's use of vulgarity, reminiscent of but more extreme than Periyar's, is attractive to his audiences precisely because he is a powerful man whose language and behavior index a commonality of interest with his audience—like the speakers of the pre-Dravidianist movement. Theepori, a man set above his audience on a stage, makes himself one of his audience, and speaks aloud the things said only among friends on familiar street corners and in tea stalls. Among people who have come to look upon their leaders with some cynicism, even when they feel bound to acknowledge their power, Theepori attacks the very norms by which others look down upon the "uneducated"—who supposedly do not even understand the speech of their leaders anyway. Theepori's fire burns the proper, ridicules the conventional; like the clowns, comics, and other social critics of the lower classes, it is exactly this inversion of the proper social evaluation of public speech that gives this speaker his drawing power and gives him the power not only to attack his political enemies but also to subvert the "standards" within "Tamil culture," which are in fact unattainable by most people in the land.

From the larger perspective of the public sphere, though, Theeporiyar embodies a reassertion of a masculine dominance, a reassertion of the gender of the public oration itself. Even as a head speaker in the original Dravidian Party, the DMK, he transcends the Dravidianist paradigm by embodying not the feminine power of *centamil*—though he can—but by its inversion in masculinist vulgarity.

AFTERWORD

DRAVIDIAN NEOCLASSICISM

THIS WORK has discussed how a particular form of language, "fine" or "beautiful" *centamil*, was deployed in political oratory during the postcolonial era of democratic politics in Tamilnadu, India. What we have called the *centamil* revolution embodied a "proper" distinction between leaders and the people, a political distinction between the DMK and the Congress Party, and a civilizational distinction between the Dravidian and the Indo-Aryan civilizations. A new, archaic, feminized, literary, and therefore "proper" mode of speech was markedly different from the ordinary speech of people in their everyday lives. It was distinguished from the plain speech of a previous generation of Congressmen and people like Periyar E. V. Ramaswamy of the DK (who was decisively not engaging in party politics). And Dravidianist orators became avatars of Tamil itself, of its purity, its virginity, and its antiquity. As far as the vast majority of Tamilians were concerned, the Dravidianist paradigm embodied Tamil tradition, and in so doing invented it.

The paradigm emerged in the early twentieth century as a mode of political action dealing with vastly changing circumstances. Tamil political oratory itself was established only in 1918–1919 as a mode of organizing a mass movement and the formation of political organizations in their struggle for Indian independence. Likewise, the shift from ordinary Tamil to an archaic literary form was associated with the transformation of a movement of Indians versus British to one in which Indians would struggle with each other for control of the political process. In the case of the Tamils (and much of South India generally), the struggle took the form of lower-caste/class groups challenging the hierarchical paradigms of the highest caste/class, Brahmins.[1] Contrary to the situation in North India, which saw a "vertical" mobilization of castes and classes in the Indian independence movement, Dravidian nationalist politics was characterized by a "horizontal" mobilization of the lower classes and castes vis-à-vis the Brahmin-controlled Congress (Rudolph and Rudolph 1967; Varshney 2000:5–6). In doing so, DMK founders Ariñar C. N. Annadurai and Kalaiñar Mu. Karunanidhi evoked an imaginary of ancient kings and gods and created a model of ancient speech that had never existed as such.

We have come to call such things "invented traditions" (Hobsbawm 1983), and we tend to associate them with the globalization of modernity. New and powerful ritual complexes form to commemorate the ancient at the very moment of creating an organic link to it in national holidays, in new flags, spectacular processions, and architecture embodying ancient grandeur; the nation is personified in new signs such as Brittania, Lady Liberty, Marianne of France, Mother India, Tamil Tay (these are often feminine signs that emblematize an organic consanguinity among a new citizenry);[2] and thus people who had no link with each other suddenly find themselves as "a people," "a nation," "brothers" (Hobsbawm 1983:6–8). In the fifteenth and sixteenth centuries Europeans "discovered" their classical roots in Greece and Rome, and began writing Latin in ancient styles and building structures (or at least facades) to resemble those of the ancient cities. As Marshall Sahlins wrote, while we tend to refer to what the Tamils (and other colonized people) did as "invented tradition," we call what the Europeans did the Renaissance (2002:3–5).[3]

But though we can find examples of this in the remote past, it is only in the past two hundred fifty years that the process has become systematized and widespread, indeed, globalized. The discovery and essentializing of "tradition" itself, what we generally call neoclassicism, is one of what Sudipta Kaviraj (2005b, 2005c) called the "new newnesses" of modernity. We usually think of modernity as something that looks forward, that embodies the future, something that speaks of the now-and-henceforth. Frank Lloyd Wright's architecture, art deco of the 1920s, the "glass box" skyscraper of Mies van der Rohe and the international style, the spectacular futurism of Dubai and the contemporary Gulf States—all embody this register of modernity in architecture. The big cities of India—New Delhi, Chennai, Kolkata, Mumbai, Bengaluru[4]—like those of China, are being turned inside out with new structures that fit this pattern. In some cases, new reinforced concrete buildings in Mumbai (Bombay) articulate not the modern but the hypermodern, a kind of not-yet-and-henceforth, a timescape that we do not believe we have yet achieved.

But modernity is perhaps even more often embodied in new things that appear very old, things that look both forward and backward, containing what Milton Singer called Janus-faced signs (1972:400). Neoclassicism and the neogothic are the standard architectural examples of this trope, styles that suggest not the now-and-henceforth, but a now that is intimately and organically connected to the past. Washington, D.C., is shot through with it, from the Doric pillars of the Lincoln Memorial to the Corinthian pillars of the U.S. Capitol Building—one might make similar claims of the entire classical motif that structures the appearance of the capitol city itself. Neoclassicism suggests an organic link between ancient Rome (and via Rome, Greece) and a nascent democratic nation state whose capitol was built *de novo* in a Virginia swamp. They were quite self-consciously building a state unlike any the world had ever seen, and they chose to embody the ideals of that newness in structures that claimed to be as old as Western civilization itself. Or consider "collegiate gothic," an architectural style that characterizes large parts of such institutions as the University of Chicago and Yale. The use of gothic architecture, dating in both cases from the 1930s, suggests an antiquity for the universities and a link to the ancient stature of Cambridge and Oxford and the most ethereal intellectual heights of the European tradition more broadly.

In the case of Indian politics, Singer was among the first to notice how one of the major diacritics of modernity was "the cultural ideology of 'traditionalism'" (1972:384). Singer specified Mahatma Gandhi's promotion of homespun *khadi*, the "traditional" spinning wheel, his pilgrimage-like Salt March of 1930, his naked body itself, as modern "Janus-faced" signs within his struggle for India's independence from Britain. Though seemingly ancient, they are quintessentially modern precisely because they are deployed *as* traditional, simultaneously traditional and meta-traditional, signs that speak of themselves *as* traditional. Indeed, we have a difficult time imagining the deployment of such items outside the context of a mass political movement within a modern empire and nascent nation-state.

The counterintuitive qualities of the Dravidianist paradigm—a populism that speaks an elite language, a femininity within a masculine public sphere, ancient content in brand-new forms—are manifestations of the Janus-faced qualities of neoclassical modernity, albeit a vernacular modernity peculiar to the Tamil situation. Dravidianist oratory, a speech genre modeled on a written form that sounds old, is an iconic index—an emblem—of antiquity deployed at the very moment when a modern institution emerges. So, too, *bhakti*, praise, temple festival–like processions, political pilgrimage, signs of feminine purity and power—all have the feel and the appearance of something old, something "traditional," within the context of something quite new. The signs and practices of neoclassical Dravidianism illustrate the general principle that tradition, in this case Dravidian tradition, is not so much a continuation of older practices as a deployment of categorically "traditional," "Dravidian" elements considered as such into the modernity that is democracy.

NOTES

INTRODUCTIONS

1. Throughout the book I use the term "Dravidianist" rather than the more common "Dravidian" to differentiate a particular aesthetic paradigm from the specific social and political "Dravidian movement." The latter was taken up as political ideology and institutionalized in such organizations as Periyar E. V. Ramaswamy's Dravidian Association (DK), C. N. Annadurai's Dravidian Progress Association (DMK), and M. G. Ramachandran and J. Jayalitha's All India Annadurai Dravidian Progress Association (AIADMK). The Dravidianist paradigm, however, was taken up more broadly, even by the Congress-I party, a decisively non-Dravidian party—indeed, the DMK's first political rival. Furthermore, the political ideology of the Dravidian movement had all but disappeared by the last decade of the twentieth century, as the major Dravidian parties (DMK and AIADMK) had abandoned much of the original cultural nationalism of its earlier years.
2. The notion of Aryan invasions of indigenous Dravidians is the essence of what Thomas Trautmann calls the "racial theory of Indian civilization" (1997). The theory is based on late nineteenth-century linkages of language families with concepts of "race." Setting aside such inclinations to interpret history in this fashion, Trautmann found that there is no evidence whatsoever of such a racial migration or invasion, despite the near-universal acceptance of such a theory. For more on the history of this theory see Trautmann 2006.
3. For a discussion on the dating of Tamil literature see Hart 2004.
4. Certeau's use of the term "proper" as a noun (i.e., the Proper) rather than its usual adjectival sense is admittedly odd. It finds a precedent in Christian (in particular Catholic and Anglican) services: the proper is that portion of the mass (or service) which varies according to the calendar year, the celebration of saints, etc.
5. "Every established order tends to produce the naturalization of its own arbitrariness. . . . When there is a quasi-perfect correspondence between the objective order and the subjective principles of organization (as in ancient societies) the natural and social world appears as self-evident. This experience we shall call doxa so as to distinguish it from an orthodox or heterodox belief implying awareness

and recognition of the possibility of different or antagonistic beliefs" (Bourdieu 1977:164).

6. Bodily hexis involves "a way of walking, a tilt of the head, facial expressions, a way of sitting and of using implements, always associated with a tone of voice, a style of speech, and (how could it be otherwise?) a certain subjective experience" (Bourdieu 1977:87).
7. From the Greek *orexis* (*n.* mental desire; effort), the biological referents, relating to desire, appetite, willing, and feeling. Turner's (1974) opposition between the ideological and the orectic parallels an earlier one he drew between the ideological and the sensory poles of culture (1967:27–29; see also 1969:125–130), an opposition paralleled again by his lifelong concern with the *societas* and *communitas*, structure and antistructure.
8. The "worst sense of the word," writes Gramsci later in his *Prison Notebooks*, is "a dogmatic system of eternal and absolute truths" (Gramsci 1971:407). Still later he notes that ideology is "an intermediate phase between philosophy and day-to-day practice" (427). Compare Gramsci's understanding with Friedrich's three "most valuable meanings of ideology" (1989:301): (1) "the more ideational, intellectual, and conceptual constituent of culture," usually regarding specific areas of thought and action, e.g., "honor or matrilineal affiliation"; (2) "a system, or at least an amalgam, of ideas, strategies, tactics, and practical symbols for promoting, perpetuating, or changing a social and cultural order; in brief, it is political ideas in action"; and (3) "a negative, usually rhetorical, self-righteous part that actually originated with Napoleon, who called ideology a misleading metaphysics as contrasted with 'laws adapted to the heart and the lessons of history.'"
9. For other recent extensions of the concept of language ideology see Charles Briggs on "communicability" (2005) and Webb Keane on "semiotic ideology" (2007). With this latter concept Keane expands on the language ideology position by extending it to the widest range of semeiosic activity in general. Expanding further on Keane's concept of semiotic ideology, we might call the widest and most encompassing term *semeiosic phenomenology*, including the sometimes articulable consciousness of semeiosic activity (semeiosic ideology) opposed to (and in interaction with) an embodied and doxic semeiosic aesthetic.
10. There is even a sense that the Tamil spoken in Tamilnadu is further away from that original Tamil still spoken by people in northern and eastern Sri Lanka, a sense shared on both sides of the Palk Strait. Of course, this perception may be due to the broadcast standard of the 1950s–1970s, when the very popular Radio Ceylon ruled Tamil airwaves in both Sri Lanka and Tamil India. The sense of Ceylonese linguistic purity was taken up in recent decades by the Liberation Tigers of Tamil Eelam who, in the 1980s and '90s embarked on a new "pure Tamil movement" (*tanitamil iyakkam*) to purge Tamil of foreign terms.
11. The great linguist P. B. Pandit was fond of recounting the question that American linguists would frequently ask upon arrival in India: How is it that so many Indians speak multiple languages? Pandit's response would invariably be that the Americans had the question backward (Uberoi and Uberoi 1977).
12. The earlier part of the twentieth century saw the Brahmin dialect as the higher-status standard (or received pronunciation) of the Tamil (as is evidenced, for instance, from early talking cinema of the 1930s and '40s). This is not the case today: Brahmin dialect in films is often presented as an element of caricature or otherwise

highly marked. The standard, unmarked, variety of Tamil in public discourse is non-Brahmin—a function, one might speculate, of the success of the non-Brahmin movement and Tamil cultural nationalism generally.

13. I have heard Urdu speakers derisively claim that Hindi is a kind of L to the Urdu H, a less sophisticated version of a language steeped in the glory and grandeur of the Mughal court. Not many folks would say such a thing out loud in mixed company, however.

14. Narges Erami (2008, chap. 5), discussing normative language ideologies in Arabic, following Steven C. Caton (1990), claims that diglossia theories found ready acceptance among higher-status scholars and others. "Normative ideologies of Arabic and Islam are mutually reinforcing in establishing the impression of a universal and stable code for linguistic and religious interaction, ostensibly unchanged since the time of the Prophet. . . . After centuries of elaboration in the Middle East by both theologians and grammarians, the hierarchical ideology elevating normative Islam and Arabic has inevitably influenced the work of social scientists analyzing language and religion. Ferguson's own work is open to criticism for an unexamined acceptance of the 'H' ideology valorizing *al-fusha*" (Erami 2008:32).

15. Of course, the particular heteroglossic configuration that we call "diglossic" is composed of what contemporary linguists call register distinctions. "A register," writes Agha (1999:216), "is a linguistic repertoire that is associated, culture internally, with particular social practices and with persons who engage in such practices." Unlike the wide range of genres marking culturally specific styles of becoming that Bakhtin focused on—such as the styles of the underclass of a particular city, elite casual banter at a countryclub, the overstuffed importance of official ceremonial discourse, the recognizable spin of a party hack on a cable news talk show—register differences have a "sociohistorical regularity" to them (Agha 2007:130) that correspond to long-term, durable socioeconomic asymmetries among groups of people. It is also the case, as in *centamil*, that only a certain segment of the population with access to the privileged institutions of cultural production may have within their linguistic repertoire the ability to animate such enregistered distinctions of "refined" social being.

16. An "accentless" proper form of language is no doubt perceived far more on the aesthetic end of the phenomenological continuum, albeit buttressed by the ideological work of grammarians and the schooling of grammar. An accentless proper, in fact, can be the result only of both ideological and aesthetic elements of language phenomenology.

1. THE DRAVIDIAN PROPER

1. Despite the pervasiveness of street-level democratic campaigning and oratory, there is very little written about it in English scholarship. In Tamil, on the other hand, there are reams and reams of newspaper articles about it, and another dozen or so books and speaking manuals (which I will discuss in chapter 2).

2. Of the many orators who welcomed me at their meetings and discussed their lives with me, special mention must be given to Solomon Poppaiya, former head of the Tamil Department at the American College, Madurai, and the dean of all *pattimandram* speakers.

3. "Have you come to spy on us?" asked a man after an interview in my neighborhood. During interviews conducted to elicit responses to political events and participation therein, I usually ended by asking the interviewee to interview me if they had any questions about me or my work. They usually did; and sometimes the richest information about what I had been asking emerged in these counterinterview sessions. In this case, when my questions came to an end, the first thing my interviewee asked was the one above. A small crowd that had gathered in his small home listened attentively as I explained what I was doing, that I wasn't a spy, etc. But his question was clearly on the minds of a great many people, including members of some political parties, in particular the CP(M), whose meetings I ceased attending.
4. My policy, at first as a matter of ethnographic ethics, was always to ask someone in charge at a meeting to be able to attend the function and use a tape recorder. I wasn't able to ask each speaker, but I felt that as long as an organizer knew I was there and had granted permission that I was "covered" ethically. When I asked simply to turn my machine on next to a loudspeaker (as opposed to plugging into the mic-set), I was refused permission, or stalled, on only two occasions. As it turned out, my abstract ethical motivation became quite concrete after I heard of the following incident: During the year following the destruction of the Babri mosque in Ayodhya (6 December 1992), various relatively unpopular (in Madurai) organizations, associated with the Hindu Right, held some prominent meetings—prominent in the event, but sparsely attended. On several occasions the stages were burnt down before the meetings took place. Several members of a civil rights organization—not known to me but known to good friends of mine as progressives,—attempted to surreptitiously record one of the meetings. Audience members, suspecting their intentions, caught the researchers in the act with tape recorders hidden away in their bags. The researchers were beaten, their cameras and recorders were smashed, and they found themselves hauled off by the police. The event emphasized to me the importance of being up-front in these matters and reinforced my ethical sensibility by means of a vivid object lesson on the proprietary nature of speech broadcast over loudspeakers at a "public" meeting.
5. The very next day someone I thought to be a plainclothes policeman came to visit me at my home to inquire about my activities. He introduced himself as coming from the police office where foreigners register, and I didn't think too much about it. I welcomed him, gave him some coffee, and proceeded to discuss what I had been doing up to that point. I showed him my collection of cassettes, which had religious, literary, and political speeches evenly represented. At the end of the interview, I told him what had happened the night before, and I confided to him that I was at a loss as to how I would proceed. He very matter-of-factly suggested that I hide my tape recorder in my bag! I explained to him that I could not do that (see the previous note). As he was leaving I discovered that he was an officer of the Central Intelligence Bureau, India's FBI.
6. Other events gave me pause and contributed to my general unease. Word had been spreading among the foreign research community of a U.S. scholar who had been denied permission to return to India as a researcher based on his unauthorized visits to the DMK headquarters in Madras. Another political researcher had been investigated rather thoroughly by the CBI, who embarrassed her by questioning friends and neighbors about her activities (thus raising serious questions in

everyone's mind). But most disturbing of all, in April 1993 a friend and fellow researcher from the University of Chicago, Raja Sundararaman, disappeared after a weekend stay along the coast outside of Madras. He was never heard from again. Raja had been studying the historical development of what he called the "Dravidian Canon," that set of texts that had become foundational to Tamil nationalism. Rumors swirled around his disappearance, all of them false. To this day his disappearance remains a mystery.

7. The use of a place (*idam*) name to refer to a person or thing in that place or space is called *idavakupeyar*, a kind of "transformed name" (*akupeyar*) that I will discuss in depth in chapter 3. But the principle extends from the ward (*vattam*) level to the district political subdivisions called *pakuti* and all the way up to the district (*mavattam*) and state (*manilam*) level. The leaders of each of those divisions were frequently referred to by means of these "transformed names of place."
8. Contrast the image of the tea-stall newspaper reading with Anderson's description of it, following Hegel, as a prayerlike activity which takes place individually "in the lair of the skull" (1991:35).
9. The publication of Caldwell's grammar is a touchstone event for politicians from local to state levels speaking on street-corner stages and praising the work of *Kaldvel Durai*, "Caldwell Sahib" (cf. Ravindran 1996). Though Caldwell is largely credited for the discovery of the Dravidian language family as distinct from Sanskrit, more recent scholarship by Thomas Trautmann on what he has called the Madras School of Orientalism demonstrates that the "Dravidian proof" was made some three decades before Caldwell by Francis Whyte Ellis and other scholars at the College of Fort St. George in Madras; see Trautmann 1999a, 1999b, and esp. 2006.
10. One of the most prodigious scholars and publishers of the era was Dr. U. Ve. Swaminatha Iyer (1855–1942), who alone transcribed and published 88 volumes in his own lifetime and 28 more posthumously. He and his contemporary, C. W. Thamotharampillai (1832–1901), are sometimes thought to have singlehandedly inaugurated the Tamil Renaissance, men equivalent to a whole generation of scholars who carried manuscripts from the fallen Constantinople in 1453, thereby ushering in the European Renaissance.
11. The British warmly encouraged the idea of an independent Dravidian civilization for a variety of reasons, not least of which was a long-standing distrust of Brahmins ("Brahminophobia") as well as the disproportionate representation of Brahmins in education and administrative organizations on the one hand, and in the Home-Rule Movement and Indian National Congress on the other (Irschick 1969; Trautmann 1997).
12. *Thirukkural*, a ca. sixth-century didactic compilation of 1,330 aphorisms, is perhaps the most widely known text of the Dravidian Canon and is emblematic of Tamil literature as a whole.
13. Compare this rumpled, lower-caste orator of literary refinement with standard images of the kinds of oratorical performances associated with democracy in the United States (Bate 2004). See Fliegelman 1993 for a discussion of the power of Patrick Henry's "natural" language in the eighteenth century; or Michael Silverstein's discussion of the image of Abraham Lincoln: "Lincoln the autodidact frontiersman had matured into the plain-speaking, practical Evangelical Christian preacher of and for this special nation's indissoluble, transcendent moral unity 'under God'" (Silverstein 2004:30).

2. THE KING'S RED TONGUE

1. "these poets / with their good red tongues" (Ramanujan 1985:125).
2. Lord Edward Bulwar-Lytton, MP, included "The Secret Way" in a volume of stories called *The Lost Tales of Miletus* (1866). A classicist, Bulwar-Lytton got the story from Athenaeus' third-century C.E. Greek text called *Deipnosophists*, or "Banquet of the Learned," 13.35 (1854:919–920). The narrator there says the story came from Chares of Mitylene, who had included it in his *History of Alexander* (now lost). Miletus was a city-state of Asia Minor on the Aegean Sea that had a relatively prosperous trading empire extending throughout the Black Sea area; its stories were considered in the middle of nineteenth century to be the ancestors of the modern novel. Chares of Mitylene says that the story was very popular "among the barbarians of Asia" and that they painted scenes from it on the walls of their temples and houses (Bulwar-Lytton 1866:2; cf. Athenaeus 1854:920 for the source of Bulwar-Lytton's quote).
3. Achariya gives the following terms for "rhetoric" in his appendix (1949:393): *vakalangaram, vakucaturyam, vacalakam, collani*. All of these terms could just as easily serve to describe "poetics."
4. Today, "rhetoric is everywhere. Never before in the history of rhetoric, not even during its glory days of the Italian Rennaissance, did its proponents claim for rhetoric so universal a scope as some postmodern neosophists do today. The rhetoric of science is simply one manifestation of this contemporary impulse to universalize rhetoric" (Gaonkar 1997:26).
5. Note that both senses—the ideological and the aesthetic—of the phenomenology of rhetoric$_1$ cut across the ancient division of *rhetorica utens*, or rhetoric as practical activity, and *rhetorica docens*, the "pedagogically motivated network of critical terms, practical devices, prudential rules, and semitheoretical formulations" regarding language (Gaonkar 1997:27; cf. also Plato's *Gorgias* [1987]).
6. *avarkaley*: *avarkal* (III-pl) + *ey* (Voc), a mode of formal address characteristic of the opening salutations (*munnilai vizhikal*) of an oration when the speaker addresses the members of the audience by name. To say "*avarkaley, avarkaley, avarkaley*," as Tho. Pa. does here, is to synecdochally represent the speech genre of a formal oration by mentioning the opening salutations. See chapters 3 and 4 for further discussion.
7. Public meeting protocol dictates that the first person addressed in the introductory salutations be the meeting leader (*talaivar*), who acts to announce speakers and maintain the schedule for the event. The *talaivar* is usually not the organizer of the meeting, nor is he the highest-ranked person. Indeed, he is usually among the lower-ranked party workers in the organization running the meeting.

3. WALKING UTOPIA

1. 1937 elections; Go. Kesavan, pers. comm., 1995.
2. A shamefully partial (and Tamil-biased) list of the vast literature that may be cited in this respect includes Appadurai 1990; Appadurai and Breckinridge 1976; Breckinridge 1976; Dirks 1989, 2001; Marriott 1976; Moffatt 1979; Narayana Rao et al. 1992; Price 1996a; Waghorne 1994. Breckenridge (1976:126) notes that the similarity between the "royal trappings" of kings and deities has been observed since at least the time of sixteenth-century Jesuit Robert DeNobili.

3. "All exchanges between donor and deity, and between deity and donor, are exchanges of honors. Thereby the deities are confirmed, however paradigmatically and however partially, as the presiding and omnipresent Lords of the temple ritual and redistribution process. The donor, in turn, is confirmed as a 'ruler' over his particular domain that is either a family, a caste, a monastery, or an estate. By confirming deities and men as rulers, puja has historically been the context for perpetual struggles" (Breckenridge 1976:123).
4. "In contrast to the ritually enclosed inside, . . . the outside, for which we have used the bazaar as a paradigm, has a deeply ambiguous character. It is exposed and therefore malevolent. It is not subject to a single set of (enclosing) rules and ritual defining a community. It is where miscegenation occurs. All that do not belong to the 'inside' (family/community) lie there, cheek by jowl, in unassorted collection, violating rules of mixing: from feces to prostitutes" (Chakrabarty 1991:25).
5. *en suyanalattil pothunalamum kalantirukkirathu* ("The general good is mixed in with my selfishness"), declares Sivaji Ganesan in a famous line from the film *Parasakti.*
6. Dravidianist politicians produced a discourse of kinship to envision their party: MGR's trademark salutation was *en rattattin rattam* ("O, Blood of my Blood"), while Kalaiñar concludes the opening salutations of every speech with the universally recognized *en uyirinum anbu udan pirappukkale* ("O, My Siblings whom I love more even than my life!").
7. "Material excesses are integral to the production of value in the kotai. Specifically . . . density—a sign of increase—is converted by worshippers into a scale of value. That scale may be understood as relative 'bigness' (*perumai*), as its degrees are displayed and compared" (Mines 1995:291; cf. 2005:149–150).
8. Thanks to Diane Mines for this observation.
9. Shawls and garlands are placed in the hand of the recipient, rather than draped over their neck or shoulder, when presented by a member of the opposite sex, to avoid association with the marriage garland. Only if a person presents a garland or shawl to his or her own spouse will the gift be placed on the recipient's shoulders.
10. Several groups keep a garland around themselves without removing it: deities, corpses, brides and bridegrooms, and white tourists who receive garlands from tourist officials when touring a temple.
11. My own efforts to gain access to an output socket on an amplifier were sometimes thwarted by my primary competition for such access, journalists and the police.
12. This procession by an opposition party, like most of the processions I witnessed, appeared to combine the rectilinear, military orderliness associated with "official" displays of state power with the vortexed multifocusedness of "unofficial" display, festival, and celebratory rebellion (Schechner 1991:46).
13. Sound-and-light contractors claim that communal harmony became a major theme in the structures of all of the major parties after the destruction of the Babri Masjid (mosque) in Ayodhya (6 December 1992) and the subsequent riots.
14. One of Madurai's evening papers on the night of Vaiko's arrival dubbed this poster, which was plastered all around the Kattabomman circle opposite the Periyar bus stand, a *ratchata*, or "titanic," poster (*Malai Murasu* 9.8.94:6). It was sponsored and designed by "Suruli" Ramesh and printed at Chola Offset Printers, Madurai-1.
15. "Life-sized pictures of Vaiko could be seen covering the walls on thatch boards. MDMK flags were tied all along the [Vagai River] Overbridge. Loudspeakers on the

roadsides broadcast Vaiko songs. Over 500 welcome arches were constructed" (*Dinakaran* 10.8.94:8).

16. New SSK (Ponnagaram, Madurai) constructed all of the serial towers and provided the mic-set.
17. Whereas a simple cloth arch may cost its sponsor some Rs. 1,000–2,000 to construct, a box arch costs Rs. 10,000–15,000.
18. My count of cutouts and arches began at the corner of Aruppukkottai Road and S. Veli Street, continued along her route on South and North Veli streets, over the main bridge ("Overbridge"), through Gorippalayam and Tallakkulam, and ended at the race course at KK Nagar, where the awards ceremony took place. The meeting site itself, which I did not personally see, was enclosed by four 60-foot images of the chief minister. This figure does not include the many other arches and cutouts outside Madurai along the Aruppukkottai Road to the south and the Melur Road to the northeast.
19. "Cutouts, which have become recognized aspects of Tamilakam's political meetings, have also become prevalent in Congress meetings too. 60-foot tall Rajiv, Sonia Gandhi, and Valappati Ramamurthy cutouts and decorative welcome arches have been constructed for today's meeting" (*Dinamalar* 15.10.94:1).

4. ON LIFE, MOONLIGHT, AND JASMINE

1. *Tolkappiyam, akattinaiyiyal* 3–4: "Those who know the grammar/nature of things say that the 'first things' are time and place."
2. In a later article, Ramanujan explicitly tied his concept of metonym to a Peircean framework: "In such a metonymic view of man in nature—man in context—he is continuous with the context he is in. In Peircean semiotic terms, these are not symbolic devices, but indexical signs—the signifier and the signified belong in the same context" (1989:50).
3. The text is written in *akaval* (Swaminathaiyar 1995 [1918]:xv), literally "calling," a meter specifically indexing the discursive interaction characteristic of teaching, i.e., the teacher "calls" to the student to listen and learn (T. S. Natarajan, pers. comm., 1995).
4. Most scholars today believe that the *Tolkappiyam* was composed sometime in the first–third centuries C.E. (Ramanujan 1967:97–98), although there are unresolved controversies that place it from as early as the third century B.C.E. to as late as the eighth centry C.E. (Hart 2004; Wentworth 2009). Unfortunately, the number of contemporary scholars with the linguistic and philological expertise to make a reasonable claim one way or another can be counted on only one or two hands. Regardless, it ranks among the world's oldest and most sophisticated linguistic treatises. Though certainly in interaction with Panini's famous Sanskrit grammar, *Tolkappiyam* contains elements of Tamil-specific material along with a Tamil-specific exegetical framework for the composition and interpretation of the poems collected in the Sangam ("Academy") anthologies. For discussion of this grammar and the Sangam poems generally, see Hart and Heifetz 1999:xv–xxxvii; Rajam 1992:1–18; Ramanujan 1967:95–115 and 1985:229–97.
5. Some earlier versions of this *sutra* (including that of Mayilainathar) are numbered 289 due to the absence of a previous one. I follow present-day versions taught in schools and universities, which number it 290.
6. "A metaphor is the transfer of a word belonging to something else, a transference

either from genus to species, from species to genus, from species to species, or to an analogy" (Aristotle, *Poetics* 1457:8–9). Note that Aristotle's *metaphor* combines several different tropological relationships, including similarity and contiguity, making this definition closer to the contemporary understanding of the general term *trope* than to present-day metaphor. The contemporary understanding of the "four master tropes" (Burke 1969 [1945])—metaphor, metonym, synecdoche, and irony—does not appear until almost two thousand years after Aristotle, in sixteenth-century European rhetoric (White 1973:31–33, note 13; cf. Sonnino 1968).

7. Linguists and philosophers of language will immediately recognize these terms as Austinian performatives, famously discussed by J. L. Austin in *How to Do Things with Words* (1962).
8. In Tamil the eye (*kan*) is frequently, and from the earliest references, a sign of dearness, love, and charm. Parents and lovers call their children or partners *kanney*, "O, Eye." And contemporary cinema songs are rife with eyes: *kannaalaney*, "O, Ruler of my Eye," begins one song by the contemporary lyricist Vairamuthu ("Bombay"); and Kannadasan, the great lyricist of the 1950s, '60s, and '70s writes of a lover: *kan pola valarttathu annai*, "she raised me as a mother regards her eye" (*Pavamanippu* ["Forgiveness of Sins"]).
9. Thanks to Dr. T. S. Natarajan, professor of Tamil, Madurai Kamaraj University, who first demonstrated this concept to me during tutorials in 1995.
10. Mu. Ka. Stalin was in fact named after Joseph Stalin. It is not uncommon (though not entirely quotidian) to meet people whose parents named them for world leaders who were admired for their strength, boldness, and/or political acumen. The European or American visitor may be startled to meet people with such names as Stalin, Lenin, Hitler, Kennedy—even Nixon! In 2003, shortly after the start of the war in Iraq, one man gleefully confronted me, the American-at-hand, with the fact that he had two sons, one named Saddam Hussein and the other Yasir Arafat. He peered keenly into my eyes as he informed me so.
11. In a song penned by Vairamuthu and set to A. R. Rahman's music for Manirattinam's film *Bombay*, the father/lover sings to the mother/lover that "this father wants a daughter" (*inta appanukku oru ponnu venum*). The mother/lover playfully responds "I won't give you a little girl for you to cuddle-speak to" (*konju peca ponnu onnu taramatten*).
12. Stalin was also the star of a TV serial on Sun TV called "*Kurinji*."
13. A. K. Ramanujan repeatedly made this point in seminars in the 1980s, and I thank Diane Mines for reminding me of this insight.
14. For a complete formal discussion of contiguity tropes in general see Friedrich 1990:34–37.

5. *BHAKTI* AND THE LIMITS OF APOTHEOSIS

1. The first two "chapters" (*attiyayam*) were "written," no doubt, by Periyar E. V. Ramaswamy and Ariñar C. N. Annadurai.
2. The concept of a "hierarchical intimacy" was first mentioned to me by A. K. Ramanujan in 1992. McKim Marriott also notes that the concept was discussed widely in seminars and classes during the 1970s at the University of Chicago (pers. comm., 15 November 1999; see also Marriott 1978.)
3. Today these same poems are recited in the evenings at major Saivite temples throughout Tamilnadu. In a lovely passage from her book on these poems, Indira

Peterson describes the experience of hearing the words of *Thevaram* from the confines of her home: "As a child, I lived for a year with my grandmother in Mylapore, the old Brahmin quarter of the city of Madras. The house was located on one of the four streets which form the square enclosing the ancient temple of Siva Kabaleeswara. In that year and in that place began my acquaintance with the *Thevaram*. . . . Every evening at the temple I heard the clear, sweet voice of the hymn singer rise in song above the voices of the devotees worshipping at the shrine. The words were in Tamil, my mother tongue; they spoke eloquently of deep emotion, of sacred places, of God in beautiful landscapes" (Peterson 1989:xi).

4. Uses, both verbal and nominative, were taken from *Madras University Tamil Lexicon*, vol. 5; *Dandiyalankaram* (*su*. 92).
5. *Angapirathachanam* is a kind of vow to the deity for a boon in return, often the good health of a loved one. The devotee promises to roll a certain number of times (usually three) around the god's temple. The rigors of the act, as well as the abject humbling of the devotee (who removes his shirt and rolls on the often muddy ground), make *angapirathachanam* a particularly dramatic vow.
6. A Tamil proverb—*intha punaiyum intha palai kudikkuma?*—wonders whether, if one is able to get away with a trick once, she perhaps can try it again with someone else.
7. The *Malai Murasu* photograph of Velmurugan struggling with his comrades to assert his right of self-immolation seems an oddly jolly scene: Velmurugan's friends are laughing, and faces in the background wear broad smiles—hardly the awe one might expect from the threat of political *sati*. The somewhat irreverent political weekly *Nakeeran* called Velumurgan's attempt at self-immolation "hypocritical pretense" (*pacanga ceyal*), and they noted that he calmed down considerably after the photographers had turned their cameras elsewhere (*Nakeeran* 12–18.7.95:24).
8. Shanmugasundaram, a reporter for *Nakeeran*, suggested that Mariyappan had staged the entire event: "Coconutshop Mariyappan was happy that he could raise the influence of his party, which had been eroding, by sending his own brother's son and other supporters to throw tar on the advertisement that he himself drew [*sic*], thereby provoking a big problem" (*Nakeeran* 12–18.1995:24). This suggestion was never confirmed.
9. This is not to claim, however, that the ideas of power are devoid of eroticism; indeed, among men (at least) in casual conversation, Kalaiñar's multiple households are praiseworthy signs of his power. Many more powerful politicians have several households, despite a public aesthetic/ideology that promotes the distinctly middle-class and publicly expressed value of *oruththanukku oruththi*, "One Woman for One Man." Regardless, I have not seen *ulas* written in praise of Kalaiñar's—or anyone else's—sexual *lilas* on posters, newspapers, or songs.

6. KAVITHA'S LOVE

1. It always struck me that many of my urban middle-class friends had no idea what life was like for people living in the "other India," just a few blocks away; the lives of the vast majority of people in India were as foreign to them as they were to me. (The same can be said of my understanding of urban underclass life in America.) It also struck me, on numerous occasions, that while middle-class folks claimed to have a clear view of what life was like for their poorer countrymen (due to their superior education), they did not go into those other neighborhoods, or sweep

their houses, or clean their latrines, or feed and love their children, etc. The poor folks, on the other hand, did all that, saw how the more fortunate lived, conducted fieldwork in their homes at the most intimate levels. Poorer folks also tended to "other" the rich far less often. Ashis Nandy's observation regarding the degradation of the colonized by the colonizer seems to apply equally well to the degradation of the lower classes/castes by the upper. "The reasoning," he writes, as to why we should attend to the visions of the slave "is simple. Between the master and the slave, one must choose the slave not because one should choose voluntary poverty or admit the superiority of suffering, not only because the slave is oppressed, not even because he works (which, Marx said, made him less alienated than the master). One must choose the slave also because he represents a higher-order cognition which perforce includes the master as a human, whereas the master's cognition has to exclude the slave except as a 'thing'" (Nandy 1983:xv–xvi).

2. The term "text" here should be read as both denotational and interactional text (Silverstein 1993; Silverstein and Urban 1996), not merely as what we might call the "text artifact" (e.g., a book, a document), the usual sense of that term.
3. She does not address the lower-ranking members of the ward organization, i.e., Durai's subordinates, in her introductions, perhaps because she has never met them before. Theepori Arumugam, one of the featured speakers for the night, is always careful to address them as *tambi*, younger brother.
4. The term *adukkumozhikal* suggests a vertical geometrical image, i.e., of one thing "stacked" upon another, as opposed to the horizontality of "folding" or the fractal imagery suggested by "refraction" in *madakku*.

7. SPEECH IN THE *KALI YUGAM*

1. Saiva Vellalas are a "forward community," by today's terminology: an economically "forward" or advanced group, traditionally landowners and members of educated professions (e.g., scholars, accountants, etc.).
2. "*Theeppori porundamal irundathu—theepporiyum neram porundathu.*"
3. "The equation of language and woman is played out on several other registers as well, so that . . . the purity and fidelity of Tamil as language comes to be metaphorically seen in terms of the (sexual) purity and faithfulness of the woman as Tamilian" (Lakshmi 1990). And: "As women themselves came to be marked as surrogate Tamilttays and as daughters of Tamil in revivalist discourse, they were burdened with the responsibility of not only producing true and pure Tamil children but also with reproducing true and pure Tamil speech" (Ramaswamy 1993:712).
4. The burden the female Tamil stage speaker bears to uphold the purity of speech and comportment is contrasted with the popular perception of female political workers as women who have fallen from the ideal status of the good mother or chaste daughter. This, of course, was a large part of Kavitha's burden.
5. Colloquial non-Brahmin Tamil will frequently break up consonant clusters such as */nkr/* with */nkir/*, thus yielding *kankiras* for "Congress."
6. Most people I spoke with used the English term "double meaning" with a sly wink to indicate that what was "doubled" was sexual innuendo. This may have been because they were speaking to a white man; or the English phrase "double meaning" may have entered Tamil. I heard the Tamil equivalent *irattai porul* on only a few occasions, used by well-educated speakers. But no one ever used the formal term *sledai*, "pun," which I attempted to elicit many times to no avail.

7. The interview with Theeporiyar took place in his home (26 February 1995) with his wife and several of his children present. During that time he refrained from quoting any of his more vulgar phrases, though he mentioned to me that he did say some "harsh things" from time to time.
8. His poem is a more stinging version of Nizzim Ezekiel's famous poem "Goodbye Party to Miss Pushba T. S." (Ezekiel 1989:190–191), which mocks the hyperbole and hyperformality of an English speech: "Friends, / our dear sister / is departing for foreign / in two three days, / and we are meeting today / to wish her bon voyage. // You are all knowing, friends, / what sweetness is in Miss Pushpa. / I don't mean only external sweetness / but internal sweetness. / Miss Pushpa is smiling and smiling / even for no reason / but simply because she is feeling. // Miss Pushpa is coming / from very high family. / Her father was renowned advocate / in Bulsar or Surat, / I am not remembering now / which place. // Surat? Ah, yes, / once only I stayed in Surat / with family members / of my uncle's very old friend, / his wife was cooking nicely . . . / that was long time ago. / Coming back to Miss Pushpa / she is most popular lady / with men also and ladies also. // Whenever I asked her to do anything, / she was saying, 'Just now only / I will do it.' That is showing / good spirit. I am always / appreciating the good spirit. / Pushpa Miss is never saying no. / Whatever I or anybody is asking / she is always saying yes, / and today she is going / to improve her prospect, / and we are wishing her bon voyage. // Now I ask other speakers to speak, / and afterwards Miss Pushpa / will do summing up."

AFTERWORD: DRAVIDIAN NEOCLASSICISM

1. For a novel discussion of how the figure of the Brahmin emerged as salient in political discourse, see Pandian 2007.
2. Note how often the generic person standing in for the nation is female. With the exception of Uncle Sam or German Michael, it is usually a specific man who stands in for a nation, and then not as "our" nation, but as "theirs"—e.g., Saddam, Hilter, Stalin, etc.—from the American point of view.
3. "What else can one say about it," quipped Sahlins, "except that some people have all the historical luck? When Europeans invent their traditions—with the Turks at the gates—it is a genuine cultural rebirth, the beginnings of a progressive future. When other peoples do it, it is sign of cultural decadence, a factitious recuperation, which can only bring forth the simulacra of a dead past" (2002:4).
4. In the 1990s and 2000s the great cities of India changed their colonial era names to ones reflecting local pronunciations or "original" names: Bombay became Mumbai, Madras became Chennai, and Calcutta and Bangalore were vernacularized to Kolkata and Bengaluru (and there are others). These are all perfect icons of the same kind of invented link to an organic, Indian past: in all four cases, there were no cities prior to the British colonial period.

Appendix

KAVITHA'S SPEECH

24 April 1995, Madurai

N. G. M. Kavitha, DMK Head Speaker and Associate Secretary, DMK Women's Wing, Kamarajar District. Photo ca. 1995.

I. Introductory Salutations

[00.00] கடமை, கண்ணியம், கட்டுப்பாடு காக்கக்கூடிய

தடா, மிசா, போன்ற சட்டங்களை எதிர்க்கக்கூடிய சக்தி வாய்ந்த திராவிட முன்னேற்றக் கழகத்தின்

இன்றைக்கு நடைபெறுகின்ற இந்த மாபெரும் பொதுக் கூட்டத்திற்குத் தலைமை,

24வது வட்ட இளைஞர் அணித் துணைச் செயலாளர் எஸ். முருகன் அவர்களே;

முன்னிலை வகித்திருக்கின்ற ஏ. ஜெயராம் அவர்களே, கணேசன் அவர்களே, பாண்டி அவர்களே, கோபால் அவர்களே சின்னமுத்து அவர்களே, ஜெயராம் அவர்களே;

கழகக் கொடியேற்றுபவர் அஞ்சா நெஞ்சன் வணக்கத்திற்குரிய அண்ணன் மு.க. அழகிரி அவர்களே;

நீங்கள் ஆவலோடு எதிர்பார்த்துக்கொண்டிருக்கும் சிறப்புரை ஆற்ற வருகை தந்திருக்கும் தலைமைக் கழகத்தின் தலைசிறந்த பேச்சாளர், அண்ணன்

நன்னிலம் நடராஜன் அவர்களே;

வணக்கத்திற்குரிய அண்ணன் தீப்பொறி ஆறுமுகம் அவர்களே;

மதுரை மாநகர் மாவட்டச் செயலாளர் கழக வழக்கறிஞர்

அண்ணன் காவேரி மணியன் அவர்களே;

[ca.1:00] முன்னாள் சட்டமன்ற உறுப்பினர்

அண்ணன் கோ. பால்ராஜ் அவர்களே;

அண்ணன் பாக்கியநாதன் அவர்களே;

மதுரை மாநகர் இளைஞரணி அமைப்பாளர்

I. INTRODUCTORY SALUTATIONS

Capable of protecting Duty, Dignity, and Self-control,

capable of opposing laws such as TADA and MISA, the powerful Dravidian Progress Association's

leader of this enormous public meeting occurring today,

to the 24th Ward Youth Wing Assistant Secretary S. Murugan;

to A. Jeyaram who stands at the head of the audience, to Ganesan, to Pandi, to Gopal, to Sinnamuthu, to Jeyaram;

to he who raised the Association's flag, the Honorable Elder Brother Braveheart Mu. Ka. Alagiri;

to the man for whom you are waiting with great interest to bestow his presence and deliver the featured speech for this evening, a most distinguished head party speaker, Elder Brother

Nannilam Natarajan;

to the honorable Elder Brother Theepori Arumugam;

to Madurai City/District Secretary, Party Advocate

Elder Brother Kaverimaniyan;

to Former Member of the Legislative Assembly

Elder Brother Cho. Balraj;

to Elder Brother Bakyanathan;

to Madurai City Youth Wing Secretary,

பாசத்திற்குரிய அண்ணன் — அவர்களே

வரவேற்புரை ஆற்ற இருக்கின்றவர்,

— வது வட்ட செயலாளர், — வது பகுதி செயலாளர்

என் பாசத்திற்குரிய அண்ணன் — அவர்களே;

மகளிரணி மதுரை மாநகர் மகளிரணி அவைத் தலைவர்

பாசத்திற்குரிய அம்மையார்

பார்வதி அண்ணாமலை அவர்களே;

செவத்தியம்மாள் அவர்களே; மற்றும் மகளிரணியைச் சேர்ந்த அருமைச் சகோதரிகளே;

நன்றியுரை ஆற்றுகின்ற அண்ணன் திரு. குரூஸ் அவர்களே;

மற்றும் கழகத்தின் கழக முன்னோடிகளே;

கழக உடன்பிறப்புகளே; இப்பகுதியில் வசிக்கும் தாய்மார்களே பெரியோர்களே, நடுநிலையாளர்களே;

இக்கூட்டத்தை ஒளிந்திருந்து ஒலிபெருக்கி மூலம் ஒட்டுக் கேட்கும் மாற்றுக் கட்சியின் அன்பர்களே;

கூட்டத்தின் பாதுகாப்பிற்கு வருகை தந்திருக்கும் காவல் துறையினரே;

[ca.2:00] உங்கள் அனைவருக்கும்:

காமராஜர் மாவட்ட மகளிரணியின் சார்பாக முதற்கண் வணக்கத்தைத் தெரிவித்துக்கொள்கிறேன்.

வணக்கம்.

beloved Elder Brother – ;

to he who will give the Welcome Address,

24th Ward Secretary, and 24th District Sectretary,

my beloved Elder Brother—;

Women's Wing—to Madurai City Women's Wing Assembly Leader,

Beloved Mother

Parvathi Annamalai;

to Cevattiyammal; and to my other dear sisters in the Women's Wing;

to Elder Brother Mr. Suresh, who will deliver the Vote of Thanks;

and to the Party's pioneers;

to the Party Siblings; to the women, to the men, and to those of the middle classes who live in this area;

to our friends from other parties who are listening to this meeting on the sly via the loudspeakers;

to the members of the police department who have come to protect this meeting;

to all of you:

on behalf of the Kamarajar District Women's Wing I offer my greetings.

Vanakkam.

II. Jayalalitha's Fears vs. Kalaiñar's Deeds

[ca.2:08] துரோகிப் படையின் சூழ்ச்சிகளைத் தூள்தூளாக்கிவிட்டுக் கழகத்தைக் கட்டி நிற்கும் எங்கள் தமிழினத் தலைவன்,

அந்தத் தலைவன் இருக்கும் இடத்தை நோக்கி வணங்கி

ஒரு சில கருத்துகளை மட்டும் உங்கள் மத்தியிலே எடுத்துவைத்து விடைபெறலாம் என்று கருதுகிறேன்.

எனக்கு முன்னால் உரையாற்றிய அண்ணன் அவர்களெல்லாம்

இன்றைக்கு ஆளுகின்ற அம்மையார் அவர்கள் ஆட்சியில் நடைபெறுகின்ற ஊழல் பட்டியலையும் விலைவாசிப் பட்டியலையும் மிகத் தெள்ளத் தெளிவாக உங்கள் மத்தியிலே எடுத்துவைத்து அமர்ந்திருக்கிறார்கள்.

ஆனால் பேரறிஞர் அண்ணா அவர்களால் அமைக்கப்பட்ட திராவிட முன்னேற்றக் கழகத்தில் ஏற்பட்டுள்ள சலசலப்புக்கு என்ன காரணம்?

சற்று எண்ணிப் பார்க்கவும் அருமைப் பெரியோர்களே.

பழநி நாடாளுமன்றத்திற்கும் இராணிப் பேட்டை சட்டமன்றத்திற்கும் இடைத் தேர்தல் நடந்ததல்லவா?

ஆனால் 1991ஆம் ஆண்டு பழநி நாடாளுமன்றத் தொகுதியில்,

[ca.3:00] 2,60,000 வாக்குகள் வித்தியாசத்தில் எங்கள் தி.மு.க. தோற்றது.

கடந்த இடைத் தேர்தலில் 2,20,000 வாக்குகள் ஈடுகட்டிவிட்டு

வெறும் 40,000 வாக்குகள் வித்தியாசத்தில் கழகம் வெற்றி வாய்ப்பை இழந்திருக்கிறதென்றால்

இடைத் தேர்தலில் திமுகவுக்கு செல்வாக்கு வந்துவிட்டது. பொதுத் தேர்தலில் திமுக வெற்றிபெறும்.

திமுக ஆட்சிக்குள் நுழைந்துவிடும் கோட்டைக்குள் நுழைந்துவிடும் என்ற பயம், பேதி

II. JAYALALITHA'S FEARS VS. KALAIÑAR'S DEEDS

[*ca.* 2:08] Our Tamil people's leader, who stands in protection of our party after chopping to pieces the plots of that cabal of traitors—

I face the place where that leader resides and honor him,

and I will put to you just a few thoughts and then take my leave.

All the Elder Brothers who have orated before me

have very clearly placed among you lists of corruption that are taking place in the administration of the woman who rules today, lists of prices, and have sat down again.

But what is the cause of the trouble/confusion that has emerged today in the Dravidian Progress Party that was founded by Perariñar [the Great Sage] Anna?

Think about it a little bit, O, my dear gentlemen.

The Palanai Parliamentary and Ranipettai Legislative Assembly by-elections occurred, right?

But in 1991, in the Palanai Parliamentary district,

[*ca.* 3:00] our DMK lost by a difference of 260,000 votes.

In the last by-election, 220,000 votes were cast,

and the party lost its chance to win by a mere 40,000 votes; [we know] therefore [that because]

the DMK has gained influence in the by-election, the DMK will achieve victory in the general election.

The DMK will gain power, and the DMK will enter the Fort; these fears, this nausea

தமிழக முதல்வர் ஜெயலலிதாவுக்கு ஏற்பட்டுவிட்டு கழகத்திற்குள்ளே கழகம் விளைவிக்கின்ற அளவுக்கு

இன்றைக்கு ஈடுபட்டு இருக்கின்றார் இந்த அம்மையார் ஜெயலலிதா.

தேர்தலுக்காகவும் அதிகாரப் பொறுப்புகளுக்காகவும் ஆடம்பரத்திற்காகவும் கொள்ளையடிப்பதற்காக பதவிகளுக்காக இருக்கக்கூடிய இந்த இயக்கம் திராவிட முன்னேற்றக் கழகம் அல்ல.

சுயமரியாதையோடு இருக்கக் கூடிய இயக்கம்தான் எங்கள் திராவிட முன்னேற்றக் கழகம்.

தமிழ்நாட்டில் எத்தனையோ கோடி மக்கள் இருக்குமிடத்திலே

தலைவர் கலைஞரை மட்டும் ஏன் தலைவனாக ஏற்றுக் கொண்டோம்.

தலைவர் கலைஞரிடத்தில் என்ன இருக்கிறது?

[ca.4:00] எழுத்தாற்றல் இருக்கின்றது, பேச்சாற்றல் இருக்கின்றது, தமிழர்களுக்காக

தமிழ்நாட்டிற்காக தமிழ் இனத்திற்காக.

தமிழ்நாட்டில் நடக்கின்ற அநியாய அக்கிரமங்களை

தட்டிக் கேட்பதற்கு தலைவர் கலைஞரைத் தவிர வேறு எந்த நாடு இருக்கின்றது? இந்தத் தமிழ்நாட்டிலே.

இந்த இயக்கத்திலே ஐம்பெரும் தலைவர்கள் இருந்தார்கள்:

தந்தை பெரியார் இருந்தார்.

பேரறிஞர் அண்ணா இருந்தார்.

அண்ணா மறைவுக்குப் பிறகு இன்று இந்தக் கழகத்தைக் கட்டிக்காத்துத்

that have emerged for Tamilnadu Chief Minister Jayalalitha, that our Party will emerge [victorious],

this woman Jayalalitha is today preoccupied.

It is not this movement, the Dravidian Progress Party, that exists only for the sake of elections, for seizing authority, for shows of pomp, for stealing, for office.

Our Dravidian Progress Party is the movement that exists with Self-Respect.

Among how many scores of people in Tamilnadu

why have we accepted only our leader Kalaiñar as leader?

What does our leader Kalaiñar have [to offer]?

[*ca. 4:00*] He has the ability to write, the ability to speak for the sake of the Tamilian,

for the sake of Tamil, for the sake of the Tamil people.

The atrocities of injustice that are occurring in Tamilnadu,

in what other country is there (such a leader) as our leader Kalaiñar? Only in this Tamilnadu.

In this movement there were five great leaders:

There was Thanthai Periyar.

There was Perariñar Anna.

Holding this movement together after the death of Anna,

தலைமைப் பொறுப்பை ஏற்று நடத்திவருகின்ற அஞ்சா நெஞ்சம்,

எதையும் தாங்கும் இதயம் கொண்ட தன்மானத் தங்கத் தலைவனைத் தான் நாங்கள் தலைவனாக ஏற்றுக்கொண்டோம்.

[பதிவு தெளிவில்லை]

உலகத்திலேயே சட்டமன்ற உறுப்பினராக ஒன்பது தடவை போட்டிபோட்டு தோல்வியே தழுவாமல்;

ஒன்பது தடவை வெற்றி பெற்று உலக சாதனை புரிந்திருக்கும் அந்தத் தலைவனை நாங்கள் தலைவனாக ஏற்றுக்கொண்டோம்.

எத்தனையோ முதலமைச்சர்கள் இந்த நாட்டை ஆண்டுள்ளார்கள்?

[ca.5:00] டாக்டர் இராதா கிருஷ்ணன் இந்த நாட்டை ஆண்டுள்ளார்.

பக்தவச்சலம் இந்த நாட்டை ஆண்டவர்தான். ஓமந்தூர் இராமசாமி ரெட்டியார் செய்ய முடியாத சாதனை,

ராஜாஜி செய்ய முடியாத சாதனை,

ராஜபாளையம் குமாரசாமி ராஜா செய்ய முடியாத சாதனை,

பெருந்தலைவர் காமராஜர் செய்யாத சாதனை, ஏன்

எம்.ஜி. ராமச்சந்திரன் செய்யாத சாதனை,

அவரது துணைவியார் ஜானகி அம்மையார் செய்ய முடியாத சாதனை,

எம். ஜி. ஆரோடு தொடர்பு கொண்டிருந்த அம்மா ஜெயலலிதா அவர்கள் செய்ய முடியாத சாதனை தலைவர் கலைஞர் அவர்கள் ஆட்சியிலே

தமிழ் மக்களுக்கு செய்த நல்லதொரு திட்டம்.

விவசாயிகளுக்கு இலவச மின்சாரத் திட்டம் கொண்டு வந்தார்.

விவசாயிகள் வாங்கிய பயிர்க்கடனை பத்தாயிரம் ரூபாய் தள்ளுபடி செய்திருக்கிறார்.

that Fearless Heart that accepts the responsibilities of leadership,

we only accepted as our leader the one who has a heart that will bear anything, who bestows self-honor.

[*recording unclear*]

In all of the world—He who competed nine times for membership in the Legislative Assembly, without losing even once;

we accepted as our leader the leader who achieved the world record of winning nine times.

How many Chief Ministers have ruled this land?

[*ca. 5:00*] Dr. Radakrishnan ruled this land,

Bhaktavachalam ruled this land, too. An achievement unattainable by Gomandur Ramaswamy Reddiyar,

an achievement unattainable by Rajaji,

an achievement unattainable by Kumaraswamy, the Raja of Rajapalaiyam,

an achievement unattainable by the Great Leader Kamarajar, why even

an achievement unattainable by M. G. Ramachandran,

an achievement unattainable by his wife Lady Janaki,

an achievement unattainable by Madam Jayalalitha, who had an affair with MGR in our leader Kalaiñar's administration.

A good scheme was done for the Tamil people.

He brought a Free Electricity Scheme for the farmers.

He wrote-off ten thousand rupees from the loans taken out by farmers for their crops.

விவசாயிகள் உபயோகிக்கும் பொருளுக்குப் பாதி விலை மானியம் கொடுத்திருக்கிறார்.

எட்டவாது படிக்கும் மாணவ மாணவிகளுக்கு இலவச பஸ்பாஸ் வழங்கியுள்ளார்.

[ca.6:00]

86 இலட்சம் சத்துணவுக் குழந்தைகளுக்கு ஊட்டச் சத்து உருண்டையோடு முட்டை அல்லது வைட்டமின் ஏ மாத்திரை வழங்கும் சட்டத்தையும் கொண்டுவந்திருக்கிறார் கலைஞர் ஆட்சியிலே.

வறுமைத் தேள் கொட்டிய நிலையில் வசந்தம் காணத் துடித்து நிற்கும்

ஏழைப் பெண்களுக்குத் திருமணச் செலவிற்காக 5,000 ரூபாய் கொடுத்திருக்கிறார்.

அவர் ஆண்ட இரண்டாண்டு ஆட்சியில் 35,000 பெண்களுக்குத் திருமணச் செலவிற்காக 5,000 ரூபாய் கொடுத்திருக்கிறார்.

கருவுற்றுள்ள ஏழைக் கர்ப்பிணித் தாய்மார்கள் வயிற்றில் குழந்தை கட்டாக வளர வேண்டுமென்பதற்காக மாதம் 200 ரூபாய் –

அவர் அந்த இரண்டு வருட ஆட்சியில் 4,00,000 கர்ப்பிணித் தாய்மார்களுக்கு 200 ரூபாய் கொடுத்திருக்கிறார்.

முதியோர், ஊனமுற்றோர், கைவிடப்பட்ட மகளிர்,

ஆதரவற்ற விதவைகள், இலட்சக்கணக்கான ஏழை எளியவர்களுக்கு நல்லது செய்தவர்தான். கலைஞர் ஆட்சியிலே

இந்தியாவிலேயே சிறந்த கடற்கரை மெரீனா பீச்சை உருவாக்கித் தந்தவர் தலைவர் கலைஞர் ஆட்சியிலே.

பெருந் தலைவர் காமராஜர் அவர்களுக்கு நினைவகம் கண்டது தலைவர் கலைஞர் ஆட்சியிலே.

ஓராண்டு வாழப்போகிறேன் என்று ஒரு விரலைக் காட்டிவிட்டு மறைந்துவிட்டுச் சென்றாரே

He gave a concession of half-price for materials used by farmers.

He has bestowed free bus passes for students studying in the 8th Standard.

[*ca. 6:00*] During Kalaiñar's administration, he even instituted a law bestowing either an egg or a vitamin A pill, along with a healthy fortified dumpling, for 8,600,000 children under the Nutritious Noon Meal scheme.

Hearts beating to see the spring time while living under the scorpion-sting of poverty,

to [these] poor women he gave 5,000 rupees for their wedding expenses.

During his two-year administration [1989–1991] he gave 5,000 rupees for wedding expenses to 35,000 poor women.

200 rupees a month for poor pregnant women because he wanted the children in their wombs to grow up healthy –

during his two-year administration he gave 400,000 pregnant women 200 rupees.

[For] old people, handicapped people, abandoned women,

he did good works for widows without support, and for hundreds of thousands of poverty-stricken people. During Kalaiñar's administration

he created the Marina Beach on India's most famous shore during our leader Kalaiñar's administration.

During our leader Kalaiñar's administration a memorial was established for Great Leader Kamarajar.

[For] he who held up one finger saying he would live for one year, [ca.7:00] எங்கள் இயக்கத் தலைவர் உத்தமத் தலைவர் பேரறிஞர் அண்ணாவிற்கு நினைவிடம் கண்டது தலைவர் கலைஞர் ஆட்சியிலே.

இரண்டு விரலைக் காட்டிவிட்டு, இன்று நாட்டைக் கெடுத்துவிட்டுச் சென்றாரே

அந்த எம்.ஜி. ராமச்சந்திரனுக்கு நினைவிடம் கண்டது தலைவர் கலைஞர் ஆட்சியிலே.

வீரபாண்டிய கட்டபொம்மனுக்கு நினைவிடம் கண்டது தலைவர் கலைஞர் ஆட்சியிலே.

95 வள்ளுவர் கோட்டம் கண்டது தலைவர் கலைஞர் ஆட்சியிலே

கடலோரத்தில் இருக்கும் கண்ணகிக்கு ஒரு சிலை, கப்பலோட்டிய தமிழனுக்கும் ஒரு சிலை அமைக்கப்பட்டது தலைவர் கலைஞர் ஆட்சியிலே.

ராஜாஜிக்கு ஒரு சிலை அமைக்கப்பட்டது தலைவர் கலைஞர் ஆட்சியிலே.

எங்கள் இயக்கத் தலைவர் பேரறிஞர் அண்ணா அவர்களிடம் மன்னிப்புப் பெற்றவர் ஜவகர்லால் நேரு.

அந்த நேருவின் மகள்

100 'மிசா' என்ற கடுமையான சட்டத்தைப் பயன்படுத்தி இந்தியாவையே குலுக்க வைத்த இந்திரா

சென்னைக் கடற்கரை சீரணி அரங்கத்திலே

பல லட்சம் பேருக்கு முன்னால் நான் செய்யும் தவறுக்கு வருந்துகிறேன். என்னை மன்னித்துக் கொள்ளுங்கள் என்று மன்னிப்புக் கேட்கவைத்தவர் தான் தலைவர் கலைஞர் அவர்கள்.

அந்த நேருவின் பேரன்,

[ca.8:00] அன்னை இந்திராவின் அருமைப் புதல்வர் அன்றைய பாரதப் பிரதமர் ராஜீவ் அவர்கள்

[*ca. 7:00*] a memorial for our movement's highest leader Perariñar Anna was established during our leader Kalaiñar's administration.

[For] he who showed two fingers, destroyed our land and died,

a memorial for that M. G. Ramachandran was established during our leader Kalaiñar's administration.

A memorial for Virapandi Kattaboman was established during our leader Kalaiñar's administration.

Valluvar's Memorial was established during our leader Kalaiñar's administration.

A statue by the sea for Kannaki and a statue for the Ship-Driving Tamilian [V. O. Chidambaram Pillai] were cast during our leader Kalaiñar's administration.

A statue for Rajaji [C. Rajagopalachari] was built during our leader Kalaiñar's administration.

Jawaharlal Nehru, who was forgiven by our movement's leader Perariñar Anna,

that very Nehru's daughter,

Indira, who threw all of India into turmoil by utilizing the cruel law MICA

in the Cirani Arangam on Chennai's shore,

our leader Kalaiñar asked forgiveness in front of many hundreds of thousands of people, saying, "I regret the errors committed by me. Please forgive me."

And that Nehru's grandson,

[*ca. 8:00*] Madam Indira's dearest son, then India's Prime Minister Rajiv,

தலைவர் கலைஞர் ஆட்சியில் எட்டுமுறை வந்திருக்கிறார் இந்தத் தமிழ்நாட்டிலே.

எந்தவொரு அசம்பாவிதமும் நடந்ததுண்டா?

தி.மு.க.ன்னா தி.மு.க.தான். இதுதான் உண்மையான தி.மு.க பெரியோர்களே.

இப்பேற்பட்ட தி.மு.க. *1976* இல் கவிழ்க்கப்பட்டதற்கு என்ன காரணம்?

சற்று எண்ணிப் பார்க்கவும் அருமைப் பெரியோர்களே!

இனிய விடுதலைக்காக பல ஆண்டு காலம் போராடிப் பல்லாண்டுகாலம் சிறைச்சாலையிலே இருந்தவர் ஜெயப் பிரகாஷ் நாராயணன் அன்றைக்குக் கைதுசெய்யப்பட்டார்.

அசோக் மேத்தா அன்றைக்குக் கைதுசெய்யப்பட்டார்.

மொரார்ஜி தேசாய் அன்றைக்குக் கைதுசெய்யப்பட்டார்.

முடிந்தால் காமராஜரைக் கைதுசெய்வாயா என்று தலைவர் கலைஞரிடத்தில் கேட்டபோது

கலைஞர் என்ன பதில் சொன்னார்?

இது ஜனநாயக நாடு.

நான் ஒருபோதும் காமராஜரைக் கைதுசெய்ய மாட்டேன்

என்று சொன்ன காரணத்தினால்

அன்னை இந்திராவால் எமர்ஜன்சி உத்தரவைப் பயன்படுத்தியது *1976*இலே

ஜனநாயகம் வாழ்க என்று சொன்ன காரணத்தினாலேயே தி.மு.க. ஆட்சி கவிழ்க்கப்பட்டது.

[ca.9:00]

அதன் பிறகு *1989*இலே அமைதியாக நடைபெற்றுக்கொண்டிருந்த தி.மு.கழக ஆட்சி *1991*இலே கவிழ்க்கப்பட்டதற்கு என்ன காரணம்?

came eight times to this Tamilnadu during our leader Kalaiñar's administration.

Did any untoward incident occur?

O, gentlemen! This DMK is the DMK—this is the true DMK!

What was the cause of this great DMK being dissolved in 1976?

Think about it a little, O gentlemen!

Jeyaprakash Narayanan, who struggled for many years for India's independence and spent many years in jail, was jailed at that time.

Ashok Mehta was jailed at that time.

Moraji Desai was jailed at that time.

When Kalaiñar was asked by Kamaraj, "Will you jail me if you can?"

what answer did Kalaiñar give?

"This is a democratic country.

I will never jail Kamarajar,"

because he said this,

in 1976 during Madam Indira's emergency order

the DMK government was dissolved for saying "Long live Democracy."

[*ca. 9:00*] Afterward, what was the reason that the peacefully conducted 1989 DMK government was dissolved in 1991?

அன்றைக்குக் கொள்கைப் பரப்புச் செயலாளர் ஜெயலலிதாவும்

தமிழ்நாட்டுக் காங்கிரஸ் தலைவர் வாழப்பாடி ராமமூர்த்தி அவர்களும் சேர்ந்து இணங்கி நின்று தமிழன் வாழ்க என்று சொன்ன காரணத்தால் 1991இலே தி.மு.க. ஆட்சி கவிழ்க்கப்பட்டது.

மீண்டும் 1991இலே பொதுத் தேர்தல் நடைபெற்ற பொழுது தி.மு.க. ஆட்சிக்கு

வராமல் இருந்ததற்கு என்ன காரணம்?

தி.மு.க.விற்கு ஏற்பட்ட மிகப் பெரிய சோதனையல்லவா?

ராஜீவ் கொலைக்கு தி.மு.க. தான் காரணம் என்று

தலைவர் கலைஞரிடத்தில் அபாண்டப் பழியைச் சுமத்திய காரணத்தினால்,

இன்றைக்கு நாடுவிட்டு நாடு வந்த நாட்டியக்காரி அம்மையார்,

உடையாருக்கு 2,90,000 கடன் கொடுக்க முடியாத ஜெயலலிதா அம்மையார்,

சந்தியாவின் மகள் அன்றைக்கு மைசூர் மகாராஜா வேலைக்காரியின் மகள் இன்றைக்கு நாட்டை ஆண்டுக் கொண்டிருக்கிறார்.

அதைப் பற்றி எங்களுக்குக் கவலை இல்லை.

III. The Party Traitor

1993, 94இல் திமுகவிற்கு ஏற்பட்ட குழப்பத்திற்கு என்ன காரணம்?

[ca.10:00] யார் அந்தக் கழகத்தின் துரோகி?

அவர் எப்போது இந்த இயக்கத்திற்கு வந்தார்?

1953இலே கள்ளக்குடி போராட்டத்திற்காகத் தலைவர் கலைஞர் இடத்திலே

Then, the [ADMK] Secretary for Propaganda Jayalalitha

and Tamilnadu Congress leader Valapadi Ramamurthy joined together, and because [the DMK] said "Long Live Tamilians!" the DMK government was dissolved in 1991.

Again, when the 1991 general election was conducted, the DMK government

did not return—what was the reason?

A very great sadness for the DMK, no?

That [people] said that Rajiv's murder was caused by the DMK,

because Kalaiñar had to bear the malicious sacrifice,

today this actress who can take or leave this land,

Lady Jayalalitha who can not give 290,000 in loans to those who deserve them,

Santhiya's daughter, the daughter of a servant of the Mysore Maharaja is ruling this land today.

But let us not fret over that.

III. THE PARTY TRAITOR

[*ca. 9:55*] What is the cause of the confusion that has arisen in the DMK in 1993–94?

[*ca. 10:00*] Who is that Party Traitor?

When did he come to this movement?

In 1953, along with our leader Kalaiñar, for the Kallakudi Agitation,

தண்டவாளத்திலே தலைவைத்துப் படுத்தவரா இந்தக் கழகத் துரோகி

62இலே விலைவாசிப் போராட்டத்திற்காகத் தலைவர் கலைஞர் அவர்களோடு சிறைச்சாலை சென்றாரா?

65இலே மொழிப் போராட்டத்திற்காக தலைவர் கலைஞர் அவர்களோடு பாளையங்கோட்டை சிறைச்சாலைக்குச் சென்றாரா?

அவர் எப்பொழுது இந்த இயக்கத்திற்கு வந்தார்?

1967ஆம் ஆண்டு

அகில இந்தியத் தலைவரை எதிர்த்து நின்ற வேட்பாளர் சீனிவாசன் —

தன்னுடைய இனத்துக்காரன் நெருங்கிய சொந்தக்காரன் என்பதற்காக

சீனிவாசனுக்கு ஏஜென்ட்டாக இந்த இயக்கத்திற்கு வந்தவர்தான் கழகத் துரோகி.

1967இலே அண்ணா முதல்வராகிறார்.

அண்ணா மறைவுக்குப் பிறகு தலைவர் கலைஞர் அவர்களை முதல்வராக்கினார்கள்.

பதவி எதிர்பார்த்து வந்த கழகத்தின் துரோகி அவர்களுக்கு

கலிங்கப்பட்டியிலே ஊராட்சி ஒன்றியப் பெருந்தலைவர் பதவியைப் பெற்றார்.

[ca.11:00] *நிலவள வங்கித் தலைவர் பதவி பெற்றார். நெல்லை மாவட்ட மத்திய கூட்டுறவு வங்கித் தலைவர் பதவி பெற்றார்.*

இத்தனை பதவிகளைப் பெற்ற கழகத்தின் துரோகி அவர்கள்

1989ஆம் ஆண்டு கழகம் ஆட்சியில் இருக்கின்றபோது,

did this Party Traitor lie down placing his head on the train tracks?

In '62 did he go to jail with our leader Kalaiñar during the Commodity Price Agitation?

In '65 did he go to the Palayamkottai jail with our leader Kalaiñar during the Language Agitation?

When did he come to this movement?

In the year 1967

Sinivasan, a candidate opposing an all-India leader—

for the sake of a close relative from his own community

the Party Traitor came to this movement as an agent of Sinivasan.

In 1967 Anna was Chief Minister.

After Anna died, our leader Kalaiñar was made Chief Minister.

Anticipating a post for himself, the Party Traitor

gained the post of Kalingapatti Panchayat Union Leader.

[*ca. 11:00*] He gained the Headship of Nilavala Bank. He gained the Headship of the Tirunelveli District Central Cooperative Bank.

The Party Traitor, after gaining all these posts

in 1989 when the Party was ruling,

கழகத்திற்கு இக்கட்டான சூழ்நிலையை உருவாக்குகின்ற வகையிலே தலைவர் கலைஞரிடத்திலே சொல்லாமல் கள்ளத் தோணியிலே

இலங்கைக்கு சென்றுவிட்டு கலைஞரிடத்தில் மன்னிப்புப் பெற்றவர் தான் இந்தக் கழகத்தின் துரோகி.

அதன் பிறகு பாராளுமன்றத்திலே திமுக வரிசையிலே அமரக் கூடாதென்று

பாராளமன்றத்தில் ஒரு பெண்மணியால் தூக்கியெறியப்பட்டவர் தான் கழகத்தின் துரோகி.

சிவகாசித் தொகுதியிலே தன் இனத்து மக்கள் இருக்கும் இடத்திலே

அண்ணன் காளிமுத்துவிடம் ஒன்னேமுக்கால் லட்சம் ஓட்டு வித்தியாசம் – அண்ணன் காளிமுத்துன்னா எங்கண்ணன்னு நினைக்காதீங்க.

பச்சோந்தி காளிமுத்துவிடம் ஒன்னே முக்கால் லட்சம் ஓட்டுவித்தியாசத்தில் தோல்வியுற்ற அந்தக் கழகத்தின் துரோகி

[ca.11:47] இன்றைக்கு மேடையிலே கருப்புத் துண்டு போட்டக்கொண்டு வீரவசனம் பேசுகிறார்

தந்தைப் பெரியாரை நேரில் பார்த்திருப்பாரா?

அண்ணாவின் குரலைக் கேட்டிருப்பாரா, நேரில் பார்த்திருப்பாரா?

[ca.12:00] இவர்களெல்லாம் தலைவர் கலைஞர் அவர்களைப் பார்த்து தமிழ் தடுமாறகிறது என்று சொல்லவில்லை.

கலிங்கப்பட்டி கழகத்தின் துரோகி சொல்கிறார், தமிழ்த் தலைவருக்குத் தமிழ் தடுமாறுகிறதாம்!

யாருக்குத் தமிழ் தடுமாறுகிறது?

சங்கத் தமிழ் விளக்கத்திற்கா தமிழ் தடுமாறுகிறது?

ஈரடி குறளுக்கு ஓவியம் தீட்டிடத் தூரிகை ஏற்றியவருக்கா தமிழ் தடுமாறுகிறது?

created a bad predicament for the party, when, without telling our leader Kalaiñar, in an illegal boat

went to Sri Lanka, and then recieved forgiveness from Kalaiñar, this Party Traitor.

Afterward, he could not sit as a DMK man in Parliament because

he was ousted from Parliament by a woman, this Party Traitor.

Among his own community people in the Sivakasi District

by a difference of one hundred fifty thousand votes with Elder Brother Kalimuthu—when I say "Elder Brother" Kalimuthu, please don't think I mean my own elder brother.

To that chameleon Kalimuthu he lost by a difference of one hundred fifty thousand votes, that Party Traitor.

[*ca. 11:47*] These days he gets up on stages wearing a black shawl and gives heroic orations.

Did he ever see Thandai Periyar in person?

Did he ever hear Anna's voice, or see him in person?

[*ca. 12:00*] All of those who saw our leader Kalaiñar never said that he stammered in Tamil.

The Party Traitor from Kalingappatti says so. The Tamil Leader stammers in Tamil, he says!

Who stammers in Tamil?

Does [one] stammer when discoursing on Sangam Tamil?

Will one raising a brush to paint a painting stammer in Tamil in poetic two-line stanzas?

சேரன் செங்குட்டுவனை பாண்டியனை சோழனை பல்லவனை பாரடா என்று

அடையாளம் காட்டிய அந்த பைந்தமிழுக்கா தமிழ் தடுமாறுகிறது?

சீவிச் சிங்காரித்து இரத்தக் காவிப் பொட்டிட்டு வாள் கொடுத்து சென்று வா மகனே போர்முனை நோக்கி என்று ரண களத்திற்கு அனுப்பிய தமிழச்சியை

நமக்கெல்லாம் அடையாளம் காட்டிய அந்தத் தலைவருக்கா தமிழ் தடுமாறுகிறது?

கலைஞர் துப்பும் எச்சிலில்கூடக் கன்னித் தமிழ் இருக்கிறது என்று கழகத்தின் துரோகிக்குத் தெரியாதா?

கலைஞர் அவர்கள் ஏறாத மலை உச்சியா, உலவாத புகழ் முகடா, அணியாத மலர் மாலையா, நடைபோடா ராஜ வீதியா?

[ca.13:00] கலைஞர் அவர்கள் அமராத சிம்மாசனமா, அணியாத கிரீடங்களா, தலைவர் கலைஞர் அவர்கள் பேசாத மேடையா, இசைக்காத தோடிகளா,

எழுதாத இலக்கியமா, எண்ணாத சிந்தனைகளா, வடிக்காத தமிழா, வார்க்காத கவிதைகளா,

கதையா, கட்டுரையா, சிறுகதையா, நாவலா, நாடகமா, சினிமாவா, கலையரங்கா, கட்டுரையரங்கா

லட்சக்கணக்கான மடல்கள், கவிதைகள், எழுதக்கூடிய தங்கத் தலைவனுக்குத் தமிழ் தடுமாறவில்லை.

அடப் பைத்தியக்காரா, கலிங்கப்பட்டி துரோகி!

தமிழ் தடுமாறும் என்றால் உனக்கும் எனக்கும் தான் தமிழ் தடுமாறும்.

என்ன காரணம்?

(தெலுகுல மாட்டாடிசி தமிழ் மாட்டாடு) தமிழ் தடுமாறும்.

நமது தாய்மொழி தெலுகு.

"Hey, Da, look at Ceran, at Senkuttuvan, at that Pandyan King, at the Colan King, at the Pallavan King,"

Will one stammer in pure, ancient Tamil when pointing [these kings] out?

Having groomed and decorated [her son], having placed a blood *thilagam* on [his forehead] and given him a sword, and turning to the battlefield sent him to war, saying, "Go and come, O, my son!"—

will one stammer in Tamil pointing this woman out to us all?

Doesn't the Party Traitor know that even Kalaiñar's spittle has Virgin Tamil in it?

Is there a mountaintop Kalaiñar has not climbed, a crown of fame not acknowledged, a flower garland he has not worn, a sacred street on which he has not walked triumphantly?

[*ca. 13:00*] Is there a throne upon which Kalaiñar has not sat, a crown he has not worn, a stage on which our leader Kalaiñar has not spoken, music not composed,

literature not written, ideas not considered, Tamil not formed, poetry not composed;

stories, essays, short stories, novels, plays, films, art competitions, debates,

hundreds of thousands of letters, poems—Does the Golden Tamilian who is able to write [all these things] stammer in Tamil?

O, you crazed fool, Kalingappatti Traitor!

If you speak of stammering in Tamil, it is only you and I who stammer in Tamil.

Why?

[A Telugu speaker who speaks in Tamil] stammers in Tamil.

Our mother tongue is Telugu.

தலைவர் கலைஞர் அவர்கள் தாய்மொழி தமிழ் மொழி. அந்தத் தங்கத் தமிழனுக்குத் தமிழ் தடுமாறவில்லை!

எனக்கு இதற்கு மேலே உன்னைப் பற்றிப் பேசுவதற்கு எனக்கு நேரமில்லை.

IV. Rape and Corruption

[ca.13:37] பெண்களுக்குப் பாதுகாப்புத் தரக்கூடிய ஒரு பெண் முதல்வர் ஆட்சியிலே,

எங்கு பார்த்தாலும் கொலை, கொள்ளை, கற்பழிப்பு, வழிப்பறிக் கொள்ளை இன்றைக்கு வழக்கமாக நடக்கிறது.

என்ன காரணம்?

லா அன்ட் பிராப்ளம் சட்டம் ஒழுங்கு கெட்டுவிட்டது அருமைப் பெரியோர்களே.

[ca.14:00] ஐ.ஏ.எஸ். பெண் அதிகாரி சந்திரலேகாவுக்கும் பாதுகாப்பு இல்லை.

அப்பாவி ஏழைப் பெண்களுக்கும் பாதுகாப்பில்லை.

எனக்கு முன்னால் உரையாற்றிய அண்ணன் அவர்கள் விடுதலை ரத்தினம் அருமையாக உங்களிடத்திலே எடுத்துச் சொன்னார்:

ஏழு வயசுப் பெண்களுக்கும்

பாதுகாப்பில்லை,

எழுவது வயதுப் பெண்களுக்கும் பாதுகாப்பில்லை.

காக்கிச் சட்டை போட்ட காவல் துறையினர் பெண்களைக் கற்பழிக்கிறார்கள்,

காவிச் சட்டை போட்ட பூசாரியும் பெண்களைக் கற்பழிக்கிறார்கள்.

ஊழல் பெற்ற மகாராணி, ஊழல் ராணி ஜெயலலிதாவைப் பார்த்து,

Our leader Kalaiñar's mother tongue is the Tamil language. That golden Tamilian never stammers!

I don't have time to speak any more about you.

IV. RAPE AND CORRUPTION

[*ca. 13:37*] In the administration of a woman chief minister, who should be able to provide protection for women,

wherever one looks murder, robbery, rape, and highway robbery today occur on a regular basis.

What is the reason?

O, my dear gentlemen, laws dealing with the law and (order) problem have been destroyed.

[*ca. 14:00*] No protection for an I.A.S. woman officer, Chandraleka;

no protection for innocent poor women either.

Viduthalai Rathinam, who spoke before me, put it to you beautifully:

For seven-year-old girls

there is no protection,

neither is there protection for seventy-year-old women.

Wearing khaki shirts, members of the police department are raping women.

Wearing a saffron shirt, a priest is raping women during the administration of the former actress Jayalalitha.

Looking at the Maharani of Corruption, the Queen of Corruption Jayalalitha,

காஞ்சி காமாட்சியே, மதுரை மீனாட்சியே, காசி விசாலாட்சியே. ஆதிபராசக்தியா? காவேரித் தாயா? வீராங்கனையா?

யாரை வாழ்த்துவது?

முன்னாள் நடிகை ஜெயலலிதா, ஊழல் ராணியா? உன்மீது ஊழல் பட்டியல் அடுக்கடுக்காய் வந்துகொண்டிருக்கிறது.

மத்தியிலே

காங்கிரஸ் ஊழல் நடைபெறுகின்றது. மாநிலத்தில் உன்னிடத்தில

ஊழல் நடைபெற்றுக் கொண்டிருக்கிறது.
எனக்கு நீண்ட நேரம் உரையாற்றுவதற்கு நேரமில்லாமல்,

V. Kalaiñar's Praise

[ca.14:55] தங்கத் தலைவனை, தமிழ்நாட்டுத் தலைவனை, டாக்டர் கலைஞர் அவர்களை வாழ்த்திவிட்டு விடைபெறலாம் என்று கருதுகிறேன்.

[ca.15:00] உடன்பிறப்பே கழக உடன்பிறப்பே என்றழைத்து உணர்வுகளை கொட்டிவைத்து உலகத்தமிழர்களின் உள்ளத்தில் நிறைந்தவரே!

பள்ளத்தில் விழுந்திங்கு பரிதவிக்கும் தமிழினத்தை துள்ளி எழுந்தோடி வந்து தூக்கிவிட துடிப்பவரே!

திருவாரூர் மண்ணில் பிறந்த தென்பாண்டி சிங்கமே!

எதையும் தாங்கும் இதயம் கொண்ட தன்மானத் திருவிளக்கே, தமிழ் குடமுழக்கே!

எந்தப் புயலிலும் விழாத திராவிடக் கொடிமரமே சூரியனை மட்டும் சுற்றும் பூமியே!

மாறாத மூலிகை வண்ணமாய் மின்னும் வானத்தின் மின்விளக்கே!

லட்சிய செயல்பாட்டில் வேகம் கொண்ட லட்சிய வீரனே வீரமறத் தமிழனே!

O, Kanji Kamachi! O, Madurai Meenakshi! O, Kashi Visalachi! Athipara-sakti? Mother Kaveri? Amazon Warrior?

Just who is being praised?

Is it former actress and Queen of Corruption Jayalalitha who is being praised? A list of corruption charges are being placed before you in stacks and stacks.

Meanwhile

Congress corruption is occuring in the state!

Corruption is occuring. Because I do not have time to speak a long time,

V. KALAIÑAR'S PRAISE

[ca. 14:55] I think I will praise the Golden Leader, the Leader of the Tamil Race, Dr. Kalaiñar, and then take my leave.

[ca. 15:00] O, he who fills the hearts of the world's Tamilians, who thrills us with emotions calling us, "O, My Siblings! O, My Party Siblings!"

O, he whose heart beats to raise us up, who comes jumps up to run to the Tamil race which suffers here having fallen into an abyss!

O, Lion of the South Pandi Land, born in the earth of Thiruvarur!

O, Sacred Lamp of self-respect, who has a heart that can bear anything! O, Holy Water of the Temple of Tamil!

O, Mast of the Dravidian Flag which no storm will fell! O, Only Earth that circles the Sun!

O, Lightning Light of the Sky that brightens with eternal colors!

O, Auspicious Hero who brings life in songs of auspicious deeds!

கலிங்கப்பட்டி வாழைமர மட்டையை, வைரம் பாய்ந்த தேக்குகளாய் விலைமதிப்பாக்கிவிட்ட வித்தகரே, முத்தமிழ் அறிஞரே!

கோழைகளையும் முட்டாள்களையும் வளைக்கின்ற உரையாற்றும் திறமை படைத்தவரே!

கற்கண்டை வெல்கின்ற சொற்கண்டுக் கவிதை தரும் தமிழினத் தலைவா!

உன் கொஞ்சு தமிழ் சொல் கேட்டால் பிஞ்சும் மலரும் துள்ளியெழுந்தோடி வரும் தமிழ்நாட்டுத் தலைவனுடைய

[ca.16:00] வைர வார்த்தைகளுக்கும் வைடூரிய வாக்கியங்களுக்கும் வற்றாத சிந்தனைகளுக்கும்,

வளையாத கொள்கைகளுக்கும், உதய சூரியன் சின்னத்திற்கும், கறுப்பு சிவப்புக் கொடிக்கும்,

திராவிட முன்னேற்றக் கழகத்திற்கும், சொந்தக்காரர் தலைவர் கலைஞர் அவர்கள் இருக்க

இன்னொருவனைத் தலைவனாக ஏற்றுக்கொள்ள தலைவர் அவர்கள் விட்டாரா? என்ன செய்தார்?

மடமையை மாய்த்து, கொடுமையைக் களைத்து, சிறுமையை சாய்த்து

அநீதி அகற்றி ஆணவத்தை இடுப்பொடித்து உருக்குலைத்து துள்ளிவந்த துரோகத்தை

கிள்ளி எறிந்துவிட்ட தமிழினத் தலைவர் டாக்டர் கலைஞர் அவர்கள்

என்றைக்கும் அண்ணா வழி நின்று நெஞ்சுக்கு நீதி நின்று அமைதியான ஆட்சி நடத்துகின்றவர்.

உலகத் தமிழர்களின் உள்ளத்தில் இடம்பெற்றிருக்கும் தன்னிகரில்லாத தானைத் தலைவர்

அறிவும், தெளிவும், திறனும்,

O, Master, O, Sage of the Three-fold Tamil who turned a Kalingappatti bannana tree into a stone of teak, who turned valuelessness to value!

O, Creator of the skills of oration which break the backs of weaklings!

O, Leader of the Tamil Race who gives poems with words sweeter than rock candy!

When hearing your child-like Tamil, budding flowers come bouncing, jumping and running. (For) the Tamil Race Leader's

[ca. 16:00] diamond words, for his sentences of precious stones, for his thoughts that do not wilt,

for his unbent principles, for the sign of the Rising Sun, for the Black and Red Flag,

and for the Dravidian Progress Party – while our leader of our kin Kalaiñar is there

will our leader allow us to accept another as leader? What has he done?

Destroying foolishness, weeding out cruelty, felling small-heartedness,

putting that which destroys justice in it's place, disfiguring the life of weakness, arrogant betraya,l

ripping and throwing (it) away, our leader Dr. Kalaiñar,

the one who conducts his administration always upholding Anna's way, upholding (the principle of) Justice for the Heart;

the peerless, honorable leader who has found a place in the hearts of Tamils the world over;

wisdom, clarity, abilty,

அளவற்ற அருளும், அளவற்ற உழைப்பும், சீரிய சிந்தனையும், சிறந்த குணமும், செம்மாந்தச் செயலும்,

[ca.17:00]

உள்ளத்தில் குடிகொண்ட கொள்கையும், தன்னை உருவாக்கிய தலைவர் பேரறிஞர் அண்ணாமீது கொண்ட

விசுவாசம் கொண்ட அந்த ஒப்பற்ற தலைவர்,

தமிழினத் தலைவர் டாக்டர் கலைஞர் அவர்கள் ஆட்சியில் விலைவாசி எப்படியிருந்தது?

இன்றைக்கு ஆளுகின்ற அம்மையார் அவர்கள் ஆட்சியில் விலைவாசி எப்படியிருக்கின்றது?

எனக்கு சொல்லுவதற்கு நேரமில்லை. நான் அடுத்த கூட்டத்தில் –

என்னென்ன பேசணுமோ நீங்கள் எதிர்பார்க்கும் அளவிற்கு இந்தக் கவிதா நான் பேசக் கற்றிருக்கிறேன்.

இனம் இனம் என்று சொல்வார்கள்

தெலுங்கு பேசுகின்ற கவிதா இன்றைக்கு மேடையிலே பேசுகின்றேன் என்றால் என்ன காரணம்?

இனம் என்றால் எனக்கு இந்த திராவிட முன்னேற்றக் கழகம் தான். இனம் என்று உங்கள் மத்தியில் எடுத்துவைத்து

VI. Conclusion

நீண்ட நேரம் உரையாடுவதற்கு நேரமும் வாய்ப்பும் இல்லை. அண்ணன் நன்னிலம் நடராஜனும்

தீப்பொறி அவர்களும் இன்றைக்கு இடியும் மின்னலும் போல் வெட்டக் காத்திருக்கிறார்கள்!

ஆகவே தமிழகத்திலே தமிழன் தலைநிமிர்ந்து நிற்க வேண்டும்.

தன்மானத் தலைவர் டாக்டர் கலைஞர் அவர்கள் ஆட்சி மலர வேண்டுமென்றால்

மதிப்பும் மரியாதைக்குரிய முத்துவேல் அஞ்சுகத்தாய் பெற்றெடுத்த மாணிக்கத்தை

unmeasurable skill, unmeasurable work, the finest thought, the highest qualities, perfect deeds,

[*ca. 17:00*]

principles that live in our hearts, the leader who formed him, Perariñar Anna,

having faith that matchless leader,

the leader of the Tamil people, in Dr Kalaiñar's administration how were the (commodity) prices?

How are commodity prices under the administratin of the woman who rules today?

I don't have time to say. I, in the next meeting –

What should I speak? I, this Kavitha, am ready to speak for as long as you expect.

A people, a people, they say.

I, Kavitha, who speaks Telegu, am speaking on this stage today. What is the reason?

I submit to you that if you say "people," the Dravidian Progress Party is my only "people."

VI. CONCLUSION

I have neither the time nor the opportunity to speak for an extended time.

Elder Brother Nannilam Natarajan and Tippori Arumugam today, like thunder and lightning, are waiting to strike!

Therefore the Tamilian must stand with his head high in our Tamil land.

If (you) want the Honorable Leader Dr. Kalaiñar's administration to blossom,

the ruby born of the esteemed and honorable Muthuvel and Anjakattay, [ca.18:00] கலைஞானம் கொண்ட விலைமதிப்பில்லா வித்தகனை வெற்றித் திருமகனை தன் அருமை மைந்தனை

சீராட்டிப் பாராட்டி வளர்த்த செல்வ மகன்தான் எங்கள் உள்ளத்திலே

மணிவிளக்காய்த் திகழும் உத்தமத் தலைவர் ஒரே தலைவர், முத்தமிழ் அறிஞர், இயற்றமிழ் அறிஞர், இசைத் தமிழ் அறிஞர்

நாடகத் தமிழ் அறிஞர், வித்தகக் கவிஞர், தத்துவத் திருவர், தமிழினத் தலைவர்

டாக்டர் கலைஞர் அவர்களுக்கும், உதயசூரியன் சின்னத்திற்கும்,

திராவிட முன்னேற்றக் கழகத்திற்கும், தளபதி ஸ்டாலின் அவர்களுக்கும் ஆதரவு தாரீர்! தாரீர்! என்று

மீண்டும் ஒருமுறை நான் காமராஜர் மாவட்ட மகளிர் அணி சார்பாகவும்

எனக்குப் பேச வாய்ப்பளித்த அண்ணன் — அவர்களுக்கும் மீண்டும் ஒருமுறை நன்றி கூறி

[ca.18:39] விடைபெறுகிறேன். நன்றி. வணக்கம்.

[*ca. 18:00*] the priceless master of the wisdom of the arts, victorious son, their dear child,

raised with elegance and praise, the beloved son, who in our hearts

glows with lustre as a bejeweled lamp, our highest leader, the one and only leader, the sage of three-fold Tamil, the sage of Literary Tamil, the sage of Musical Tamil,

the sage of Dramatic Tamil, the Master Poet, the Sacred One of Philosophy, the Leader of the Tamil People,

to Dr. Kalaiñar, to the Rising Sun Flag,

to the Dravidian Progress Party, to Talapathi Stalin, give your support! Give your support!

And again, once more, I, on behalf of the Kamarajar District Women's Wing

express my thanks to Elder Brother – for giving me the opportunity to speak,

[*ca. 18:39*] and I take my leave. Thank you. *Vanakkam.*

GLOSSARY

This List includes proper names, terms, and phrases as they are spelled in the book according to common conventions in Tamilnadu. The terms are followed by a more precise transcription using the *University of Madras Tamil Lexicon* transcriptional schema.

ADI (*aṭi*): base, foundation.

ADUKKUMOZHIKAL (*aṭukkumoḻikaḷ*): "stacked utterances."

AKUPEYAR (*ākupeyar*): trope; "transformed word" (*ākuvākum peyar*), the opposite of "natural words" (*iyalpeyar*); the hyponym for sixteen named varieties of contiguity tropes. See chapter 3.

ANGAPIRATHACHANAM (*aṅkapiṟataṭcaṇam*): a vow to the deity for a boon in return, often the good health of a loved one; the devotee promises to roll on the ground a certain number of revolutions (usually three) around the god's temple. The rigors of the act, as well as the abject humbling of the devotee (who removes his shirt and rolls on the often muddy ground), make *angapirathachanam* a particularly dramatic vow.

ANGATHAM (*aṅkatam*): satire.

ANI (*aṇi*): adornment, a literary adornment, a figure (e.g., *akupeyar*) or formal trope (e.g., *maṭakku*).

ANMIGAM (*āṉmīkam*): religion, worship.

ARACIYAL (*araciyal*): politics.

ASINGAM (*aciṅkam*): "dirty," "disgusting," "shameful."

AVARKALEY (*avarkaḷē*): 3-person plural vocative; used as a formal mode of hailing people from the speaking stage.

BHAKTI (*pakti*): devotional love, worship; the name of several counterstructural religious movements over the past 1,300 years.

CENTAMIL (*centamiḻ*): "refined," "pure," "beautiful," or "literary" Tamil; distinguished from *koccai-* (vulgar), *kodun-* (bent), or *naṭimuṟai-* (everyday) Tamil.

DANDORA POTTU (*tanṭōra poṭṭu*): use of a drum to announce some event to the society at large.

DRAVIDA KAZHAGAM (*tirāviṭak kaḻakam*): the Dravidian Association, or DK, the organization founded by Periyar E. V. Ramaswamy in 1944, and the single most important intellectual center of the Dravidian movement generally.

DRAVIDA MUNNETRA KAZHAGAM (*tirāviṭa muṉṉēṟṟak kaḻakam*): the Dravidian Progress Association, or DMK, the political party founded by C. N. Annadurai in 1949.

EETRADIKKURAL (*īṟṟaṭikkuṟaḷ*): two-line stanza, couplet; the poetic form of the *Thirukkural.*

INAM (*iṉam*): "people," "community"; akin to the term *jati* (see entry below).

JATI (*jāti*): "caste"; a named, endogamous group; any one of a set of categories, e.g., a "genus" or "species."

KALACHARAM (*kalāccāram*): culture, civilization.

KARUTHARANGAM (*karuttaraṅkam*): discourse, or symposium, among learned people.

KATHAKALAKSHEPAM (*katāk kalāṭcēpam*): performance genre featuring religious discourses interspersed with songs, usually featuring a single *othuvar* (singer/reciter). The most prominent of the *othuvars* of this genre during the second half of the twentieth century was Kiripananda Variyar (1906–1993).

KAZHAGAM (*kaḻakam*): lit. "association," but refers to political organizations or "parties," especially in the language of the Dravidian parties (e.g., Dravida Munnetra Kazhagam, DMK.)

KEDAIYAM (*kēṭaiyam*): ceremonial "shield" given as a formal gift on special occasions. In the public meeting the *kedaiyam* is the highest-profile gift a local person can give to his leader.

KIRAMAM (*kirārāmam*): village.

KOCHAITAMIL (*koccaittamiḻ*): spoken or "vulgar" (*kochai*) Tamil.

KODUNTAMIL (*koṭuntamiḻ*): "bent" Tamil, homonymous with *kochai-*, or "vulgar," Tamil.

KOTTAI (*koṭṭai*): fort; or The Fort, the Chennai office of the Legislative Assembly and Secretariat of Tamilnadu.

KOYIL (*kōyil, kōvil*): temple, lit. the "place" (*il*) of the "king" (*kō*).

KUDICAI (*kuṭicai*): traditional mud-walled and thatched house, common in villages. In urban areas it has more the sense of "hut" or "hovel," an informal dwelling that stands opposed brick and mortar houses with "proper" (*pakka*) tile or cement roofs.

KURALADI VANJIPPA (*kuṟaḷaṭi vañcippā*): a poetic metre consisting of a five-syllable foot composed of two short metremes (*niṟai*) and one long metreme (*nēr*).

LILA (*līla*): play, sports; (in Saivism) the Lord Siva's divine play of world creation.

MADAKKU (*maṭakku*): a formal trope bearing the sense of "folding," "refraction," "repetition of a word, foot, or line of poetry in a stanza, each time in a different sense" (*Dandiyalankaram, su.* 92).

MALAI (*mālai*): garland of flowers, given to deities, leaders, brides and bridegrooms, corpses, white tourists, and other honored beings.

MANAM (*maṇam*): fragrance, a smell.

MANAM (*maṉam*): heart or mind.

MANIKKODI (*Maṇikkoṭi*): journal (1933–1939) that featured modernist writers, most famously Puthumaippithan (1906–1948).

MANONMANIYAM (*Maṉōṉmaṇīyam*): Sundaram Pillai's 1891 play featuring the first "heroic oration" in Tamil literature.

MAPATHAGAM (*māpātakam*): great crime; (in religous contexts) sacrilege.

MARIYATHAI (*mariyātai*): distinction, honor, respect.

MARUMALARCHI DRAVIDA MUNNETRA KAZHAGAM (*marumalarcci tirāviṭa muṉṉēṟṟak kaḻakam*): the Rennaissance Dravidian Progress Association, or MDMK, a breakaway party from the DMK founded in 1994 by Vai. Gopalswamy (Vaiko).

MATHAM (*matam*): lit. "frenzy" or "madness"; religion.

MEDAITAMIL (*meṭaittamiḷ*): oratory; literally "stage Tamil"; sometimes distinguished as oratory using *centamil.*

MEL (*mēl*): top, up, above; North.

MEY (*mey*): the body; truth.

MEYKEERTHI (*meykīrtti*): the Tamil equivalent of *prashasti,* a Cola period (ca. ninth–twelfth century C.E.) genre of inscriptions in which great men praise the king.

MEYMAI (*meymai*): truth as expressed in the body and in actions, the third form of truth (see also *unmai, vaymai*).

MUNNILAI VIZHIKAL (*muṉṉilai viḷikkaḷ*): introductory salutations; the first part of a formal speech in which the speaker addresses specific individuals and groups present.

MUTAL MARIYATAI (*mutal mariyātai*): "first honors"; the position of primacy during worship or any other formal ritual action; to be honored first before others.

NADAIMURAITAMIL (*naṭaimuṟaittamiḷ*): the language of "ordinary," or everyday (*naṭaimuṟai*) life.

NADU (*naṭu*): center, the middle.

NADU (*nāṭu*): country, land, as in Tamilnadu; the cultivated lands occupied by human beings (vs. *kadu* [*kāṭu*], "waste lands," forests, places occupied by the dead, by ghosts, etc.).

NADUVAR (*naṭuvar*): mediator, the central figure in formal debates such as *pattimanram* or *pattimandabam.*

NAVALAR (*nāvalar*): orator; a title given to a great orator, such as Arumuga Navalar (1821–1879).

NAVANMAI (*nāvaṉmai*): "tongue power" or "tongue-strength"; eloquence.

NEETHIPATHI (*nītipati*): judge, mediator; the judge of a speech competition or formal debate.

NUL (*nūl*): text; textual artifact.

PAHUTHARIVU (*pakuttaṟivu*): rationalism, the root philosophy of Periyar E. V. Ramaswamy and the Dravidian Association (DK).

PANBADU (*paṇpāṭu*): culture. A neologism of the "pure Tamil movement" of the 1930s and '40s.

PARIVATTAM (*parivaṭṭam*): a piece of cloth, ideally a shawl, given to an honored guest or on ceremonial occasions.

PATTIMANDRAM, PATTIMANDABAM (*paṭṭimaṉṟam, paṭṭimaṇṭipam*): a form of literary or social debate involving two sides and a "mediator" or "judge."

PASAM (*pācam*): attachment, love, affection.

PECHU KALAI (*pēccuk kalai*): the "speaking arts," rhetorical skills.

PERIYA PEN (*peṟiya peṇ*): lit. "big woman/girl"; a teenage girl who has reached puberty.

PERUMAI (*peṟumai*): greatness, renown; distinction.

PIRACHARAM (*piraccāram*): political campaigning; propaganda.

PONGAL (*poṅkal*): Tamilnadu's harvest festival featuring a sweet rice preparation (*poṅkal*) which boils over, embodying abundance and plenty.

POTHUKUTTAM (*potuk kūṭṭam*): "public meeting," usually reserved for political events.

PRASHASTI (*piraṣasti*): praise poems inscribed in Sanskrit used by precolonial kingdoms. (See *meykeerthi*).

PUJA (*pūca, pūcai, pūjai*): worship, paying homage; a formal ritual worship of the deity in a temple officiated by priests.

PURAM (*puṟam*): the exterior; one of the two main genres of Sangam Tamil poetry, opposed to *akam*, the "interior."

PURANAM (*puṟāṇam*): Purana, a traditional, sometimes sacred, narrative; the old stories of places and gods; a tale.

PUHAZHA PUHAZH (*pukaḻāp pukaḻ*): lit. the "praise that does not praise"; ironic or sarcastic praise; satire.

SANGAM (*caṇkam*): "academy"; the academies of ancient Tamil, by tradition said to be located in Madurai; the poems and grammar, Tolkaappiyam, of classical Tamil, ca. first–third centuries C.E.

SILAPPATHIKARAM (*Cilappatikāram*). "The Tale of the Anklet," or the tale of Kannaki, ca. sixth–eight century C.E.

TALAIMAI PECHALARKAL (*talaimai pēccāḷarkaḷ*): "chief speakers"; the highest rank of paid orators in a political party.

TAMILAKAM, THAMLIZHAGAM (*Tamiḻakam*): the Tamil lands. "Tamilnadu" refers to the tate, whereas "Tamilakam" has more of a sense of the people, of "the nation" in the sense of a group of people rather than the demarcation of a political cum bureaucratic entity. In some respects it partakes of the same opposition that Valentine Daniel (1984, 1996) draws between two words for town or village: the *ūr*, which has the sense of a substantive connection of people, place, deity, etc., vs. the *kirāmam*, a bureaucratic and geographical entity. The *ūr*, writes Daniel, is an ontic place whereas the *kirāmam* is an epistemic space.

TAPPATTAI (*tappaṭṭai*): also called *tappu* (*tappu*), mentioned as the type of drum that used to announce public speakers in the 1930s. See *dandora pottu*.

THIRUKKURAL (*Tirukkuṟaḷ*): "the Sacred Kural"; ca. 6th century C.E. A text of 1,330 couplets (*kural*) organized according to the three aims of life (*trivārga*): *dhārma* (right conduct), *ārtha* (material gain), and *kāma* (romantic love).

THIRUVIZHA (*tiruviḷā*): temple festival (as opposed to *paṇṭikai*, or festivals of the home, such as Pongal).

ULA (*ulā*): a genre of Cola period (ca. ninth–twelfth century C.E.) literature extolling the virtues, beauty, desirability, etc., of the king as he is processing through the streets.

ULLAM (*uḷḷam*): inside; heart/mind, the interior of a person's being.

UNMAI (*uṇmai*): truth as expressed from the heart/mind (*uḷḷam*), the most 'internal' of truths (see also *vaymai, meymai*).

VATTAM (*vaṭṭam*): lit. "circle." Ward, the smallest organizational unit in the political geography. Through tropic extension, this is also the title given to the leader of a ward.

VANJA PUHAZHCHI (*vañcap pukaḻcci*): a named trope of satire, lit. the "praise that blames," a kind of ironic hyperbolic praise.

VARAVERPURAI (*varavēṟpurai*): "welcome address"; a performance genre of oratory that, as the name suggests, welcomes and praises an honored guest to a special occasion.

VAY (*vāy*): mouth.

VAYMAI (*vāymai*): truth as expressed in the mouth (*vāy*), the middle form of truth (see also *unmai, meymai*).

VEERAM (*vīram*): virility, manliness, potency.

VEERAVASANAM (*vīravacaṉam*): heroic discourse, kingly oration.

VERI PACAM (*veṟip pācam*): "frenzied love."

VESHTI (*vēṣṭi*): a *dhoti*. Worn with a white shirt, and perhaps a shoulder cloth (*tuṇṭu*), this is the standard uniform of a male Tamil politician in public.

YAPPU (*yāppu*): meter or prosody.

REFERENCES

TAMIL NEWSPAPERS

Dinakaran
Dinamalar
Dinathandi
Malai Malar
Malai Murasu
Nakeeran
Tharasu

BOOKS AND ARTICLES

Abrams, P. 1988. "Notes on the Difficulty of Studying the State (1977)." *Journal of Historical Sociology* 1.1:58–89.

Achariya, Devasigamani. 1949. *Medaitamil* (Platform Tamil).

——. 1987 [1949]. *Medaitamil* (Platform Tamil). Reprint, chapters 1–18. Chennai: Palms Printers.

Agha, Asif. 1999. "Register." *Journal of Linguistic Anthropology* 9.1:216–219.

——. 2007. *Language and Social Relations*. Cambridge: Cambridge University Press.

Ali, Daud. 1996. "Regime of Pleasure in Early India: A Genealogy of Practices at the Cola Court." Diss., Department of History, University of Chicago.

——. 2004. *Courtly Culture and Political Life in Early Medieval India*. Cambridge: University of Cambridge Press.

Amin, Shahid. 1988. "Gandhi as Mahatma: Gorakhpur District, Eastern U.P., 1921–22." In *Selected Subaltern Studies*, ed. Ranajit Guha and Gayatri C. Spivak, 288–348. New York.

Anderson, Benedict. 1991 [1983]. *Imagined Communities*. New York: Verso.

Andronov, M. S. 1969. *A Standard Grammar of Modern and Classical Tamil*. Madras: New Century Book House.

Annamalai, E. 1976. "Discussion Over Standard Spoken Tamil." In *Studies in Dialectology* 1.2, ed. B. Gopinathan Nair. Trivandrum: University of Kerala.

——. 1980. "Simplification as a Process of Modernization." In *Sociolinguistics and Dialec-*

tology, ed. S. Agesthialingom and K. Karunakaran, 1–12. Annamalai Nagar: Annamalai University Press.

Appadurai, Arjun. 1990. "Topographies of the Self: Praise and Emotion in Hindu India." In *Language and the Politics of Emotion*, ed. C. A. Lutz and L. Abu-Lughod, 92–112. Cambridge: Cambridge University Press.

——. 1996. *Modernity at Large*. Minneapolis: University of Minnesota Press.

——. 2003. "The Still Life of Empire." Keynote address for *Representing the Raj*, a symposium and exhibit, Yale Center for British Art, 17 October 2003.

——. 2006. *Fear of Small Numbers: An Essay on the Geography of Anger*. Durham, NC: Duke University Press.

Appadurai, Arjun, and Carol Breckenridge. 1976. "The South Indian Temple: Authority, Honour, and Redistribution." *Contributions to Indian Sociology* 10.2:187–210.

Aravanan, Ka. Pa. 1994. *Tamizhar Tadangal* (Complaints of a Tamilian). Puthucheri: Tamizhkottam.

Aristotle. 1961. *Aristotle's Poetics: Translation and Analysis*. Ed. K. A. Telford. Chicago: Regnery.

Arnold, David. 1977. *The Congress in Tamilnad: Nationalist Politics in South India, 1919–1937*. New Delhi: Manohar.

Arokianathan, S. 1982. "Language Use in Mass Media with Special Reference to Tamil Radio Programs." Diss., University of Washington.

Arooran, Nambi. 1980. *Tamil Renaissance and Dravidian Nationalism, 1895–1944*. Madurai: Koodal Publishers.

Asad, Talal. 1993. *Genealogies of Religion: Discipline and Reasons of Power in Christianity and Islam*. Baltimore: John Hopkins University Press.

——. 2003. *Formations of the Secular: Christianity, Islam, Modernity*. Stanford: Stanford University Press.

Athenaeus. 1854. *The Deipnosophists; or, Banquet of the Learned of Athenaeus* III. Trans. C. D. Yonge. London: Henry G. Bohn.

Austin, J. L. 1975 [1962]. *How to Do Things with Words*. Cambridge, MA: Harvard University Press.

Babb, Lawrence A. 1986. *Redemptive Encounters: Three Modern Styles in the Hindu Tradition*. Berkeley: University of California Press.

Baker-Reynolds, Holly. 1987. "Madurai: Koyil Nagar." In *The City as a Sacred Center*, ed. B. Smith and H. Baker-Reynolds, 12–44. New York: Brill.

Bakhtin, M. N. 1981. *The Dialogic Imagination*. Ed. M. Holquist. Trans. C. Emerson and M. Holquist. Austin: University of Texas Press.

——. 1986. "The Problem of Speech Genres." In *Speech Genres and Other Late Essays*, 60–102. Austin: University of Texas Press.

Balagangadhara, S. N. 1994. *"The Heathen in his Blindness. . ." Asia, the West, and the Dynamic of Religion*. Leiden: Brill.

Bate, Bernard. 2002. "Political Praise in Tamil Newspapers: The Poetry and Iconography of Democratic Power." In *Everyday Life in South Asia*, ed. Diane Mines and Sarah Lamb, 308–325. Bloomington: Indiana University Press.

——. 2004. "Shifting Subjects: Elocutionary Revolution in Eighteenth-Century America and Twentieth-Century India." *Language and Communication* 24.4:337–352.

——. 2005. "Arumuga Navlar, Saivite Sermons, and the Delimitation of Religion, c. 1850." In *Language, Genre, and the Historical Imagination in South India*. Special issue, *Indian Economic and Social History Review* 42.4:467–482.

Bateson, Gregory. 1958 [1936]. *Naven*. Stanford: Stanford University Press.

Beck, Brenda. 1976. "The Symbolic Merger of Body, Space, and Cosmos." *Contributions to Indian Sociology,* n.s. 10.2:213–243.

Beschi, Constantine G. 1822 [1730]. *A Grammar of the High Dialect of the Tamil Language, Termed Shen-Tamil: To Which Is Added, an Introduction to Tamil Poetry.* Trans. Benjamin Guy Babington. Madras: College Press.

——. 1831 [1728]. *A Grammar of the Common Dialect of the Tamulian Language, Called Koduntamij.* Trans. Christopher Henry Horst. Madras: Vepery Mission Press.

Bloch, Maurice. 1975. "Introduction." In *Political Language and Oratory in Traditional Society,* 1–28. London: Academic Press.

——. 1989. *Ritual, History, Power: Selected Papers in Anthropology.* Atlantic Highlands, NJ : Athlone Press.

Bourdieu, Pierre. 1977. *Outline of a Theory of Practice.* Cambridge: Cambridge University Press.

Brass, Paul. 1974. *Language, Religion, and Politics in North India.* London: Cambridge University Press.

——. 1990. *Politics of India Since Independence.* Cambridge: Cambridge University Press.

Breckenridge, Carol A. 1976. "The Sri Minakshi-Sundaresvarar Temple: Worship and Endowments in South India, 1833–1925." Diss., University of Wisconsin, Madison.

——. n.d. (a). "Risking Incorporation: Worship and Social Forms in Peninsular India."

——. n.d. (b). "Urban Capitals and Peninsular Indian Landscapes: The Case of the Sixteenth and Seventeenth Centuries."

Briggs, Charles L. 2005. "Communicability, Racial Discourse, and Disease." *Annual Review of Anthropology* 34:269–291.

Britto, Francis. 1986. *Diglossia: A Study of the Theory with Application to Tamil.* Washington, DC: Georgetown University Press.

Buhler, Karl. 1982 [1934]. *Sprachtheorie.* Stuttgart: Fischer.

Bulwar-Lytton, Sir Edward, Bart., M.P. 1866. *The Lost Tales of Miletus.* London: John Murray.

Burke, Kenneth. 1957 [1941]. *The Philosophy of Literary Form.* Rev. abr. ed. New York: Vintage.

——. 1969 [1945]. *A Grammar of Motives.* Berkeley: University of California Press.

——. 1969 [1950]. *A Rhetoric of Motives.* Berkeley: University of California Press.

Caldwell, Robert. 1981 [1856]. *A Comparative Grammar of the Dravidian, or South Indian, Family of Languages.* Delhi: Gian Publications.

Caton, Steven C. 1990: *"Peaks of Yemen I Summon": Poetry as Cultural Practice in a North Yemeni Tribe.* Berkeley: University of California Press.

Certeau, Michel de. 1984. *The Practice of Everyday Life.* Berkeley: University of California Press.

Chakrabarty, D. 1991. "Open Space/Public Place: Garbage, Modernity, and India." *South Asia* 14.1:15–31.

Chandrababu, B. S. 1993. *Social Protest and Its Impact on Tamil Nadu.* Madras: Emerald Publishers.

Chatterjee, Partha. 1993. *The Nation and Its Fragments: Colonial and Post-Colonial Histories.* Princeton: Princeton University Press.

Chidambaram. 1987. "Cultural Entrepreneurs and Language Strategists: DMK in Tamil Nadu." *Indian Journal of Political Science* 48.3:418–427.

Cohn, B. 1987. *An Anthropologist Among the Historians and Other Essays.* New Delhi: Oxford University Press.

——. 1996. *Colonialism and Its Forms of Knowledge: The British in India*. Princeton: Princeton University Press.

Crocker, J. Christopher. 1977. "The Social Functions of Rhetorical Forms." In Sapir and Crocker 1977:33–66.

Cutler, Norman. 1987. *Songs of Experience: The Poetics of Tamil Devotion*. Bloomington: Indiana University Press.

——. 2003. "Three Moments in the Genealogy of Tamil Literary Culture." In *Literary Cultures in History: Reconstructions from South Asia*, ed. Sheldon Pollock, 271–322. Berkeley: University of California Press.

Daniel, E. Valentine. 1984. *Fluid Signs: Being a Person the Tamil Way*. Berkeley: University of California Press.

——. 1996. *Charred Lullabies: Chapters in an Anthropography of Violence*. Princeton: Princeton University Press.

——. 2002. "The Arrogation of Being and the Blind Spot of Religion." In *Discrimination and Toleration*, ed. K. Hastrup and G. Ulrich, 31–53. Great Britain.

Daniel, E. Valentine, and J. M. Peck, eds. 1996. *Culture and Contexture: Explorations in Anthropology and Literary Studies*. Berkeley: University of California Press.

Dasan, Vi. Ma. 1984. *Pechchu: Medaippechchin Muulangal* (Speech: The Bases of Stage Speaking). Dindugal: Beschi College.

Davis, R. 1985. "Chola Meykkirttis as Literary Texts." *Tamil Civilization* 3.2–3:1–5.

——. 1991. *Rituals in an Oscillating Universe*. Princeton: Princeton University Press.

Deleuze, Gilles, and Félix Guattari. 1987. *A Thousand Plateaus: Capitalism and Schizophrenia*. Trans. Brian Massumi. Minneapolis: University of Minnesota Press.

Dhamotharan, A. 1980. *Nannul Muulamum Kulangaittambiran Uraiyum* (*Nannul* Original and Kulangaithambiran's Commentary). Wiesbaden: Steiner.

Dickey, Sara. 1993a. "The Politics of Adulation: Cinema and the Production of Politicians in South India." *Journal of Asian Studies* 52.2:340–372.

——. 1993b. *Cinema and the Urban Poor in South India*. New Delhi: Cambridge University Press.

Dirks, N. 1987. *The Hollow Crown: Ethnohistory of an Indian Kingdom*. Bombay: Cambridge University Press.

——. 1989. "The Original Caste: Power, History, and Hierarchy in South Asia." *Contributions to Indian Sociology* 23.1:59–78.

——. 2001. *Castes of Mind: Colonialism and the Making of Modern India*. Princeton: Princeton University Press.

Duranti, Alessandro, and Charles Goodwin, eds. 1992. *Rethinking Context: Language as an Interactive Phenomenon*. Cambridge: Cambridge University Press.

Eck, Diane. 1981. *Darshan: Seeing the Divine Image in India*. Chambersburg, PA: Anima Books.

Egnor, Margaret. 1978. "The Sacred Spell and Other Conceptions of Life in Tamil Culture." Diss., University of Chicago.

Erami, Narges. 2008. "The Soul of the Market: The Social World and Effective History of Persian Rugs and Their Bazaar." Diss., Columbia University.

Errington, J. Joseph. 1998. *Shifting Languages: Interaction and Identity in Javanese Indonesia*. Cambridge: Cambridge University Press.

——. 2007. *Colonial Linguistics: A Story of Language, Meaning, and Power*. Oxford: Blackwell.

Ezekiel, Nizzim. 1989. *Collected Poems, 1952–1988*. Delhi: Oxford University Press.

Ferguson, Charles F. [1959]. "Diglossia." *Word* 15.2: 325–340. Reprinted in Hymes and Dell 1964:429–439.

Fernandez, James W. 1974. "The Mission of Metaphor in Expressive Culture." *Current Anthropology* 15.2:119–145.

——. 1982. *Bwiti: An Ethnography of the Religious Imagination in Africa*. Princeton: Princeton University Press.

——. 1986. *Persuasions and Performances: The Play of Tropes in Culture*. Bloomington: Indiana University Press.

——. 1990. *Beyond Metaphor: The Theory of Tropes in Anthropology*. Stanford: Stanford University Press.

Fishman, Joshua, ed. 1967. "Bilingualism With and Without Diglossia; Diglossia With and Without Bilingualism." *Journal of Social Issues* 23.2:29–38.

Fliegelman, Jay. 1993. *Declaring Independence: Jefferson, Natural Language, and the Culture of Performance*. Princeton: Princeton University Press.

Francis, W. 1906. *Madura*. Madras District Gazetteers. Madras: Government Press.

Frazer, James George. 1940. *The Golden Bough*. Abridged ed. New York: Macmillan.

Freud, Sigmund. 1961. *The Interpretation of Dreams*. Trans. and ed. James Strachey. New York: Science Editions..

Friedrich, Paul. 1979a. "Poetic Language and the Imagination: A Reformulation of the Sapir Hypothesis." *Language, Context, and the Imagination*, 441–512. Stanford: Stanford University Press.

——. 1979b. "The Symbol and Its Relative Non-Arbitrariness." In *Language, Context, and the Imagination*, 1–61. Stanford: Stanford University Press.

——. 1989. "Language, Ideology, and Political Economy." *American Anthropologist* 91.2:295–312.

——. 1990. "Polytropy." In *Beyond Metaphor*, ed. James W. Fernandez, 17–55. Stanford: Stanford University Press.

——. 2006. "Maximizing Ethnopoetics: Fine-Tuning Anthropological Experience." In *Language, Culture, and Society: Key Topics in Linguistic Anthropology*, ed. Christine Jourdan and Kevin Tuite, 207–228. New York: Cambridge University Press.

Friedrich, Paul, and James Redfield. 1979. "Speech as a Personality Symbol: The Case of Achilles." In *Language Context and the Imagination*, 403–440. Stanford: Stanford University Press.

Gal, Susan, and Judith Irvine. 1995. "The Boundaries of Languages and Disciplines: How Ideologies Construct Difference." *Social Research* 62.4:967–1001.

Ganesan, Pi. Ci. 1981. *Ningalum Pechchaalaraakalaam* (You Too Can Become an Orator). Chennai: Vanathi Pathipaham.

——. 1992. *Pecungal, Vettri Perungal* (Orate and Achieve Success). Chennai: Gangai Puththaha Nilaiyam.

Gaonkar, Dilip P. 1997. "The Idea of Rhetoric in the Rhetoric of Science." In *Rhetorical Hermeneutics: Invention and Interpretation in the Age of Science*, ed. Alan Gross and William Keth, 25–85. Albany: State University of New York Press.

Geertz, Clifford. 1973. *The Interpretation of Culture; Selected Essays*. New York: Basic Books.

Geetha, V., and S. V. Rajadurai. 1995. "Eighth World Tamil Conference: Of Cardboard History and Discursive Space." *Economic and Political Weekly* 30.4:201–203.

——. 1998. *Towards a non-Brahmin Millennium: From Iyothee Thass to Periyar*. Calcutta: Samya.

Gnanakoothan. 1994. *Meendum Avargal* (Them Again). Chennai: Maiyam Publishers.

Gnanasundaram, V. 1980. "Standard Spoken Tamil: What and How?" In *Sociolinguistics and Dialectology*, ed. S. Agesthialingom and K. Karunakaran, 66–97. Annamalai Nagar: Annamalai University Press.

Goffman, Irving. 1974. *Frame Analysis: An Essay on the Organization of Experience*. Cambridge, MA: Harvard University Press.

——. 1983. *Forms of Talk*. Philadelphia: University of Pennsylvania Press.

Gramsci, Antonio. 1971 [1929–1935]. *Prison Notebooks*. New York: International Publishers.

Gupta, Akhil. 1995. "Blurred Boundaries: The Discourse of Corruption, the Culture of Politics, and the Imagined State." *American Ethnologist* 22.2:375–402.

Hanks, William. 1987. "Discourse Genres in a Theory of Practice." *American Ethnologist* 14:668–693.

Hardgrave, Robert. 1965. *The Dravidian Movement*. Bombay: Popular Prakasan.

——. 1975. *When Stars Displace the Gods: The Folk Culture of Cinema in Tamil Nadu*. Austin: Center for Asian Studies, Occasional Paper 3.

Hart, George. 2004. "Review" of Herman Tieken, *Kavya in South India: Old Tamil Cankam Poetry* (Groningen: Forstein, 2001). *Journal of the American Oriental Society* 124.1:180–184.

Hart, George, and Hank Heifetz. 2000. *The Four Hundred Songs of War and Wisdom: An Anthology of Poems from Classical Tamil, the Purananuru*. New York: Columbia University Press.

Herzfeld, M. 1992. "History in the Making: National and International Politics in a Rural Cretan Community." In *Europe Observed*, ed. Joao de Pina-Cabral and John Campbell, 93–122. London: Macmillan.

——. 1996. "National Spirit or the Breath of Nature? The Expropriation of Folk Positivism in the Discourse of Greek Nationalism." In *Natural Histories of Discourse*, ed. Michael Silverstein and Greg Urban, 277–298. Chicago: University of Chicago Press.

——. 1997. *Cultural Intimacy: Social Poetics in the Nation-State*. New York: Routledge.

Hill, Jane. 1992. ""Today there is no respect": Nostalgia, 'Respect,' and Oppositional Discourse in Mexicano (Nahuatl) Language Ideology." *Pragmatics* 2.3:263–280.

Hobsbawm, Eric. 1983. "Introduction: Inventing Traditions." In *The Invention of Tradition*, ed. Eric Hobsbawm and Terrence Ranger, 1–14. Cambridge: Cambridge University Press.

Hudson, D. 1992a. "Arumuga Navalar and the Hindu Renaissance Among Tamils." In *Religious Controversy in British India: Dialogues in Asian Languages*, ed. Kenneth W. Jones, 27–51. Albany: SUNY Press.

——. 1992b. "Winning Souls for Siva: Arumuga Navalar's Transmission of Saiva Religion." In *A Sacred Thread: Transmission of Hindu Traditions in Times of Rapid Change*, ed. Raymond B. Williams, 23–51. New York: Columbia University Press.

——. 1994. "Tamil Hindu Responses to Protestants: Nineteenth-Century Literati in Jaffna and Tinnevelly." In *Indigenous Responses to Western Christianity*, ed. Steven Kaplan, 95–123. New York: New York University Press.

Hughes, S. P. 1991. "Spectacular Strategies and Crowd Signs in the 1989 Tamilnadu Elections." Unpublished manuscript.

Inden, Ronald. 1990. *Imagining India*. Oxford: Blackwell.

Irschick, E. 1969. *Politics and Social Conflict in South India: The Non-Brahmin Movement and Tamil Separatism, 1916–1929*. Berkeley: University of California Press.

Irvine, Judith, and Susan Gal. 2000. "Language Ideology and Linguistic Differentiation." In Kroskrity 2000:35–84.

Jakobson, Roman. 1956. "Two Aspects of Language and Two Types of Aphasic Disturbances." In *Fundamentals of Language*, ed. R. Jakobson and Morris Halle, 67–96. The Hague: Mouton.

——. 1959. "Overlapping of Code and Message in Language." *American Anthropologist* 61.5:139–145.

——. 1960. "Concluding Statement: Linguistics and Poetics." In *Style in Language*, ed. T. Sebeok, 350–378. Cambridge, MA: MIT Press.

Jeffrey, R. 1997. "Tamil: Dominated by Cinema and Politics." *Economic and Political Weekly* 32:254–256.

Kailasapathy, K. 1986. *On Art and Literature*. Madras: New Century Bookhouse.

Kailasa Pillai, T. 1955 [1918]. *Arumuga Navalar carittiram* (The Life of Arumuga Navalar). Madras.

Kaliyappa, Kovai. 1955. *Medaiyil Pecuvathu Yeppadi* (How to Speak on a Stage). Chennai: Prem Prasuram.

Kalyanasundaram, Thiru. Vi. 1982. *Vazhkai Kurippukkal* (Notes on My Life). Chennai: Saiva Siddhantham.

Karunanidhi, Mu. 1981. *Pecum Kalai Valarppom* (We Will Cultivate the Speaking Arts). Chennai: Bharathi Pathipaham.

Kaviraj, Sudipta. 1993. "The Imaginary Institution of India." In *Subaltern Studies* VII: *Writings on South Asian History and Society*, ed. Partha Chatterjee and Pandey Gyanendra, 1–39. Delhi: Oxford University Press.

——. 2005a. "On the Enchantment of the State: Indian Thought on the Role of the State in the Narrative of Modernity." *European Journal of Sociology* 46.2:263–296.

——. 2005b. "Outline of a Revisionist Theory of Modernity." *European Journal of Sociology* 46.3:497–526.

——. 2005c. "The Sudden Death of Sanskrit Knowledge." *Journal of Indian Philosophy* 33:119–142.

Keane, Webb. 2007. *Christian Moderns: Freedom and Fetish in the Mission Encounter*. Berkeley: University of California Press.

Kelly, John. 1988. "Bhakti and the Spirit of Capitalism in Fiji: The Ontology of the Fiji Indians." Diss., University of Chicago.

Kersenboom, Saskia. 1995. *Word, Sound, Image: The Life of Tamil Texts*. Oxford: Berg Publishers.

King, Richard. 1999. *Orientalism and Religion: Postcolonial Theory, India, and "Mythic East."* London: Routledge.

Kramrisch, Stella. 1996 [1946]. *The Hindu Temple*. 2 vols. New Delhi: Motilal Banarsidass.

Kroskrity, Paul, ed. 2000. *Regimes of Language: Ideologies, Politics, Identities*. Santa Fe: School of American Research Press.

Kumari, Anandan. 1977. *Ningalum Pechchaalaraakalaam* (You Too Can Become a Speaker). Chennai: Vanathi Pathipaham.

Lakshmi, C. S. 1990. "Mother, Mother-Community, and Mother Politics in Tamil Nadu." *Economic and Political Weekly*, October 20–27: WS-72.

Leavitt, John. 2005. "Linguistic Relativities." In *Language, Culture, and Society: Key Topics in Linguistic Anthropology*, ed. Christine Jourdan and Kevin Tuite, 47–81. Cambridge: Cambridge University Press.

Lelyveld, David. 1993. "Colonial Knowledge and the Fate of Hindustani." *Comparative Studies of Society and History* 35.4:665–682.

Levi-Strauss, Claude. 1968. *The Savage Mind*. Chicago: University of Chicago Press.

Lewandowski, Susan. 1977. "Changing Form and Function in the Colonial Port City in India: An Historical Analysis of Madurai and Madras." *Modern Asian Studies* 2.2:183–213.

Lorenzen, David N. 2006. *Who Invented Hinduism: Essays on Religion in History*. New Delhi: Yoda Press.

Lucy, John. 1992. *Language Diversity and Thought: A Reformulation of the Linguistic Relativity Hypothesis*. Cambridge: Cambridge University Press.

Lutz, Catherine A., and L. Abu-Lughod, eds. 1990. *Language and the Politics of Emotion*. Cambridge: Cambridge University Press.

Lynch, Owen. 1990. *Divine Passions: The Social Construction of Emotion in India*. Bekeley: University of California Press.

Marriott, McKim. 1976. "Hindu Transactions: Diversity Without Dualism." In *Transaction and Meaning: Directions in the Anthropology of Exchange and Symbolic Behavior*, ed. Bruce Kapferer, 109–142. Philadelphia: ISHI Publications.

——. 1978. "Intimacy and Rank in Food." Unpublished manuscript, paper delivered at the Tenth ICAES, New Delhi.

——. 1989. "Constructing and Indian Ethnosociology." *Contributions to Indian Sociology* 23.1:1–39.

Marriott, McKim, and Ronald Inden. 1977. "Toward an Ethnosociology of South Asian Caste Systems." In *The New Wind: Changing Identities in South Asia*, ed. KennethDavid, 227–238. The Hague: Mouton.

Mbembe, Achille. 1992. "Provisional Notes on the Postcolony." *Africa* 62.1:3–37.

Meenakshisundaram, T. P. 1958. "Thiru T. V. K.,Äîthe Living." *Tamil Culture* 7.1:16–21.

Messick, Brinkley. 1993. *The Caligraphic State: Textual Domination and History in a Muslim Society*. Berkeley: University of California Press.

Mines, Diane P. 1995. "Making and Remaking the Village: The Pragmatics of Social Life in Rural Tamilnadu." Diss., University of Chicago.

——. 2005. *Fierce Gods: Inequality, Ritual, and the Politics of Dignity in a South Indian Village*. Bloomington: Indiana University Press.

Mines, Mattison. 1994. *Public Faces, Private Voices: Community and Individuality in South India*. Berkeley: University of California Press.

Mishra, Pankaj. 2004. "The Invention of the Hindu." Axess 2004/02 (online magazine), http://www.axess.se/english/2004/02/theme_inventionhindu.php.htm (accessed 8 June 2007).

Moffatt, Michael. 1979. *An Untouchable Community in South India: Structure and Consensus*. Princeton: Princeton University Press.

Moore, Robert. 2000. "Coyote Occasions." In "'The People Are Here Now': The Contemporary Culture of an Ancestral Language: Studies in Obsolescent Kiksht (Wasco Wishram Dialect of Upper Chinookan),"2:271–391. Diss., University of Chicago.

Munn, Nancy D. 1992 [1986]. *The Fame of Gawa: A Symbolic Study of Value Transformation in a Massim (Papua New Guinea) Society*. Durham, NC: Duke University Press.

Nandy, Ashis. 1983. *The Intimate Enemy: Loss and Recovery of Self Under Colonialism*. Delhi: Oxford University Press.

Narayanan, Arandhai. 1994. *Meedaiyil Peecalaam Vaarunkal* (Come, We Shall Speak on the Stage). Chennai: New Century Bookhouse.

Narayana Rao, V., David Shulman, and Sanjay Subrahmanyam. 1992. *Symbols of Substance: Court and State in Nayaka Period Tamil Nadu*. Delhi: Oxford University Press.

——. 2003. *Textures of Time: Writing History in South India, 1600–1800*. New York: Other Press.

Nataraja Sarma, T. 1971. *Simile in Tamil: A Comparative Study of Tolkappiyam* uvamai iyal *and Thandiyalankaram* uvamai ani. Nagarkoil: Jayakumari.

Paley, Julia. 2002. "Toward an Anthropology of Democracy." *Annual Review of Anthropology* 31:469–496.

Pandian, M. S. S. 1992b. "Jayalalitha: 'Desire' and Political Legitimation." *Seminar* 401:31–34.

——. 1992a. *The Image Trap: M. G. Ramachandran in Film and Politics*. New Delhi: Sage Publications.

——. 1994. "Notes on the Transformation of 'Dravidian' Ideology: Tamilnadu, c. 1900–1940." *Social Scientist* 22.5–6:104.

——. 1996a. "Denationalizing the Past: 'Nation' in EV Ramaswamy's Political Discourse." *Economic and Political Weekly* 28.42:2282–2287.

——. 1996b. "Towards National-Popular: Notes on Self-Respecters' Tamil." *Economic and Political Weekly* 31.51:3323–3329.

——. 2007. *Brahmin and Non-Brahmin: Genealogies of the Tamil Political Present*. New Delhi: Permanent Black.

Pandian, M. S. S., S. Anandi, and A. R. Venkatachalapathy. 1991. "Of Maltova Mothers and Other Stories." *Economic and Political Weekly* 26.16:1059–1064.

Parandhamanar, A. Ki. 1989. *Pechchaalaraaka* (To Become a Speaker). Chennai: Bharathi Nilaiyam.

Parthasarathy, R. 1992. *The Cilappatikaram of Ilanko Atikal: An Epic of South India*. Translations from the Asian Classics. New York: Columbia University Press.

Peirce, Charles Saunders. 1955. "The Principles of Phenomenology" (1940). In *Philosophical Writings of Peirce*. Ed. Justus Buchler. New York: Dover.

——. 1960. *Collected Papers of Charles Saunders Peirce*. 2 vols. Cambridge, MA: Harvard University Press.

Pennington, Brian K. 2005 *Was Hinduism Invented? Britons, Indians, and the Colonial Construction of Religion*. Oxford: Oxford University Press.

Peterson, Indira V. 1989. *Poems to Siva: The Hymns of the Tamil Saints*. Delhi: Motilal Banarsidass.

Plato. 1987. *Gorgias*. Trans. Donald J. Zeyl. Indianapolis: Hackett.

Pollack, Sheldon. 1996. "The Sanskrit Cosmopolis, 300–1300: Transculturation, Vernacularization, and the Question of Ideology." In *Ideology and Status of Sanskrit: Ccontributions to the History of the Sanskrit Language*, ed. J. E. M. Houben (Leiden: Brill), 198–248.

——. 2006. *The Language of the Gods in the World of Men: Sanskrit, Culture, and Power in Premodern India*. Berkeley: University of California Press, 2006.

Price, P. 1996a. *Kingship and Political Practice in Colonial India*. New York: Cambridge University Press.

——. 1996b. "Revolution and Rank in Tamil Nationalism." *Journal of Asian Studies* 55.2:359–383.

Ram, N. 1977. "Prehistory and History of the DMK." *Social Scientist* 6.5:59–91.

Ramanujan, A. K. 1967. *The Interior Landscape: Love Poems from a Classical Tamil Anthology*. Bloomington: Indiana University Press.

——. 1971. "Towards an Anthology of City Images." In *Urban India: Society, Space, and Image*, ed. Richard G. Fox. Durham, NC: Duke University Program in Comparative Studies on Southern Asia.

——. 1973. *Speaking of Siva*. Harmondsworth: Penguin.

——. 1985. *Poems of Love and War*. New York: Columbia University Press.

——. 1989. "Is There an Indian Way of Thinking? An Informal Essay." *Contributions to Indian Sociology* 23.1:41–58.

——. 1992 [1981]. *Hymns for the Drowning: Poems for Visnu by Nammalvar*. New York: Penguin.

Ramaswamy, Sumathi. 1992. "Daughters of Tamil: Language and the Poetics of Womanhood in Tamilnad." *South Asia Research* 12.1:38–59.

——. 1993. "En/gendering Language: The Poetics of Tamil Identity." *Comparative Studies of Society and History* 35:683–725.

——. 1997. *Passions of the Tongue*. Berkeley: University of California Press.

——. 1999. "The Demoness, the Maid, the Whore, and the Good Mother: Contesting the National Language in India." *International Journal of the Sociology of Language* 140:1–28.

Ravindiran, V. 1996. "The Unanticipated Legacy of Robert Caldwell and the Dravidian Movement." *South Indian Studies* 1:83–110.

Rebhun, Linda-Anne. 1999. *The Heart Is Unknown Country: Love in the Changing Economy of Northeast Brazil*. Stanford: Stanford University Press.

Redfield, Robert, and Milton Singer. 1954. "The Cultural Role of Cities." *Economic Development and Cultural Change* 3:57–77.

Rudolph, Lloyd, and Susanne Rudolph. 1967. *The Modernity of Tradition: Political Development in India*. Chicago: University of Chicago Press.

Sadakoparamanujancariyar, Vai. Mu., Ce. Krishnamasariyar, and Vai. Mu. Kopalakrishnamasariyar. 1972. *Nannul Kandikaiyurai* (*Nannul* Critical Commentary). Chennai: Vai. Mu. Gopalakrishnamasariyar.

Sahlins, Marshall D. 1976. *Culture and Practical Reason*. Chicago: University of Chicago Press.

——. *Waiting for Foucault, Still*. Chicago: Prickly Paradigm Press.

Sambandan, M. S. 1997 [1944]. *Ciranta Pechchaalarkal* (Great Orators). Chennai: Manivasagar Pathipaham.

Sapir, Edward. 1995. "The Unconscious Patterning of Behavior in Society" (1927). In *Language, Culture, and Society: A Book of Readings*, ed. Ben Blount, pp. 29–42. Prospect Heights, IL: Waveland Press.

Sapir, J. David, and J. Christopher Crocker, eds. 1977. *The Social Use of Metaphor: Essays on the Anthropology of Rhetoric*. Philadelphia: University of Pennsylvania Press.

Schechner, R. 1991. "The Street Is the Stage." *The Future of Ritual: Writings on Culture and Performance*. London: Routledge.

Schieffelin, Bambi, Kathryn Woolard, and Paul Kroskrity, eds. 1998. *Language Ideologies: Practice and Theory*. New York: Oxford University Press.

Schiffman, Harold F. 1974. "Language, Linguistics, and Politics in Tamilnad." In *Studies in the Language and Culture of* South Asia, ed. Edwin Gerow and Margery Lang, 125–134. Seattle: University of Washington Publications on Asia of the Institute for Comparative and Foreign Area Studies 23.

——. 1997. "Diglossia as a Sociolinguistic Solution." In *Handbook of Sociolinguistics*, ed. Florian Coulmas, 205–216. Oxford: Blackwell.

Shanmugam Pillai, M. 1965. "Caste Isoglosses in Kinship Terminology." *Anthropological Linguistics* 7:59–66.

Silverstein, Michael. 1976. "Shifters, Linguistic Categories, and Cultural Description." In *Meaning in Anthropology*, ed. Keith Basso and M. Selby, 11–56. Albuquerque: University of New Mexico Press.

——. 1979. "Language Structure and Language Ideology." In *The Elements: A Parasession on Linguistic Units and Levels*, ed. Paul Clyne, William Hanks, and Carol Hofbauer, 193–247. Chicago: Chicago Linguistic Society.

——. 1993. "Metapragmatic Discourse, Metapragmatic Function." In *Reflexive Language*, ed. John Lucy, 33–58. Cambridge: Cambridge University Press.

——. 1998. "The Uses and Utility of Ideology." In *Language Ideologies: Practice and The-*

ory, ed. Bambi Schieffelin, Kathryn Woolard, and Paul Kroskrity, 123–145. New York: Oxford University Press.

——. 2000. "Whorfianism and the Linguistic Imagination of Nationality." In *Regimes of Language: Ideologies, Polities, and Identities*, ed. P. Kroskrity, 85–138. Santa Fe, NM: School of American Research Press.

——. 2004. *Talking Politics: The Substance of Style from Abe to "W"*. Chicago: Prickly Paradigm Press.

Silverstein, Michael, and Greg Urban. 1996. *Natural Histories of Discourse*. Chicago: University of Chicago Press.

Singer, Milton. 1972. *When a Great Tradition Modernizes*. Chicago: University of Chicago Press.

——. 1991. *Semiotics of Cities, Selves, and Cultures: Explorations in Semiotic Anthropology*. Berlin: de Gruyter.

Sivathamby, K. 1979. "Hindu Reaction to Christian Proselytization and Westernization in the Nineteenth Century Sri Lanka." *Social Science Review* (Colombo)1.1:41–75.

——. 1995. *Understanding Dravidian Movement: Problems and Perspectives*. Madras: NCBH.

Sonnino, L. A. 1968. *A Handbook to Sixteenth-Century Rhetoric*. London: Routledge and Keegan Paul.

Subramanian, Narendra. 1999. *Ethnicity and Populist Mobilization: Political Parties, Citizens, and Democracy in South India*. New Delhi: Oxford University Press.

Sundaramoorthy. 1974. *Early Literary Theories in Tamil (in Comparison with Sanskrit Theories)*. Madurai: Sarvodia Ilakkiya Pannai.

Sundaram Pillai. 1968 [1891]. *Manonmaniyam*. Coimbatore: Tamilnadu Mokkuri Puththaka.

Swaminathaiyar, U. Ve. 1991 [1925]. *Nannul Mulamum Sankara Namachivayar Uraiyum* (Nannul Original and Sankara Namachivayar's Commentary). Chennai: Doctor U. Ve. Swaminathaiyar Book Trust.

——. 1995 [1918]. *Nannul Mulamum Mayilainathar Uraiyum* (Nannul Original and Mayilainathar's Commentary). Chennai: Doctor U. Ve. Swaminathaiyar Book Trust.

Tambiah, Stanley. 1985. "The Galactic Polity in Southeast Asia." In *Culture, Thought, and Social Action: An Anthropological Perspective*, 252–286. Cambridge, MA: Harvard University Press.

Telford, K. A. 1961. *Aristotle's Poetics: Translation and Analysis*. Chicago: Regnery.

Tennekoon, N. Serena. 1988. "Rituals of Development: The Accelerated Mahavali Development Program of Sri Lanka." *American Ethnologist* 15.2:294–310.

Thamizhvanan, Lena. 1978. *Pechchaalaraavathu Yeppadi* (How to Become an Orator). Chennai: Manimegalai Pracuram.

Tocqueville, Alexis de. 1969 [1848]. *Democracy in America*. Trans. George Lawrence. Ed. J. P. Mayer. Garden City, NY: Doubleday Anchor.

Trautman, Thomas. 1997. *Aryans and British India*. Berkeley: University of California Press.

——. 1999a. "Hullabaloo About Telegu." *South Asia Research* 19.1:53–70.

——. 1999b. "Inventing the History of South India." In *Invoking the Past: The Uses of History in South Asia*, ed. Daud Ali, 36–54. Oxford: Oxford University Press.

——. 2006. *Languages and Nations: The Dravidian Proof in Colonial Madras*. Berkeley: University of California Press.

Trawick, Margaret. 1990. *Notes on Love in a Tamil Family*. Berkeley: University of California Press.

Turner, Victor. 1967. "Symbols in Ndembu Ritual." In *The Forest of Symbols: Aspects of Ndembu Ritual*, 19–47. Ithaca: Cornell University Press.

——. 1969. *The Ritual Process: Structure and Anti-Structure*. Chicago: Aldine.

——. 1974. *Dramas, Fields, and Metaphors: Symbolic Action in Human Society*. Ithaca: Cornell University Press.

Uberoi, Patricia, and J. P. S. Uberoi. 1977. "Towards a New Sociolinguistics: A Memoir of P. B. Pandit." In *Parole and Langue: Studies in French Structuralism*, ed. H. S. Gill, iii–xvii. Patiola: Punjabi University.

Van der Veer, Peter. 2001. *Imperial Encounters: Religion, Nation, and Empire*. Princeton: Princeton University Press.

Varshney, Ashutosh. 2000. "Is India Becoming More Democratic?" *Journal of Asian Studies* 59.1:3–25.

Venkatachalapathy, A. R. 1994. "Reading Practices and Modes of Reading in Colonial Tamilnadu." *Studies in History* 10.2:273–290.

——. 1995a. "Dravidian Movement and Saivites: 1927–1944." *Economic and Political Weekly* 30:761–768.

——. 1995b. "Coining Words: Language and Politics in Late Colonial Tamilnadu." *Comparative Studies of South Asia, Africa, and the Middle East* 15.2:120–129.

——. 1996. "Subramania Bharati and the Modernization of Tamil." *South Indian Studies* 1:136–143.

——. 1997. "Domesticating the Novel: Society and Culture in Inter-War Tamil Nadu." *Indian Economic and Social History Review* 34.1:53–67.

——. 2005. "'Enna Prayocanam?' Constructing the Canon in Colonial Tamilnadu." *Indian Economic and Social History Review* 42.4:535–553.

——. 2006. *In Those Days There Was No Coffee: Writings in Cultural History*. New Delhi: Yoda Press.

Volosinov, M. L. 1973. *Marxism and the Philosophy of Language*. Austin: University of Texas Press.

Waghorne, Joanne. 1994. *The Raja's Magic Clothes: Re-Visioning Kingship and Divinity in England's India*. University Park: Pennsylvania University Press.

Wagoner, Philip. 2003. "Precolonial Intellectuals and the Production of Colonial Knowledge." *Comparative Studies in Society and History* 45.4:783–814.

Washbrook, David. 1989. "Caste, Class, and Dominance in Modern Tamil Nadu: Non-Brahminism, Dravidianism, and Tamil Nationalism." In *Dominance and State Power in Modern India: Decline of a Social Order*, ed. Francine R. Frankel and M. S. A. Rao, 204–264. New Delhi: Oxford University Press.

——. 1991. "'To Each a Language of His Own': Language, Cultur,e and Society in Colonial India." In *Language, History, and Class*, ed. Penelope J. Corfield, 179–203. Oxford: Blackwell.

Weber, Eugen. 1976. *Peasants Into Frenchmen: The Modernization of Rural France, 1870–1914*. Stanford: Stanford University Press.

Weber, Max. 1946. "The Sociology of Charismatic Authority." In *Max Weber: Essays in Sociology*, ed. H. H. Gerth and C. Wright Mills, 245–264. New York: Oxford University Press.

Wentworth, Blake. 2009. "Yearning for a Dreamed Real: The Procession of the Lord in the Tamil Ulaa." Diss., University of Chicago.

Wheatley, P. 1969. *City as Symbol*. London: University College.

White, H. 1973. *Metahistory: The Historical Imagination in Nineteenth-Century Europe*. Baltimore: Johns Hopkins University Press.

Whorf, Benjamin Lee. 1956. "The Relation of Habitual Thought and Behavior to Language" (1939). In *Language, Thought and Reality: Selected Writings of Benjamin Lee Whorf*, ed. John Carroll, 134–159. Cambridge, MA: MIT Press.

Williams, Raymond. 1977. *Marxism and Literature*. Oxford: Oxford University Press.

Woolard, Kathryn. 1998. "Introduction: Language Ideology as a Field of Inquiry." In *Language Ideologies: Practice and Theory*, ed. Bambi Scheiffelin, Kathryn Woolard, and Paul Kroskrity, 3–47. New York: Oxford University Press.

Woolard, Kathryn, and Bambi Schieffelin. 1994. "Language Ideology." *Annual Review of Anthropology* 23:55–82.

Young, R. F., and S. Jebanesan. 1995. *The Bible Trembled: The Hindu-Christian Controversies of Nineteenth-Century Ceylon*. Vienna: Sammlung der Nobili.

Zvelebil, Kamil. 1963. "Dialects of Tamil IV." *Archiv Orientalni* 32:237–264.

——. 1992. *Companion Studies to the History of Tamil Literature*. Leiden: Brill.

INDEX

GPSR Authorized Representative: Easy Access System Europe, Mustamäe tee 50, 10621 Tallinn, Estonia, gpsr.requests@easproject.com

www.ingramcontent.com/pod-product-compliance
Lightning Source LLC
Chambersburg PA
CBHW030825310726
48980CB00006B/644/J

* 9 7 8 0 2 3 1 1 4 7 5 6 9 *